HUMAN–COMPUTER INTERACTION

*Psychology, Task Analysis
and Software Engineering*

Professor P. Johnson

McGRAW-HILL BOOK COMPANY

London · New York · St Louis · San Francisco · Auckland
Bogotá · Caracas · Hamburg · Lisbon · Madrid · Mexico
Milan · Montreal · New Delhi · Panama · Paris · San Juan
São Paulo · Singapore · Sydney · Tokyo · Toronto

Published by
McGRAW-HILL Book Company Europe
Shoppenhangers Road · Maidenhead · Berkshire · SL6 2QL · England
Tel: 0628 23432; Fax 0628 770224

British Library Cataloguing in Publication Data

Johnson, Peter
Human computer interaction: psychology, task analysis and software engineering
I. Title
004.019

ISBN 0-07-707235-9

Library of Congress Cataloging-in-Publication Data

Johnson, Peter
Human computer interaction: psychology, task analysis, and software
engineering / P. Johnson
    p.   cm.
Includes bibliographical references and index.
ISBN 0-07-707235-9
1. Human-computer interaction.   I. Title.
QA76.9.H85J64 1992   91-33969 CIP

2345   CL   95432

Typeset by Computape (Pickering) Ltd, Pickering, North Yorkshire
and printed and bound in England at Clays Ltd, St Ives plc

This book is dedicated to my mother and father,
Edith and Ernest Albert Johnson and to my wife Hilary.

CONTENTS

Trademarks   xi
Preface   xiii

1 **Introducing human–computer interaction**   1
   HCI, ergonomics and human factors   2
   Psychology and HCI   3
   HCI and computer science   3
   HCI, users and organizations   4
   The user interface   5
   A framework for HCI   7
   Overview of the book   9

2 **An introduction to human memory**   11
   Fundamental memory structures and processes   13
   Short-term memory experiments   16
   Chunking   20
   Working memory   21
   Long-term memory   23
   Recall from categories   24
   Consistency and coherence   26

3 **Memory, organization and structures**   28
   Recall and recognition   29
   Propositional networks   30
   Facilitation and priming   32
   Coherence   33
   Spreading activation   34
   Interference effects   35
   Elaborated memory structures   37
   Inference and memory recall   39
   Memory for gist   41

4 **Knowledge representation**   43
   Representations and knowledge   43
   Three representational families   44
   Conclusion   58

5   Expertise, skill and skill acquisition   **60**
Stages of skill acquisition   61
An example of skill acquisition   62
Practice effects   64
Positive and negative transfer   65
Programming as a skill   66
Conclusion   67

6   Developing interface designs   **69**
Perspective on user-interface design   70
Software-engineering methods and HCI design   72
Formal methods   74
Three softeware-engineering paradigms   75
Prototyping   77
Pressman's model of system development   80
Generic phases in software development   81
Conclusion   82

7   Evaluations of interactive systems   **84**
Evaluation and design procedures   85
Experimental methods   87
Experimental methodology   88
Experimental design   93
Statistical treatment of the data   97
Conclusion   99

8   User-interface design: environments, managements systems and toolkits   **100**
User-interface design environments   101
User-interface management systems   104
User-interface toolkits   107
Conclusion   112

9   Early attempts at modelling human–computer interaction   **114**
A classification of early models in HCI   115
Command language grammar   117
Task action language   125
Goals, operators, methods and selection rules   127
Summary of early models in HCI   133

10 Interaction and user modelling in human–computer interaction   **134**
Introduction   135
Task action grammar   135
Cognitive complexity theory   139
Interactive cognitive subsystems as a basis for a cognitive task analysis   143
Programmable user models   148
Conclusion   149

11 Task analysis and task modelling   **151**
Early approaches to task analysis   152
Task analysis and task modelling in HCI   154

Why use task analysis in HCI? 155
A theory of tasks—task and knowledge structures 156
Task knowledge structures and HCI 157
Transfer of knowledge between tasks 158
Tasks, task structure and task knowledge 160
Task knowledge structures 161
A summary of task knowledge structure theory 162

12 Knowledge analysis of tasks **165**
A method of task analysis—knowledge analysis of tasks 165
Identifying knowledge 166
Collecting task data: applying knowledge-gathering techniques to task analysis 167
Identifying task knowledge structure components using knowledge analysis of tasks 170
Identifying representative, central and generic properties of tasks 172
Task models 174

13 Task analysis applied to interactive system design **177**
Task analysis and system design—a brief review of design practices 177
An application of task analysis to interaction design 183
Summary of case studies 192

14 Informal and formal specification of user-interaction task scenarios **193**
Informal specifications of tasks and user intefaces 193
The generalized task model 194
The specific task model 198
The specific interface model 198
A formal specification approach for task-based design 201
Task-object specification and semantics of procedures 204
Conclusion 205

References and Bibliography **207**

Author Index **213**

Index **215**

TRADEMARKS

MacWrite is a trademark of Claris.

MsWord is a trademark of the Microsoft Corporation.

SuperPaint is a trademark of Aldus Corporation.

Apple Macintosh, Macintosh II and *HyperCard* are trademarks of Apple Computer Inc.

PostScript is a trademark of Adobe Systems Inc.

UNIX is a registered trademark of AT&T Bell Laboratories.

PREFACE

Human–computer interaction is an exciting and important area of computer science. In fact it was through the problems of human–computer interaction (HCI) that I became more widely interested in computer science. I first became aware of some of the issues in HCI when I was attending an undergraduate course in statistics in which we were required to use some of the standard statistical packages such as SPSS. This was in the early seventies and the versions of these packages we were using were non-interactive, which meant we had to submit jobs made up of data and instructions to the computer and wait to see if our complete job was executable (often it was not) and performed the analysis we wanted. To make matters worse, we had to submit our jobs through a card reader, and we had no interactive editing facilities available to create our data and instructions. These early experiences may sound archaic in the present day, however, the problems we had are often still found today in different forms. For example, the instruction language we had to use to tell the computer how our data were organized and what statistical tests we wanted to perform was a very low-level language that had to be learned and remembered. The language bore no meaningful relation to the tasks we were trying to instruct the computer to perform. To us it was a language made up of seemingly arbitrary symbols. Today many novice programmers find similar problems when they first try to master UNIX. Other problems were that because of the input and output devices we were using (output was by a line printer) we had no immediate feedback, furthermore when an error occurred the feedback provided by the program was non-diagnostic and so did not help us to understand or learn from the mistake.

Human–computer interaction requires an understanding of the people who would use the computer program (the users), the domain and institutional structures that might affect how or when they would use the program, the tasks that are carried out, and the software and hardware solutions that could be offered. Human–computer interaction is very much concerned with design, by providing designed solutions to identified problems taking full account of all the constraints and requirements. The design aspect of HCI is important and does not just apply to the software or hardware. In HCI it is a system that includes the users, the software and the hardware that is designed. The purpose of the design is to enable work and other activities to be performed more effectively, efficiently and, when performed by people, with more enjoyment and satisfaction. Since work gives rise to tasks then task modelling and task analysis form a central part of HCI design.

HCI design can be seen as involving mappings between the various constraints and requirements of users (and their institutional contexts), tasks (and the situations they give rise to), and software/hardware to provide solutions that meet these constraints and requirements with known cost and performance consequences. Cost and performance include both user and software/hardware aspects. A user cost might be the skill level and amount of training required of the user before the computer can be used to complete a known task, to a given standard, in a specified time. A software/hardware cost would include the amount of effort required to produce the program and the amount of machine memory and processing capacity required to run the program. Hardware and software performance would include the speed with which the program, when running on a given machine, could execute benchmark tasks, such as the time taken to redraw the cursor position on the screen as the mouse is moved around.

The issue of the relationship between users, tasks and hardware/software needs to be considered from theoretical, methodological and practical perspectives. It is tempting to argue for user-centred design rather than software/hardware-centred design since it is believed (e.g. Norman and Draper, 1986) that user-centred design will produce better systems. However, to ignore the contribution of the hardware and software designer in creating both new ways of doing things and new things we can do is a regressive step. For this reason, it is more sensible to think of both user and software/hardware coming together in a task-oriented system. That is to say, the user and the computer work together to perform tasks. To say that design is task oriented does not mean that we are concerned only with the tasks of design (although these are addressed as part of any design method), nor does it mean that we are concerend with designing systems that mirror the way that people currently perform tasks or that are limited to just those tasks which people currently perform. What task-oriented design means is that tasks are seen as being the central focus of the design, in that it is through understanding the tasks that people currently do perform or try to perform that the designer is going to come up with a new and better way of performing those tasks and have ideas as to how people might be helped to perform tasks that are currently beyond them. In this respect, the designer needs to situate the design in the context of what people were previously able or trying to do in order to assess if the design has improved task performance at all and at what costs. Also, the designer needs to be able to reflect upon the scope their design has for changing the very things that people do. For example, early text editors allowed more people to produce typewritten quality documents with more ease and less effort than was previously involved in using a typewriter. From this, people started to experiment with producing their own layouts and page settings; this in turn led to the development of word processors that now enable more people to produce print-quality documents with different fonts, styles and layout facilities available. In this way, word-processor design has changed the tasks that we now associate with producing documents and allowed us to produce far more imaginative documents than were previously possible.

This book is based upon the belief that HCI requires consideration of user, hardware/software and task requirements, and that good design is not just something that occurs by accident or is to be achieved only by a few gifted individuals. It represents an attempt to provide some steps towards a more systematic and considered approach to HCI design. Theory, methods and practice frequently come into sharp conflict in HCI, precisely because of the lack of any clear understanding of what the relationships between the three are. Throughout this book theory and methods are introduced and put into the context of practical problems. For example, in the case of task analysis, it is possible to show how a theory of Task Knowledge Structures has led to a method of task analysis, and to show further how this method has been applied to HCI design issues. Of course, it is often the case that practical problems and current practice give rise to new research problems and to the development of more applicable and useful theories and methods. An example of this is the application of formal methods to HCI. At present, there are many attempts to utilize the power of formal methods in HCI design problems, and these attempts to use formal methods in HCI practice are giving rise to the development of more appropriate and applicable formal methods.

This book arose largely out of an undergraduate course in Human Factors for Interactive Systems Design that I developed and continue to teach to second-year undergraduate computer science students at Queen Mary and Westfield College (QMW), University of London. I first taught the course in 1985/6 and have been further developing it each year since then. With no texts available, and strong views about what I thought should be included, I set about producing course notes. As these notes grew and grew (and the course became more and more overcrowded with material) it began to seem that a book was emerging. The course lasts for 11 weeks and comprises 33 hours of lectures, 11 hours of tutorials and has four intensive courseworks that are each planned to take the students between two to three weeks to complete. Additional material came from an opportunity to contribute to a software engineering course also given to second-year computer science students at QMW. This formed a six-week block of lectures on design processes, requirements, evaluation and user-interface architectures. The final source for the book was the research that has taken place on Task Knowledge Structures and task analysis in design in the HCI laboratory at QMW since 1984. I have always felt guilty about teaching my own research findings and views to students, since I feel they should form their own views and ideas and not be subjected to a biased selection. However, I gradually realized that this was discrediting the students. In 1986, we started an M.Sc. in HCI and this gave me the opportunity to pass on the research work on Task Knowledge Structures and task-oriented design to these students. This proved to be an exciting and rewarding activity, since the students began to apply and develop Task Knowledge Structures in more ways than would otherwise have been possible.

The book is largely aimed at computer science students of second-year undergraduate and M.Sc. levels with no knowledge of HCI or psychology. However, the book can also be used by students from other disciplines taking conversion courses in computer science or information technology. While the book is not aimed primarily at researchers, research students in HCI may also find it of use. The sections on Task Knowledge Structures and task-oriented design may be of interest to researchers in HCI, but I am afraid that researchers who want a more detailed coverage of our research will have to consult the now many papers published by the researchers at the QMW HCI laboratory. I promised myself I would finish this book before starting upon a full exposé of our research on task-oriented design.

There are many people whom I must acknowledge and thank for their help and support leading to this book. In particular, I thank George Coulouris, Richard Bornat and the staff in the Computer Science Department at QMW for the continuous support and encouragement they have given me. Andy Ware at McGraw-Hill has given me great encouragement throughout. I would also like to thank the research staff and students, past and present, who have worked with me over the years in the HCI laboratory at QMW. In particular, Mark Keane, Ray Waddington, Paul Buckley and Emma Nicolosi, who have now left QMW, helped with the early work on task analysis. Christine Knowles and Victoria Bellotti have helped form my views on design processes and the use of task analysis and other HCI techniques in design. Steph Wilson has helped me understand more about user-interface management systems. Stathis Gikas has helped me come to terms with formal methods in HCI. Other staff and research students at QMW who deserve an acknowledgement are Steve Reeves, Kieron Drake, Mel Slater, Eliot Miranda, Joe Borkoles, James Pycock and Panos Markoplos, who have all allowed me to discuss my ideas with them and have given me useful feedback and criticism. I am indebted to Chris Hyde for letting me talk about his work on CHOICE and InTouch. The undergraduate and master's students who have suffered the development of this book over the years have my deepest sympathy and greatest thanks. Many of my ideas have grown from long and enjoyable discussions with John Long at UCL, as usual I have probably got all his ideas wrong. Marylyn Whaymand and Henry Bloomfield helped me correct and format the manuscript and figures. My final and greatest thanks go to Hilary Johnson for her contributions to our research on task analysis and to the general quality of the HCI laboratory; her guidance and criticisms of my ideas, and her help has been invaluable.

Peter Johnson
Queen Mary and Westfield College
University of London

1 INTRODUCING HUMAN–COMPUTER INTERACTION

Summary

- Human–computer interaction (HCI) is the study of the interaction between people, computers and tasks. It is principally concerned with understanding how people and computers can interactively carry out tasks, and how such interactive systems are designed.

- HCI is a multidisciplinary subject drawing on knowledge derived from the subject areas of science, engineering and art. There is much to be learned about how these different disciplines can contribute to the production of computer systems so that people will be able to use them effectively and easily in their working and social environments.

- HCI also involves the development and application of principles, guidelines and methods to support the design and evaluation of interactive systems.

- An important concern of HCI is the demands made by the computer on people's knowledge and understanding, and on the amount of problem solving and learning required.

- The user interface is more than what the person can see, touch or hear. The user interface includes the concepts the user needs to know about the computer system and how it can be used to carry out different tasks.

- Interaction involves task-oriented dialogues between the user and the program running on the computer. The program must communicate to the user the results and feedback of activities that are being, or have been, carried out, as well as requests for further actions, while the user must instruct or program and enter data or information into the computer system.

- A task-based approach is essential to the design of interactive systems. Tasks that users want to achieve as well as the tasks involved in using the computer must be understood. Most important is understanding the way that the computer can influence and change the tasks that people are able to do. This task–design–task cycle of change is a central feature of HCI.

1

HCI is a subject which makes use of relevant theory and methods from many disciplines, including the physical and social sciences as well as engineering and the arts. Important contributions to HCI have come from computer science and psychology. As the discipline of HCI has progressed, further contributions have been made from mathematics, graphic art, sociology and artificial intelligence. There is also much to be gained from considering the contributions that linguistics, philosophy, anthropology and the creative and performing arts can make to HCI.

The study of HCI requires knowledge of which aspects of the contributing disciplines are applicable to particular problems. While HCI research is very much concerned with theoretical and methodological advances in the development of new technologies, there is also much interest in learning how to apply the research to practical situations, and understanding from the problems and practices that occur.

HCI, ERGONOMICS AND HUMAN FACTORS

'Human factors' is one of the many terms used to describe the study of people and their behaviour in the context of using machines, tools and other technological developments to carry out work. The term originated in the USA: in the UK the same areas of concern are addressed by the study of ergonomics. However, in the USA ergonomics is much more narrowly defined, and is largely concerned with ensuring that a machine's design takes account of the physical characteristics of the intended population of users. For example, the size and force requirements of a key on a keyboard are tested to ensure that it is within the optimum range to enable a population of users with known finger sizes and strengths to depress the key comfortably and easily. While this kind of input to design is important, the size and force requirements of a key are not the only characteristics that are likely to affect a person's use of the keyboard. Other influential factors might include the colour, labelling, position and function of the key, in addition to the person's experience with other keyboards and their knowledge of the task being performed.

Ergonomists in the UK are concerned with these and many other factors that are known to affect how people use machines. When the machine or tool is a computer system, the factors that affect the use of that computer include the way that information is presented on the screen, the command language through which the person communicates with the computer, the instruction manual and training provided, in addition to the physical characteristics of the input and output devices (e.g. keyboard and display monitor).

Human–computer interaction includes appropriate parts of human factors and ergonomics. It is concerned with understanding how computers and people can interactively carry out both existing and new tasks. HCI is concerned with all aspects of the design and use of computers. Research in HCI is focused towards obtaining a better understanding of how computers can be designed and used efficiently and effectively. This research is intended to lead to the formation of principles, guidelines, methods and tools to improve the design and development of good interactive computer systems. There is great concern in HCI about how the research findings are put into practice, and about the kinds of problems and solutions that practitioners (e.g. designers and evaluators) are facing.

PSYCHOLOGY AND HCI

Psychological theory and methods form a major contribution to our understanding of HCI. Psychology is concerned with understanding, modelling, predicting and explaining what is perhaps the most complex phenomenon of all, namely human behaviour. Psychology approaches the study of human behaviour from the perspective of attempting to identify the mental structures and processes that must exist in order to account for behaviour.

Psychological methods include observations, surveys, laboratory experiments, case studies, simulations and other forms of investigating the many different aspects of human behaviour. Psychological theories cover a wide range of topics including, motivation, emotion and cognition; social, biological and organizational aspects; human development and maturation from birth to death; and aspects of normal and abnormal human behaviour. It is difficult to say which areas of psychology are the most relevant for HCI since all aspects of human behaviour may, on occasion, have some effect on a person's interaction with a computer and a computer may affect human behaviour in many ways. Designers and developers of computer systems are commonly required to make decisions based on assumptions about the user's prior knowledge, experience and ability to learn. These assumptions directly influence the quality of the interaction between the person and the computer. Consequently, much emphasis is placed on understanding how people acquire, store and use knowledge, and on how they use this knowledge in the many and complex tasks that people perform.

HCI AND COMPUTER SCIENCE

HCI is a subdiscipline of computer science. Computer science is concerned with the theory, methods and practice of computing. Its central concern is with constructing and programming computers, and as such, it considers languages for writing programs, machines upon which programs can be executed, structural properties of programs, architectures for designing programs and much more. HCI is concerned with all of the issues of computer science. It raises special concerns for computer science; for example, the user interface has to be programmed to anticipate different kinds of input, and to produce sophisticated outputs. This leads to the design of a language through which the user can control and make use of the rest of the program. Many other issues arise from HCI problems such as the requirement for fast response times, advanced forms of graphical displays, the use of logics and mathematics to specify the complex nature of user interaction, and the development of new programming environments to allow user interfaces to be constructed more easily.

User-interface design must form part of system design; to this end the process of system design must be understood and possibly changed to allow due consideration of the various requirements of designing user interfaces. This involves developing techniques and methods of software engineering that can accommodate and influencially improve the design of user interfaces. Design is very much about identifying requirements and ensuring that those requirements have been met. Consequently, HCI must identify the special and extra requirements of interactive systems, and must ensure that there are adequate and reliable ways of knowing that the design meets those requirements.

HCI, USERS AND ORGANIZATIONS

HCI is concerned with the design, development and support of computer systems with people (users) in mind. This requires, among other things, a clear understanding of how well the design matches the needs of users and their tasks. Matching the design to users' needs and tasks involves many of the analytical and investigative methods of psychology and computer science. For example, surveys and protocol analyses are employed to identify who are the users; observations and interviews are used to identify what the user tasks are; experiments and prototyping are conducted to assess which design option best satisfies both user needs and user task requirements, and specifications are used to describe and check the resultant designs.

There is, on occasion, confusion about what or who is meant by the term 'user'. Distinctions are sometimes made between 'end-users' and 'users'. In some contexts the 'user' is thought of as the person or organization who commissions the system. For example, in these terms the 'user' might refer to a chain of travel agents or perhaps the Stock Exchange. In this book, the term 'user' will be used to refer to the person who directly interacts with the computer to carry out tasks in a given domain. The term 'user-organization' is used to refer to the organization, institution or other organizational structure in which the person who directly interacts with the computer is situated. The term 'client' refers to the person or organization who may order or commission the design of the computer system.

Design normally involves some form of design requirement, and in the case of computer design, these often include 'user requirements' and the 'clients' requirements'. The clients' requirements may not address, completely or partially, the user requirements. The user requirements should give the designer guidance or information about the users of the system. The clients' requirements may provide some information about what constraints and organizational needs the design for the system will have to meet.

Engineering approximations

When it comes to identifying the needs and requirements of the user, it is often said that users are all different and therefore it is impossible to take account of all their individual needs. Individual differences and an inability to translate user needs into design recommendations are, of course, real problems. They are, however, problems that can be and are solved by HCI. For example, psychological theories attempt to understand human behaviour in terms of the mental structures and processes that all members of a given population are assumed to possess. In applying a theory to make predictions about a particular person's behaviour on a given task, the theory has to be sufficiently robust to allow for deviations and yet still provide sufficient sensitivity to predict behaviour. In applying psychological and other theories to problems in HCI, we are often faced with the task of applying theories developed to explain behaviour observed on artificial tasks carried out in laboratories to problems of a much more complex nature found in the 'real world'. One way of accommodating the added complexity of the real world is to take an engineering approach and approximate to some acceptable level of tolerance. This is not unusual or unacceptable in engineering subjects where, for example, the stress factors of concrete might be determined in the laboratory and then approximations are made to predict the stress tolerance of a design for a new motorway bridge. However, the risks involved in doing this are sufficiently large that wide safety margins are built into any predictions. Much research in HCI has been aimed at testing the applicability of existing psychological theories of behaviour and, where necessary, developing new theories to account for the rich and complex behaviour that occurs in HCI. The goals, operators, methods and selection (GOMS) approach of Card, Moran and Newell (1983) is one example of an engineering approach to modelling user task behaviour in HCI.

THE USER INTERFACE

The interface between the user and the computer is known as the user interface. Simplistically, it might be thought that the computer begins at the keyboard and screen or other forms of input and output devices, and the user finishes at that point. The interaction between the user and computer does indeed occur through input and output devices such as these, but the user interaction is influenced by many things that are often hidden from the user's view. Consequently, the user interface is more than what is visible or touchable at the various input and output devices that the person uses. For example, a user of a computer system is required to understand the meaning of commands and replies, to anticipate the effects of commands on what the computer program will do, and to relate and translate their own task goals and plans into system-specific commands that will allow those goals to be achieved. The interface between the user and computer is unclear. There is not just a physical separation of person and machine.

The person must at the very least do the following:

- Recognize that the computer system can be used to achieve a particular goal.
- Identify the necessary procedures to be carried out in using the computer to achieve the desired goal.
- Know the necessary commands to give to the computer system to access the required computer functions as part of carrying out their tasks.
- Identify and understand the various states that the program is in and the replies that are issued by the program.
- Possess the necessary skills, for example, typing, pointing, or speaking, to be able to input commands to the computer system.

There is a shared responsibility between the person and the computer for achieving the task goal. The user and computer share responsibilities for doing different activities that together contribute to the achievement of the task goal. Thus, the nature of the interactions between the user and the computer is one in which they together form an interactive system for carrying out tasks. That is, the user and computer interact with each other to produce some desired end state that constitutes the task goal.

Dialogues and tasks

The person and the computer must interact by communicating with each other to allow the user to achieve an identified goal. This communication can be thought of as a kind of dialogue. The communication is not just a set of discrete commands and responses, but a structured set of statements, requests, questions and answers which are directed towards achieving a common goal. In this sense, dialogues between users and computers are open to investigation using approaches from linguistics. The dialogue can be investigated using discourse analysis techniques, and modelled using grammars and other linguistic devices.

Of course, dialogues are most successful between partners with shared and common knowledge. This implies that the user must have adequate and appropriate knowledge of the computer, and the computer or computer-system designer should have adequate and appropriate knowledge of the user. In addition, since users and computers interact to achieve task goals, there must be some way for the designer to understand the different kinds of tasks that users might want to carry out. Tasks do not exist of themselves. They are not waiting to be discovered. People create tasks as ways of achieving goals. The designer can create new goals and tasks for the user and can also enable the user to create and achieve new goals.

A key problem for interactive system design is identifying what information the user needs, and finding ways of representing the necessary information to the user. There are two broad classes of tasks that are relevant to HCI; the tasks that the user must perform to use the computer, and the tasks that the user can perform with the computer. The former are known as *internal tasks*, and the latter as *external tasks*. For example, an internal task is the particular sequences of keystrokes and button presses that the user has to carry out to select a particular printer to send a document file for printing, and to specify the number of pages and copies of the document to be printed. Examples of external tasks are the activities of writing, reading, correcting and rewriting that a person would carry out in producing a document. Of course, there is a strong connection between the internal and the external tasks because of the decisions made by the designer of the computer. The designer can directly influence both the internal and external tasks.

If users and computers are to form an efficient interactive system that can perform tasks, then the user must know how to perform the internal tasks that are required to carry out the external tasks. Through the design of the computer system, the designer is making choices about what the user must know. To make these choices the designer must have some way of finding out what it is that users know already, and how difficult it will be for them to learn something new that might be necessary to use the computer system.

Interaction between people and computers involves some form of dialogue. Dialogues involve the taking of turns and the exchanging of information while achieving a given goal. In some cases, dialogues can be like conversations in which the utterances (for example, commands and responses) are almost immediate. In contrast, other dialogues can be more like literary correspondences in which the time between the exchanges is hours or days rather than seconds or minutes. For example, batch processing of large amounts of data for statistical or numerical analyses are tasks that are often undertaken through a dialogue that more closely resembles a literary correspondence than a conversation. The type of task being undertaken is one determinant of whether or not a conversational or correspondence style of dialogue between the user and the computer is required. For example, booking an airline seat requires a conversational style of dialogue involving questioning and answering, requests and statements. The user of such a system typically wants to know if there is a flight, if there is a seat, and the price/class of the seat. The airline typically wants to know if a no-smoking seat is required, if there is any special meal requirement, the method of payment and the name of the passenger. To design an interactive system involves recognizing what constitutes an optimum dialogue and then providing the necessary structures. The dialogue must support external tasks such as booking an airline seat, and it will give rise to internal tasks such as selecting options from a menu, keying in text, etc.

A FRAMEWORK FOR HCI

If we are to understand both the contributions to be made to HCI from the many different disciplines and the problems that HCI must solve, some form of framework is required. Long and Dowell (1989) have proposed a framework for HCI that abstractly deals with the different representations and processes that occur in applying knowledge from an appropriate discipline to a particular applied problem. This general framework is not particular to HCI, and can be used for other areas of research requiring the development of theories taken from a core discipline which needs to be transformed and made relevant to particular application problems. For example, Diaper and Johnson (1989) show how the design of an information technology training syllabus can be understood in terms of this framework.

Carroll (1990) has developed a more useful and particular framework for HCI that encompasses and shares the perspective of HCI that permeates this book. Carroll's framework is essentially a task–artefact cycle that views HCI as requiring an understanding of tasks and designs, and the way the two cyclically influence each other.

A task implicitly sets design requirements for the development of artefacts (computer systems are one form of artefact), and the use of artefacts redefines the task for which the artefact was originally designed (Fig. 1.1). As Carroll (1990) points out, typewriting altered office tasks, word processors altered them again, and desktop publishing altered them even further. In each case, changed tasks themselves suggested new needs and opportunities for further changes. To design more useful artefacts we must better understand the tasks people are undertaking and better apply our understanding of tasks to the process of design. Carroll further refines the

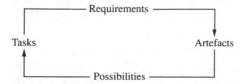

Figure 1.1   Task–artefact cycle (after Carroll, 1990)

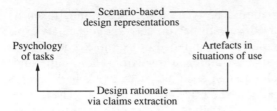

Figure 1.2   An elaboration of the task–artefact cycle (after Carroll, 1990)

task–artefact cycle to include the design activities of computer science and the psychological basis for understanding tasks (Fig. 1.2).

Carroll argues that the psychology of tasks provides an appropriate scientific basis for understanding tasks in HCI. Thus it is just those aspects of psychology that can help us generate a psychological understanding of task behaviour that is required (this is discussed in Chapters 2, 3 and 4). A psychological theory of tasks is described in Chapters 11 and 12 known as task knowledge structures.

Design rationale provides a detailed description of the issues, positions and reasons given for designs. MacLean, Bellotti and Young (1990) provide examples of this. In Chapter 6, the methods and process of design are considered together with the requirements and specifications used in software engineering.

User-interaction scenarios provide generalized or decontextualized descriptions of tasks that people do and would like to accomplish. A method of analysing these tasks is given in Chapter 11. Through the process of design, the task scenarios are elaborated to become device- or computer-application specific, and describe how those tasks will be accomplished. In Chapter 12, models and notations for describing tasks and elaborating designs in terms of task scenarios are provided.

'Artefacts in use' provides a detailed description of the computer-system design in terms of its effects on the tasks, users and other features of the domain. In carrying out a design–artefact analysis there must be some evaluation of the design and its usage. Chapter 7 discusses methods of evaluation in HCI. One weakness of Carroll's framework is that it does not provide any space for the tools and methods that are used in design and the effects these may have on our capabilities for developing new artefacts. Moreover, the structure of a user interface and its links to other parts of software can also be modelled and reasoned about. To this end, models of user-interface designs are discussed in Chapter 8 together with environments that support those models.

Consequently, the structure of this book reflects a conceptualization of HCI that emphasizes a psychological approach to understanding users and their tasks, together with a concern for the methods, processes and tools to support design. This elaborated framework (Fig. 1.3) reflects the relation between users, tasks and designs and the different forms of process that are involved in relating these three components in HCI. It includes various forms of representation including formal specifications, computational models, prototypes and informal models. It requires methods and tools to support it—some of which exist, others do not and have yet to be developed. The advances that have been and are being made in each of these areas are discussed in subsequent chapters.

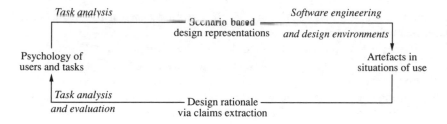

Figure 1.3   An elaborated framework for a task–design cycle

OVERVIEW OF THE BOOK

This book presents a particular approach to HCI that focuses on the three main topics, *users, computers* and *tasks*. To this end, first some of the fundamental issues of human psychology are considered to allow some understanding of how users learn, represent and remember facts and procedures. The computer is considered from the perspective of the processes of designing interactive computer systems and the special considerations necessary for designing user interfaces. Having considered some of the more fundamental aspects of users and user interfaces, the different types of model that have been used in HCI are discussed in detail. These models build upon the fundamental issues of users and user interfaces to provide sophisticated approaches to designing and evaluating various aspects of an interactive computer system. Through these sophisticated models, the perspective of tasks becomes a predominant issue. This leads to a detailed consideration of how to analyse tasks and how to consider the internal and external task as part of the design for the interactive system.

In the next four chapters, an overview of some fundamental aspects of cognitive psychology are provided, which introduce the reader to the theoretical and empirical findings about human memory, learning, knowledge representation and skill acquisition. These are chosen from the vast field of psychology to provide an awareness of how our knowledge of the psychological structures and processes can explain and help us predict human behaviour. The coverage of these topics is related to HCI by providing examples and illustrations of user-interface designs.

Chapter 2 considers basic memory structures and processes including the following: short-term memory experiments, chunking, working memory and retrieval from working memory, long-term memory, and recall from categories. In Chapter 3, memory processes and knowledge structures, recall and recognition, facilitation and priming, interference effects, elaborated memory structures, inference memory recall, and memory for gist are considered. The fundamentals of user psychology are continued in Chapter 4 with the consideration of knowledge and knowledge representation. Discussions about propositional representations, analogical representations and procedural representations are covered. Chapter 5 provides a discussion of the nature of expertise and skill acquisition, including the stages of skill acquisition, and the differences between experts and novices.

Chapter 6 considers the process of design from a software engineering perspective. Chapter 7 describes the methods of evaluation that can be used in the context of interface design. Chapter 8 considers the models and architectures of user interfaces and user-interface management systems.

Having considered users and user-interface design, the range of models that have been developed in HCI are considered. These include models of users, tasks and interfaces. Examples are given of where these models have been used, and the strengths and weaknesses of the various approaches are discussed. From this we begin to see what kind of models are useful in HCI and how they can be applied to user-interface design. These models are considered in Chapters 9 and 10. Chapter 9 provides an overview of models in HCI and outlines three early forms of model, namely: Command Language Grammar; Goals, Operations, Methods and Selection rules; and Task Action Language. Chapter 10 continues to discuss HCI models including the more recent ones such as Task Action Grammar and Cognitive Complexity Theory.

Chapters 11 and 12 provide a review of approaches to task analysis and present a theory of tasks known as Task Knowledge Structures and a method of task analysis known as Knowledge Analysis of Tasks. This method includes techniques for collecting task data, carrying out the analysis, constructing the task model and using the task model to make user-interface design decisions.

After detailing how to analyse tasks, Chapter 13 considers how to develop and elaborate designs based on task scenarios. The use of task-based models are considered with respect to design specifications, design methods and design environments.

2 AN INTRODUCTION TO HUMAN MEMORY

Summary

- Fundamental structures and processes of human memory are introduced. Memory was thought to be comprised of two related structures: *short-term memory* and *long-term memory*. Short-term memory appears to be a transient store in which information is temporarily encoded. Long-term memory appears to be a more permanent store in which information is maintained over long periods of time.

- A more appropriate analogy of memory is to think not in terms of two separate stores but of two functional states of the same system. Short-term memory is now thought of as a form of *working memory* in which information is temporarily placed in an active state so that other cognitive processes can be brought into operation.

- The capacity of working memory is limited, but it seems that this is not an absolute limit; instead, the capacity varies as a function of the meaningfulness of the information that is currently active.

- Long-term memory contains *knowledge* that is normally stored in an inactive state. To be used, this knowledge must be activated. Thus retrieving and using our knowledge requires activating information in long-term memory. Once the item has been activated, it enters working memory. Knowledge is retrieved from memory by search processes. *Serial search processes* are hypothesized to account for the fact that, as the number of items to be searched through increases, the time to retrieve an item also increases. An alternative hypothesis proposes that searching is a *parallel process*, with finite activation correlated to the size of the set to be searched.

- *Retrieval* of knowledge already in working memory is quicker than retrieval of knowledge in long-term memory. Furthermore, familiar or well-known information is retrieved from long-term memory quicker than unfamiliar or poorly known information. Knowledge is *structured* in memory. One form of structuring is in terms of *categories* or *classes*. Retrieval is quicker if the category of

11

which an item is a member has recently been activated. Conversely, as the delay between the prior activation of a category and current retrieval increases, retrieval time increases. It takes us longer to activate weaker memories. *Forgetting* can be thought of as extremely long retrieval times.

This chapter is the first of three chapters which together provide an overview of important psychological theories of human behaviour and their consequences for HCI. The ability of people to remember, recognize and recall information is taken for granted. Without this facility we would find it impossible to function normally in the world. It would be impossible to remember your name, who you knew, where you lived, where you had been or what you had done. Cases of memory loss do occur and have severe disabling effects. Sufferers of the various forms of amnesia and memory disorders must keep constant records in the form of notes and reminders; in severe cases even these notes and reminders are useless because the person cannot even remember writing them.

Much research has been carried out on the nature of human memory from philosophical, anatomical, physiological and psychological perspectives. Psychologists have developed theories of the structures, processes and functions of human memory, and have carried out many different types of empirical investigation to test predictions about human behaviour.

An understanding of human memory has much to contribute to HCI, since it can help us to design computer systems that would assist people to overcome the limitations of human memory. More importantly, an understanding of human memory could prevent the design of computer systems that place even greater loads on our memories. like having a big subject to remember 25 things

Unfortunately, most computer systems presently available often do place unnecessary loads on human memory. Consider a typical non-interactive program running on a dumb terminal linked to a remote computer. The user types in obscure commands, often more difficult to learn than a conventional programming language and bearing little relationship to a natural language. No immediate meaningful feedback about the effects of those commands is given to the user, who consequently has no way of knowing either what the computer is doing or what to do next, until, if they are lucky, the results of the previous command appears on the screen. In these kinds of environment the user is ultimately trying to perform some task, such as writing a computer program, carrying out a mathematical calculation or writing a letter, which itself may place a demanding 'cognitive load' on the user. As a consequence of the *extra* load brought about because of the poor user-interface, the user finds it difficult to concentrate and proceed with the main task (i.e. writing the program, etc.) because they have to remember the command set for instructing the program editor to open the file, to display its contents, to position the cursor at a particular point in the program text, and so on. It is surprising that lengthy programs were ever written in these conditions.

The point is that the computer system must be designed to complement and extend our capabilities, not to place additional burdens on people, and to do this we should be aware of what these capabilities are and what affects our performance.

Immanuel Kant popularized a threefold categorization of mental faculties: cognitive, affective and conative; or knowing, feeling and willing. The study of cognition is primarily concerned with knowing and includes the nature of human intelligence, understanding and problem solving. It also includes the study of how we learn and develop skills and use our knowledge. It is far too easy to overlook or be unaware of the sophisticated mental processes that must operate to allow us to perform tasks such as understanding or writing a computer program or using a word processor. The inner workings of the human mind are far more sophisticated than the most complex and advanced computer systems. The most complex machine is, by definition, not as complex as the mind that created it.

It would be impossible to cover the whole of cognitive psychology even at a very cursory and introductory level in just a few chapters of this book. However, cognitive psychology plays a major role in our understanding of people. Rather than attempt a quick summary of cognitive psychology, this and the following chapters provide a more detailed account of some of the fundamental cognitive processes relevant to understanding human–computer interaction. These include memory processes and structures, knowledge representation and processing, problem-solving strategies, learning and skill acquisition.

FUNDAMENTAL MEMORY STRUCTURES AND PROCESSES

The world we perceive and know is very different from the inanimate universe of physics and chemistry. People and animals interpret the physical world and develop some *symbolic representation* of the colours, sounds, objects, spaces, actions and events that are *perceived*. Thinking is the manipulation of internal representations of the world. Furthermore, people attach values to occurrences of objects and events in the world and attribute intentions to actors. In short, we interpret the physical world to form some understanding of that world. The interpretations we make are themselves influenced by those we have made in the past. More precisely, our perception of the world largely is determined by our existing knowledge of the world. For example, consider the way in which a musician perceives a sequence of notes drawn on a score sheet. To the non-musician these are simply dots arranged in some seemingly arbitrary pattern on a series of lines. However, to the musician these dots have a meaning in terms of tunes and melodies. The musician uses existing knowledge of music and notation to interpret these marks as notes and further to interpret these notes as tunes. The musician also builds up expectancies of what note or sequence of notes are likely to come next. Hence, the expert musician's reading time for music notation is far less than that of the inexperienced musician. A more common example is in reading English words and sentences. Reading involves predicting or having expectancies about what letters, words, phrases or sentences are likely to come next. For example, in English, at the letter level we normally expect the letter 'u' to follow 'q'. Similarly, knowledge about the world also helps us to interpret the meaning of sentences by giving us a *context* in which to interpret the words.

In a similar manner, the programmer is able to interpret a program as a sequence of instructions to enable a certain sort of machine to carry out some act. People

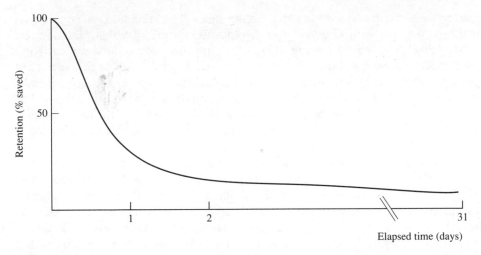

Figure 2.1   Amount retained after varying amounts of elapsed time (Ebbinghaus 1885)

construct and store internal representations of the world in memory. These memorial representations contain knowledge of the world derived from past experiences. Knowledge is stored in memory and accessed when it is needed to direct and interpret current and future actions and perceptions. Thus, our memory forms an important part of our everyday life. It enables us to interpret the world and to acquire new knowledge through learning processes, and also to plan and control our actions in the world. Memory is constantly processing information to retrieve, acquire and reorganize our knowledge of the world.

Human memory has been the subject of enquiry for many years. Plato, (427–347 BC), was among the first to theorize about the nature of human memory. Considerably later, Ebbinghaus (1885) undertook a series of experiments, using himself as a subject, in which he learned and subsequently attempted to recall lengthy lists of words. Some of the results of Ebbinghaus's early study on memory are shown in Fig. 2.1. He found that as the time since his original learning of a list of words increased, his ability to remember the list decreased. Two features of this are worth mentioning: first, the amount of forgetting was large and rapid at first but this rate of forgetting soon decreased; second, the amount remembered even after 31 days was much greater than zero and did not decrease much after the sixth day.

Ebbinghaus's early experiments correctly identified that the delay between learning and recall of information and the amount of information to be remembered are two important factors influencing memory performance. From this single experiment it would be difficult to make any generalizations, however many replications of these results in a variety of contexts have been carried out using much more rigorously controlled experiments. From these studies we can generally conclude that memory retains information without decay over long periods of time. However, much information may be lost from memory.

There are many implications of these conclusions for HCI. For instance, we should not expect people to be able to remember every piece of information they are presented with. A particular example of this would be in the design of menus and

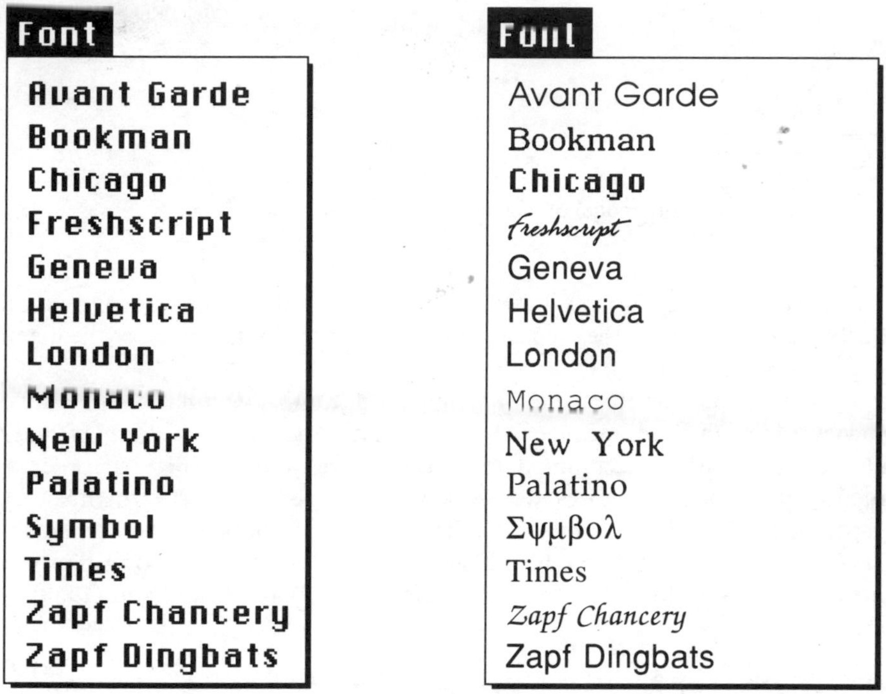

Font	Font
Avant Garde	Avant Garde
Bookman	Bookman
Chicago	Chicago
Freshscript	Freshscript
Geneva	Geneva
Helvetica	Helvetica
London	London
Monaco	Monaco
New York	New York
Palatino	Palatino
Symbol	Σψμβολ
Times	Times
Zapf Chancery	Zapf Chancery
Zapf Dingbats	Zapf Dingbats

Figure 2.2   Font menus shown written in a common font and in the font type

command sets. For example, in word processing applications such as MacWrite or MsWord there are many fonts that can be selected. The menus provide the names of each font but the user must remember what each font looks like. Consequently, people tend to examine all the fonts and then choose one or two that they prefer and continually use these, to the exclusion of others. After some time the appearances of other fonts listed on the menu will have been forgotten. A better option might be to write each menu item on the font menu in the font itself (Fig. 2.2), or alternatively to provide an example of two or three characters to accompany each menu item.

Ebbinghaus's experiments were largely concerned with memory over long periods of time (hours and days) as opposed to memory over shorter periods of time (seconds and minutes). At an early stage in memory research, it was recognized that memory over short periods of time seemed to have different characteristics from memory over longer periods of time. The classic example of differences between memory over long and short periods is readily exhibited in our memory for telephone numbers. Most normal people have little problem in holding a 7-digit telephone number in their memory long enough to dial it. However, unless the telephone number is *rehearsed* it is extremely likely that after a period of time the number will be forgotten. Rehearsal can occur through many processes, perhaps the most common is repeating the number over and over to yourself.

Similarly, for example, in using a word processor with multiple menus through which the different functions for inserting, deleting, moving text, etc., are accessed, the user is required to remember what menu items are available and on which menu

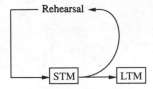

Figure 2.3   An early two store model of memory

they can be found. The inexperienced user may forget what functions were present on a previously seen menu unless they *rehearse* the items, or unless the name of the menu acts as a good retrieval cue.

Phenomena such as forgetting and rehearsal led to the postulation of a two structure view of memory storage; one to accommodate data from *short-term memory* experiments, and another to accommodate data from *long-term memory* experiments. Consequently, two memory stores were postulated, one for short-term memory (STM) and one for long-term memory (LTM). LTM was assumed to be permanent while STM was assumed to be more transient (Fig. 2.3). The distinction between STM and LTM was developed in the work of Hebb (1949) and Broadbent (1958).

SHORT-TERM MEMORY EXPERIMENTS

Experimental investigations of STM were numerous during the late fifties and most of the sixties. Some of the earlier and now classical experiments of this era were those of Brown (1958), Peterson and Peterson (1959) and Murdock (1962). These experiments demonstrated that under certain conditions memory has a transient storage capability.

Typically, subjects in these experiments were asked to study lists of nonsense items each containing three letters and then to recall the list over varying periods of time, ranging from immediate recall to, for example, 18 seconds delay.

The experimenters discovered that, when the subjects were prevented from rehearsing the letters by having to count backwards in threes from some random number (e.g. 574, 571, 568, etc.), recall deteriorated as a function of the duration of the retention interval, to the extent that after nine seconds only one in three of the letters were correctly recalled (Fig. 2.4). This demonstrated that information presented in this way is subject to rapid decay from memory if people are unable to rehearse the material.

Further experiments by Glanzer and Cunitz (1965) demonstrated that two storage mechanisms could be postulated under conditions of free recall, in which subjects were allowed to recall the material in any order they chose. Glanzer and Cunitz presented subjects with fifteen, 15-word lists of monosyllabic nouns (e.g. dog). Each word was presented for one second with a two-second interval between successive words. After the last word in each list, the subject was required either to write out the list immediately or to count aloud from a random number for either 10 or 30 seconds before writing out the list.

The results of this experiment demonstrated that items appearing later in the list of

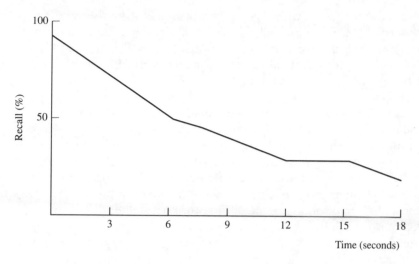

Figure 2.4 Short-term memory is subject to rapid decay (from Murdock 1962)

items to be memorized are subject to forgetting when the recall period is delayed (Fig. 2.5). However, the earlier items were not affected by the delay between the initial presentation of the list and subsequent recall. This suggests that the early items of the list were somehow easier to recall than the later items. Interestingly, with immediate recall (0-second delay), the proportion of correct recall of items at the end of the list and those at its start was almost the same. It seemed that with the delay, only those items from the end of the list were forgotten. The researchers assumed that these differences in recall reflected characteristics of short-term memory. These and other experiments by Brown (1958), Peterson and Peterson (1959), Murdock (1962) and others suggested that short-term memory store was of limited capacity, transient in nature and subject to interference, and that items would be lost from memory if not rehearsed.

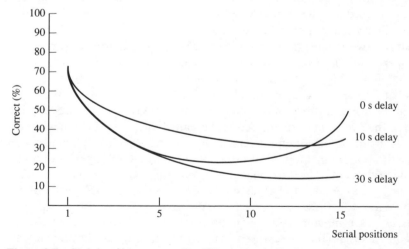

Figure 2.5 Serial position curve for different periods of recall delay (from Glanzar and Cunitz 1965)

The nature of the experiments which led to this theory of memory were largely similar. Subjects were typically presented with a list of items and required to recall items from the list in the same order or position in which they had appeared in the original list. Later we shall consider in more detail what happens when people are free to recall items in any order they choose.

Consider the implications of these limitations of memory on HCI. We have seen that people can only be expected to remember small amounts of newly presented information and that if the order of items is important this presents extra problems. It will be those items towards the end of a list or ordered sequence that are remembered well for short periods of time (this is known as the *recency effect*) but will be forgotten over longer periods of time. The earlier items will be remembered better throughout (this is known as the *primacy effect*), and the items in the middle of the sequence are most likely to be poorly recalled for both short and long recall periods.

In many programs the user is required to interact with the application by using a command language or by complex menu structures. Help, when provided, might be on the syntax of the command (if the user knew what the command was) or on the function of a particular menu item. Clearly, there is much load being placed on the user's memory by this kind of interface. Users frequently forget the command and its syntax and cannot therefore access the help. When they can remember the command, the syntactic string may be so long that users forget parts of it and leave out important arguments or parameters. This is not the users' fault but that of the design of the command language itself and/or the design of the help facilities provided (usually it is both the language and the help that are at fault).

In other interactive programs there may be less load placed on the user's memory than the above kind of designs. However, even with the kind of direct-manipulation interface currently popularized by the Apple Macintosh user interface, it is rare that a user can have the help facility of an application displayed at the same time as the area in which they are currently working. Consequently, the number of times users have to access help before they are able to complete a particular operation correctly is greater than need be. Also, notwithstanding the benefits of clearly labelled menus which can be pulled down, dragged across, or otherwise accessed, the user must still remember under which label a particular item is to be found.

Figure 2.6 shows two menus: (a) is taken from MsWord (Version 4.0) and (b) is taken from SuperPaint. Both are commercial applications that run on the Apple Macintosh. The first thing to notice is that both menus contain some similar command labels that the user can select. Those selectable items that are similar in name are, in fact, similar in function (i.e. they do the same things). However, note that the names of the two menus are different; (a) is called the Format menu while (b) is called the Style menu. So the user must remember that items such as 'plain text' can be found under the Format menu in MsWord (Version 4.0) but in SuperPaint 'plain text' is under the Style menu. The differences go beyond this: positioning items on the page can be done by the commands 'left justify', 'center' and 'right' in SuperPaint but in MsWord (Version 4.0) these are done by first selecting 'show ruler' and then selecting icons. A user moving between applications, a common activity when producing documents that contain text and figures or tables, would have problems remembering what items were on a particular menu, and could easily select the wrong

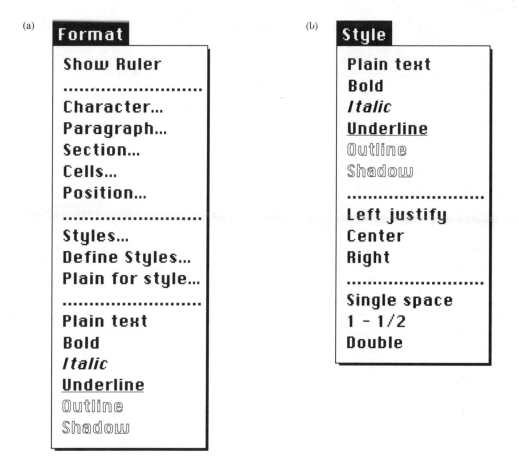

Figure 2.6 Menus adapted from current applications showing the inconsistency between structure of the menus

menu. This kind of design error could be overcome if some consideration had been made to assist users in their need to remember where items could be found by having some consistency between the two menu structures of the application packages. This kind of error in design is not unique to these particular application packages.

The problem of providing a consistent and coherent structure in menus can be related to classical research on human memory and, in particular, to the limitations of memory, such as its capacity, transience and potential for interference between items. Remember that the limitations on memory capacity identified earlier were largely taken from serial position recall experiments in which items had to be recalled in the same order as their position in the list. A further range of experiments, in which people were free to recall items in any order they chose, revealed some rather different results, especially when the lists were themselves structured or chunked together in meaningful ways.

CHUNKING

It is not useful to think of memory as two separate stores. Classic experiments by Miller (1956) showed that the STM store was not limited by the number of physical units but by the number of *chunks* or meaningful units of information.

For example, take the following string of numbers

    0 7 1 6 7 6 9 1 5 3

Are there ten units of information?

    0 7 1–6 7 6–9 1 5 3

Or are there three units of information?

If we store it as 'Mary's telephone number' then it might be treated as a single 'chunk' of information. The capacity of memory seems to vary with the meaningfulness of the information.

These are the kind of everyday experiences with which we are all familiar. It is easy to remember a telephone number but hard to remember a list of nine numbers. In the case of telephone numbers the order is important, but the list is broken down into a number of subparts, each of which has a meaning: area code (071), district code (676), subscriber number (9153). The task of remembering the number can be simplified if there is some inherent meaning in or associated with the items to be remembered. The task can be further simplified if the meaning of the structure to the items can be perceived and exploited by the user.

From studying how people performed in free-recall experiments, Miller (1956) and other psychologists since have found that people, when left to their own free choice about the order in which they recalled items from a list, remembered more items if they were able to identify some structure, meaning or relation between the items in the list. Consequently, it now seemed that the previously observed capacity limitations of memory were not always prevalent in everyday memory tasks.

Consider a further example: recalling six nonsense syllables such as

    PID LOM KIF GAN SAH TIB

may be difficult under the conditions of a short-term memory experiment. However, six monosyllabic words might be easier to recall under similar experimental conditions:

    PILE GATE ROAD PUMP BELL LIME

But, nine monosyllabic words might be more of a problem:

    HAT SAINT RUN GAIN FAN NAIL RICE LAKE TREE

However, a 27-word sentence might be less of a problem:

    Billy the kid was shocked when he saw the lawman approaching from behind the livery stable, for it was none other than his old friend, Pat Garret.

In all of the above examples, the units to be remembered are different in each case (letters, words, phrases). The units or chunks are defined as meaningful.

The two menus shown earlier in Fig. 2.6 each have some structure, which makes it easier for users to remember them than might otherwise be the case. Each menu is structured first of all under a main topic heading, format and style, and then subdivided into three further categories of menu selections. This structure helps relieve the load on user's memory by chunking into three the total number of items in each menu. However, is the structuring one that users themselves would have chosen, i.e. are the chunks meaningful to the user? While each menu may have a structure, it may not be the optimum for allowing users to find and access readily the available functions referred to by the menu item labels. In subsequent sections of this chapter, we shall consider the effects of category structure on recall. Understanding the structure of information both in the world and in the memory of a person is one of the most crucial aspects of ensuring a usable design.

WORKING MEMORY

There appears to be a contradiction between the results of the free-recall experiments and the serial-recall experiments. The contradiction centres around the effects of structure and meaning in improving recall. The root of the contradiction lies in the rather simplistic two-store model of memory as depicted in Fig. 2.3. Doubts were raised about the separateness of the two stores, STM and LTM. Memory can be improved by chunking together items that are similar and by identifying a common meaning. But how does the person have access to the meaning of the items and the chunks? Is the meaning of the chunk which unifies the individual items stored in STM? Clearly not, since that is transient, subject to interference, and limited in size. The answer seems to be that we store meaning or knowledge in LTM. This meaning must be accessed at the time the items in a list are being studied and when they are recalled. Accessing information from LTM in order to store information in STM was not included as part of the original two-store model of memory. Eventually, a new theory of memory emerged that postulated a single store with two different states, *active* and *inactive*. The active state of memory corresponds to the old concept of STM, but functions as a working memory (rather like a scratch pad). The inactive state of memory corresponds to the old concept of LTM.

When people are recalling units of meaningful information they are placing items from LTM in an *active state*. Consequently, we should think of STM not as a separate store but as a form of *working memory* in which information is held in an active state.

In summary, short-term memory characterizes a type of memory experiment. Working memory is a functional definition of a process of memory. Activation is the state in which information is held in working memory. There is a limited number of units of information that can be held in an active state at any one time. Furthermore, the duration for which we can hold information in an active state is limited. Finally, information, while active, may still be subject to interference from other information activated in working memory.

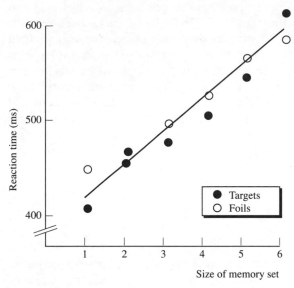

Figure 2.7   Reaction time to targets and foils as a function of the size of the memory set

Retrieval from working memory

If working memory is a functional state of our single-memory system then we must consider how information that is active is subsequently recalled. Sternberg (1969) showed that the rate of accessing memory was determined by the amount of information currently held active in working memory. Sternberg presented subjects with a set of digits, for example {2 7 9 5 4}, to be held in memory. He then presented a test or probe digit, for example {3}, and required the subject to say whether or not the probe digit was in the previous set (now held in memory). He varied the size of the set held in memory from one to six digits and recorded the time people then took to recognize targets and reject foils. For example, in the set {5 4 8 2 9 1 7}, a probe of {2} would be a target to be recognized and the probe {6} would be a foil to be rejected.

   The results (see Fig 2.7) showed that judgement or reaction time increased by about 38 ms. for every item in the memory set. Similar effects were found for letters, colours, shapes and words. The theory proposed by Sternberg was that searching through memory is a *serial* activity, and that the time for the search would therefore increase as the number of items to be searched through was increased. However, it is possible to think of an alternative, parallel mechanism that could function to produce similar results. For instance, if the speed of recognition were determined by the level of activation of the item, and if there were only a finite amount of resource for activating items available and furthermore, if we assume the number of items currently held in working memory to be negatively correlated with the level of activation of any one item, it would then follow that recognizing an item from a large set would take longer than recognizing an item from a smaller set because the level of activation of each member of the larger set was lower than in the smaller set. In such a system the search could be parallel and be influenced (decreased) by the size of the memory set to give slower recognition times for increased memory set sizes.

LONG-TERM MEMORY

Information can be retained in memory for longer periods than just the seconds or minutes of a short-term memory experiment, unless the person has suffered some form of brain damage through illness or injury. It is possible to remember events from our early childhood as well as facts that we learned many years ago. If it is the case that working memory is simply the area of memory that is currently activated then all the information that is held in memory but not currently activated is a form of long-term memory.

Information is normally held in an inactive state in memory. To use information it must first be activated. Retrieval of events and facts from memory is therefore a process of activating information. Once that information has been activated it is held in a working memory. However, the process of activation takes time and therefore the recall of information already in working memory is quicker than the recall of information from LTM. This can easily be demonstrated by a simple experiment involving immediate recall of presented material and delayed recall, where the time taken to recall information is then measured. For example, suppose that people in the experiment were presented with pairs of information to learn such as

DOG—3

and were required to learn this pair so that when later asked what word had been associated with 3 they would be expected to recall DOG. The time between being prompted with 3 and the recall of the word DOG can then be measured. Independently of this, the time between the original learning of the list and the subsequent prompting with one item of the list can be varied to give different conditions of immediate or delayed recall. It is assumed that delayed recall involves LTM and not working memory, and that immediate recall involves predominantly working memory and not LTM, since in immediate recall the items are still activated and therefore in working memory, while in delayed recall the items are no longer activated and therefore not in working memory. In which case, we would expect the delayed recall to have a longer recall time than the immediate recall condition, if recall from LTM is slower than recall from working memory, since items in LTM first have to be activated while items in working memory do not.

These two conditions were investigated in an experiment reported by Anderson (1985). Condition 1 involved immediate recall, in which the subjects were presented with two paired associates for 2 seconds and then immediately presented with one item of one pair and required to recall the other item of the same pair. In condition 2, the recall period was delayed by 48 seconds during which time subjects performed simple arithmetic operations. For example, following an initial 2-second presentation of

elephant—9
yellow   —4

Immediate recall:

Prompt with elephant → recall 9

Delayed recall:

48 seconds of mental arithmetic → prompt with elephant → recall 9

The results showed that 98 per cent correct recall was achieved under the immediate-recall condition while only 48 per cent recall was achieved when recall was delayed. This shows that under the immediate-recall condition subjects were recalling items from working memory, while in the delayed condition recall was only from LTM. The time to recall the item was also recorded and these data showed that under immediate recall the average time per item recalled was 1.31 s, while in the delayed-recall condition the average time per item recalled was 1.96 s. The results led Anderson to suggest that the time to recall information from LTM to working memory is about 0.65 s.

The relevance of this to HCI is that where the recall of information, such as command names, or function keys, etc., is required from LTM then we should expect users to take longer to recall that information than if they were able to hold it in working memory, perhaps with the aid of a help field or prompt. Also, we should expect people to recall items that are currently activated in working memory relatively quickly and with a high degree of accuracy.

RECALL FROM CATEGORIES

Recalling well-known information is not necessarily the same as recalling artificial and arbitrary information such as paired associates. We have already mentioned the fact that people structure information into meaningful units or chunks. One form of chunking is in terms of *categories*. A category is some grouping of similar objects or events. Categories can be hierarchically organized so that there is some structure to the information within a category. Consequently, categorization is very important to our understanding of how people structure and organize information into meaningful chunks. As we have seen, in free recall, where people are free to recall information in any order they choose, recall is improved. Furthermore, the order they choose to recall information is far from random. Their recall is organized so that related items are recalled together. The organization of information into categories is clearly something that people do when they recall information. The effect of information that is already structured into categories must also be considered. Information that is well structured is easier to learn and to recall, provided that the structure is one that is known and understood by the people required to recall the information. Consequently, we might expect people to recall information that is well structured into known categories better than information that is unstructured. One way that we might expect the recall of structured information to be better than the recall of unstructured information is in terms of the time it takes people to recall that information. Furthermore, one form of structuring that might have such an effect on the speed of recall is if the information is structured in terms of categories. For example, objects such as shoes, coats or hats, might be categorized as clothes or as a particular subcategory of clothes, like outdoor clothes.

Loftus (1974) investigated the time it took people to retrieve well known information about categories of natural objects. In Loftus's study the categories were, for example, 'dogs', 'fruit' and 'furniture'. The subjects in the experiment were required to recall an instance of a category after being told the name of the category and the first letter of the instance. For example:

    category—*dog*
    letter—*B*
    Instance recalled—*Boxer*

The time to recall an item under these conditions was on average 1.53 s.

Hence, recalling well-known items from memory appears to be faster than recalling artificial items such as paired associates (1.53 s for recall from categories as compared with 1.96 s for paired associates).

In her experiments, Loftus further investigated the time taken to recall other items from the same category after varying periods of delay. For example, a sequence of recall tasks that were as follows:

    recall task 1 = letter C from category furniture
    recall task 2 = letter B from category fruit
    recall task 3 = letter S from category furniture

would produce a one-item delay between first accessing the category, furniture, and then accessing the same category again for another instance. Again she recorded the time it took people to recall the instance of the category. Among the results Loftus found

    1-item delay = 1.21 s (on average)
    2-item delay = 1.28 s (on average)
    3-item delay = 1.33 s (on average)

This shows that recall from the same category is faster when the category has previously been accessed (1.21 s as compared with 1.53 s). This suggests that information about the category has been activated and is being held in an active state in working memory. This kind of effect, in which recalling one item from memory improves the recall of subsequent related items, is known as a *facilitation effect*, inasmuch as recalling one piece of information facilitates the recall of other pieces of information.

The categories of the sort described above were of natural objects, and those objects and their categories were very familiar to all who took part in the experiments. These experiments demonstrate how recall of information that is organized into categories is easier to recall than information that is less well organized. In addition, the experiments also show how information that is well known is quicker to recall than information that is novel or less well known.

The amount of learning affects the speed with which information can be retrieved from memory. As shall be seen in subsequent chapters, practice continues to affect the speed of recall over long periods of time. It seems that the stronger the memory trace is, the quicker it can be activated, and the more people practise recalling a piece of information, the stronger the memory trace appears to become.

This leads us to postulate further that forgetting may, in fact, be due to an inability to activate the correct trace (record) in memory. Rather than information being removed from LTM, it is possible that forgetting is due to accessing the wrong memory record or to a weak activation of a memory trace that is swamped by other currently activated traces. In this view, forgetting is more like very long retrieval times than deletion of information.

Categorization and its effects on human memory and learning is one of the most interesting aspects of human behaviour. Theoretically, it appears that one function of the various processes assumed to operate upon the information we store and retrieve is to organize that information into some form of structure that enables similar information to be related together through a membership relation (is a). This is just one of the many relations that are assumed to be used to represent our knowledge of the world in memory.

CONSISTENCY AND COHERENCE

In HCI the advantages, in terms of easier learnability and usability, that result from a well-structured design are only just beginning to be investigated. What it means to have a well-structured design, from the point of view of the user, is to ensure that the relations between the various real-world objects and operations represented by the computer with which the user interacts maximize the user's existing knowledge of those real-world objects and operations. As we have seen, information that is well known is easier (and quicker) to recall than novel or unfamiliar information. Consequently, we might predict that a design of a user interface which represents real-world objects and events in a faithful manner will be easier to use than one which uses novel or unfamiliar objects and operations, and which represents real-world objects and operations in an unfaithful manner.

The design of interactive systems is not restricted to simply reflecting what people currently know or do. If this were so, technology would never have advanced people's capabilities. However, in designing new ways of carrying out tasks and transforming the tasks that people can perform, it is important to recognize and consider the demands that are being made of the user. It is known that people find things easier to remember if there is a meaningful structure that the person can easily identify and learn. The designer can make it easier for the user to learn to use a program by developing a consistent and coherent structure to the user interface. Consistency can be achieved by having a categorical structure to the user interface.

Consistency is not a simple concept. You will come across different aspects of consistency throughout this book. What is or is not consistent is very much dependent upon the user's knowledge, the domain and the tasks. A fundamental property of consistency is that users are able to identify some common property or feature that exists between some or all aspects of the user interface. This enables them to develop a generalization that can be applied to all instances that possess the particular feature, and consequently reduce the number of different things that the user has to remember.

In the next chapter, the structure of knowledge and its organization in memory is considered. The special characteristics of memory for events and scenarios are also discussed.

Exercises

1 What is the distinction between short-term memory and working memory?
2 How is memory searched—in serial or in parallel?
3 What happens when people are allowed to recall things in any order?

4 When the items to be recalled are well known to the subject, how does this affect their recall?

5 Analyse the structure of the menus on any interactive program to identify how many different groupings and subgroupings there are.

6 Design a simple user interface, using just pen and paper, that has consistency and good categorical structuring.

3 MEMORY, ORGANIZATION AND STRUCTURES

Summary

- Memory organization can be thought of in terms of *propositional networks*. One model of memory makes use of the concept of *spreading activation* to explain the way in which information in memory is organized and related. Knowledge is assumed to be represented in terms of propositions, and individual items are linked together via an associative network of relations. Activation spreads through this network such that when a knowledge item is activated, other associated items of knowledge are also activated by a process known as *priming*.

- The structuring of knowledge in memory has consequences for the way activation spreads through the network. Activation of one node may *facilitate* the activation of another related node; however, in certain contexts additional information may *interfere* with existing knowledge. Thus we can consider each item of knowledge as part of an elaborated network to which new items of knowledge can be added; but adding new items may have facilitation and interference consequences for existing items in the network.

- Memory is not a static store. New information is added and existing information is reorganized. Two processes of memory reorganization are considered; *elaboration* and *inferencing*. Elaboration is where existing knowledge is used to elaborate the content of memory for a particular fact or event. Inferencing is where a number of related facts allow the person to arrive at a plausible conclusion.

- People are able to remember much more than the surface characteristics of a piece of information (e.g. what font a word is written in). Indeed, people are often better at recalling the meaning rather than anything else. One example of recalling meaning is *memory for gist*, in which a person ignores non-relevant or *redundant information* in a piece of text.

In this chapter we begin to consider models of how memory organizes information and the processes that operate on that information. In doing this, we also introduce some aspects of knowledge representation. Since memory is where our knowledge of the world is represented when we are modelling memory and memory processes, we are to some extent considering the form of knowledge representation. The format of knowledge representation and the processes of memory are not completely separable. To understand the kinds of memory phenomena that have been observed, we need to hypothesize both the form of representation and the processes that operate on that representation. However, the main concern of this chapter is to consider how the representation and organization of knowledge in memory is processed, and how such phenomena as recall, interference, facilitation and recognition, occur.

RECALL AND RECOGNITION

Recall is where we have remembered something; for example, remembering your login name and password. It can be contrasted with recognition, which occurs when you are presented with the item you are trying to remember, as, for example, when you list all the files in your directory to help you remember, by recognizing the name of the file you were looking for. 'Recognize' means to bring back into cognition or awareness—'re-cognize'.

Suppose you were presented with the following sentences:

1 The boxer chewed the meat.
2 The Siamese stole the meat.
3 The boxer chased the Siamese.

and, then at a later date (say after one week) you were asked to recall the same sentences. You might find it difficult to remember the exact words and sentence order that were originally presented. However, you would find it easier to *recall* the gist or *meaning* of each sentence.

It is much easier for people to recall the meaning of something than it is for them to recall the exactness of the event. This has many implications for human behaviour, such as, for example, in eyewitness testimonies, where the witness often finds it difficult to remember the details of an event, and may ignore or forget crucial evidence.

In using a computer, it is usually not adequate only to remember the meaning of things; the recall must often be veridical. The computer will usually only recognize correct commands or statements from the user. Consequently, if the user knows the meaning of the command required but cannot remember the correct command word, and the computer will not accept anything other than the correct command word, then the user will not be able to make the computer do what they want it to do. With this in mind, attempts have been made to provide multiple commands for the same function, and to tolerate misspellings.

In some areas of HCI, the lack of exactness in human memory has caused frequent usability problems to arise, to the extent that designers have now devised improved forms of user interfaces, with richer help facilities and forms of interaction which make allowances, or compensate, for the lack of exactness in human memory. For example, icons that are designed to closely resemble the thing (operation or data entity) that they represent are more easily recognized than obscure icons or meaning-

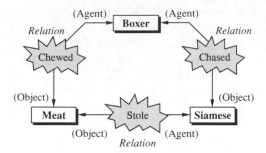

Figure 3.1   A propositional network representation for sentences 1, 2 and 3

less command names. Similarly, facilities that allow a user to search for the best match spelling of a particular item allow for the fact that the user may have forgotten how to spell the name or has mistyped it. Some help facilities allow the user to access the same section of the help from a number of alternative points. Designs that allow users to access the same information or function from a number of different routes are likely to be easier to use than those where there is only one access route to the information or resource, as we shall see below when we consider further the issues of recall.

Referring back to propositions 1, 2 and 3 above, if asked a question of the sort 'who chewed the meat?' you might find it harder to answer than if you were asked 'did the boxer chew the meat?' These two questions differ in that the first requires you to *recall* 'boxer' while the second requires you to *recognize* that the 'boxer' chewed the meat. In general, psychological experiments have shown that recognition is easier than recall, and that the amount of information that can be correctly remembered is far greater under conditions of recognition than of recall.

PROPOSITIONAL NETWORKS

The semantic structure of the three propositions 1, 2 and 3 above can be represented in a *propositional network*. A propositional network is one form of representation which identifies the types of relation between propositions. Each of the sentences are propositions and express some fact. Taken together the three sentences express relations between those facts. The complete set of relations in the three sentences can be modelled by a propositional network such as that in Fig. 3.1.

In a recall task such as answering the question, 'who ate the meat?', the person would have to access the appropriate memory structure (network) and search for links from 'meat' to 'boxer' before they could answer the question. However, in a recognition task the person is *cued* or *primed* in the question, as for example, 'did the boxer eat the meat?', with the node for 'boxer' and the node for 'meat'. Consequently, the person has more access points to the network and is therefore able to confirm or reject the truth of the supposed relation between the boxer and the meat by recognizing the existence of the relation between the concepts, 'meat' and 'boxer'.

Similarly, in the design of a computer system, the more opportunity that can be given to the user to access the correct node in their mental representation of the

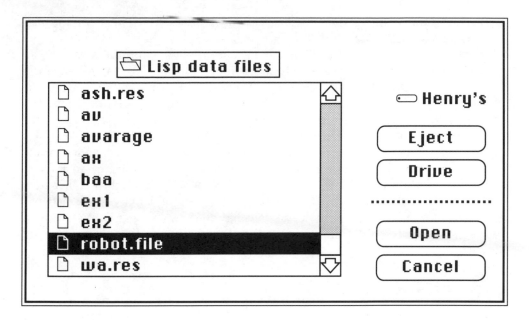

Figure 3.2   A selection window similar to the ones used in a typical Macintosh application

system, the more chance there will be that the user will remember how to use the system. Icons and labels in menus or on other parts of a display are one current mechanism for cueing a user's memory of what functions and information are available. Dialogue boxes that ask users to select from a list, button or proforma, help prevent the user from being unable to recall the names and syntax of the commands.

In Fig. 3.2 a particular form of screen representation is used to provide the user with a number of selections. This particular example, taken from the Apple Macintosh, is one that would be found under the 'open' menu item in the 'file' menu set. It is relevant to the present discussion since it uses labels and icons to help the user recognize the name and type of item that is available to be opened. The icons on the far left of the figure indicate that the labelled items 'ash.res', 'av', etc. are all files. The icon and the label 'Lisp data files' indicate that these are in the folder (a folder is the same as a directory), Lisp data files. The icon to the far right indicates that these files and this folder are on the disk named Henry's. The labelled boxes, 'eject', 'drive', 'open', and 'cancel', down the right of the figure are button options that can be selected.

In the example in Fig. 3.2, the names of files and folders do not have to be remembered in order to be opened because they are visible to the user at all times. The user is able to search the available files and folders and have the search constrained by the type of application that was used to create the file. Furthermore, the user can choose to open any of the files or cancel the search and return to the document or file currently being worked on. The user can easily see both what is available and what can be done next in this segment of the dialogue. Unfortunately, the user still has to remember by which application the file was created, since this particular form of interaction does not allow the user to view all of the files independent of their type.

In the next section the effects of cues on memory recall are introduced. A cue can be anything which triggers or activates information in memory. Icons are one form of cue to recall. Other forms of cueing are provided by prompts and reminders. The effect of these cues on memory is that they prime other items of information such that their subsequent recall is facilitated. Priming is the term used to refer to the effect a memory cue has on knowledge stored in memory. One way to think of this effect is that a cue primes recall from memory by increasing the activation of the items in memory above some ambient level of noise, and this increased level of activation makes it more likely that that information will be recalled rather than some other non-activated item. Noise refers to the level of activity in the network independent of any stimulation. Neural units have three states, inhibition—with no 'firing', with increased 'firing', and rest state—with noise-levels of activation (firing).

FACILITATION AND PRIMING

Recall of information from memory is improved if the task provides the person with alternative ways of accessing the required information. One theory of how this is achieved assumes that *priming* involves activating part of the *associative network* (Anderson, 1985) for the represented information. Information is assumed to be represented in a set of propositional networks (such as in Fig. 3.1) and these networks are connected by relational links. A process of activation is assumed that can spread through the network via the connecting relations. This view of priming has its origins in a theory of human associative memory (HAM) (Anderson and Bower, 1973), and has been further elaborated as an architecture for cognition and a computer simulation of human memory known as ACT* (Anderson, 1983). The theory accommodates much of the data from experiments on recall and recognition of facts and propositions.

An interesting experiment by Meyer and Schraneveldt (1971) showed that priming can facilitate the rate at which words are read. In the experiment, subjects were required to judge if pairs of items were both words or not. If either item in the pair was a non-word the subject was required to respond 'no'. The pairs were similar to the following examples:

| dog | house | grijk | boat | tyong |
| bone | bone | draft | frong | wrdot |

The results showed that subjects seemed to judge from top to bottom of a pair and that they were faster at discarding a pair if the first item in the pair was a non-word than if only the second item was a non-word. More interestingly, they found that the time to respond to positive pairs (i.e. when both items in the pair were words) varied systematically depending upon how closely related the items in the pair were. For example, the response to the pair 'dog and bone', would be faster than to the pair 'house and bone'. On average, the related pairs were judged to be 85 ms faster than were the unrelated pairs.

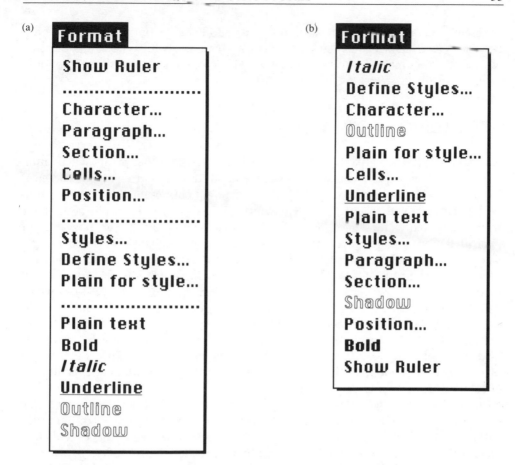

Figure 3.3   Menus that are coherent and well structured give rise to priming effects that can make reading quicker

COHERENCE

It is assumed that activation spreads from the first word in the pair to prime the second. This suggests that associative priming can facilitate the rate at which words are read. More importantly, it suggests that people can read material which has a strong *coherence* more easily than material with a weak or no coherence. The implications of this are far reaching. In the context of user-interface design, consider the design of a set of menu options. On the basis of this hypothesis, we would expect users to be able to read the list of menu items faster if there were a strong coherence between the items in the menu list than if they were randomly or arbitrarily chosen to appear together.

  In Fig. 3.3, two pulldown menus are shown; menu (a) has a more coherent structure to it than menu (b), in that it has clear separations between the different topics of the menu, which make use of division lines. We might expect that since the more coherent menu has exploited the relations between items in the menu by placing them together, then each item should prime subsequent items. Whereas, in the less coherent menu (b), any opportunity for the user to benefit from priming effects has been decreased since related items do not occur immediately together. Consequently, we might expect menu (b) to be slower to read, slower to search through and more prone to incorrect selections than menu (a).

SPREADING ACTIVATION

Ratcliff and McKoon (1981) investigated the time it took for the spread of activation to occur. In their experiment, subjects were required to commit to memory sentences like 'the elephant carried the log'. The subjects were then presented in a recognition-type experiment with nouns from the sentences and asked to report if the nouns were from the sentences they had previously seen. On some occasions the experimenter presented a priming noun from the same sentence (e.g. 'elephant' followed by 'log'). The results showed that subjects responded faster (624 ms) in the primed condition than in an unprimed condition (667 msec). A further manipulation of the experiment involved the delay period between the prime (elephant) and the target (log) which varied from 50 to 350 ms. In this condition it was found that recognition time decreased as the delay period increased (Fig. 3.4).

Priming begins almost immediately, within 50 ms of the prime occurring. Over the next 200 ms the strength of the priming effect on the speed of recognition of the target increases. This implies that there is an optimum period during which the facilitating effect of a prime on a target is strongest.

In the context of user interface design, this suggests that if the delay in presentation between related items is greater than 300 ms then the facilitating effect of the prime will be less than optimum. Consequently, in Fig. 3.3, with regard to the less coherent menu (b), related items that are separated by non-related items are less likely to be primed. This would lead us to expect that 'italic' would not prime 'plain text' or any

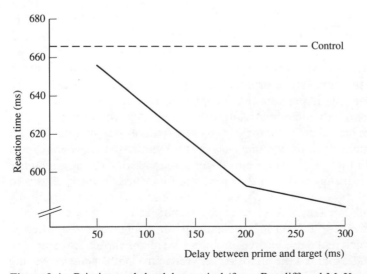

Figure 3.4 Priming and the delay period (from Ratcliff and McKoon, 1981)

other style item in the less coherent menu because it is separated from these by other non-style items, assuming that people read the menu from top to bottom.

INTERFERENCE EFFECTS

Unfortunately, the consequences of activation spreading through a network from one concept (or node) to another may not always be to our advantage. There is strong evidence that *interference* effects can occur which prevent the desired item from being easily recalled from memory. One form of interference occurs when items of information are linked together in memory to form new units and incorrect inferences are then made as a consequence. A further form of interference occurs when the number of possibly relevant facts or units of information is large. In this case it takes people longer to recall the actual fact, and sometimes they recall the wrong fact. One hypothesis of why this latter type of interference occurs, which is in keeping with the activation theory of memory, suggests that the more nodes that are activated in a network, the greater the probability of an incorrect or delayed recall.

In HCI there are a number of occasions when it is possible to identify interference effects that lead to errors of recall. It is a little more difficult to detect delays in recall because of interference without carrying out more sophisticated observations of user behaviour than are normally made. Incorrect recall that can be ascribed to interference is perhaps most common when people switch between applications or systems. For instance, the same function might be available in two applications running on the same system, but how the user accesses them may be quite different. It would not be surprising to find that a user who is familiar with both systems, on occasion, attempts to access the desired function by the wrong method, i.e. the method which is not relevant for that application but is relevant for another. For example, in Microsoft Word 4.0, aligning text as left, right, or centre justified are functions that are available on the ruler and from a 'position' option on the format menu, which enters the user into a dialogue box. However, in MacWrite 5.0 aligning text can be done either from the ruler or as separate commands under the 'format' menu, or by typing command keystrokes. Users who are familiar with both applications and use the command keystroke method for justifying text in MacWrite may, by mistake, use the same command keystrokes in Microsoft Word, which have a different effect. Such an error would be due to interference in memory caused by the number of different methods for accessing the same function.

Various factors appear to affect the amount of activation that spreads to a particular conceptual node or structure of a propositional network. Anderson (1974) demonstrated that the number of links to a node in the network and the number of alternative links activated will affect the activation of a particular node, and will in turn affect the recall of that item. In Anderson's study, subjects were required to memorize 26 facts of the sort 'an X is in a Y'. Some of the Xs were related to only one Y and some were related to two Ys (Fig. 3.5).

The subjects in the experiment had to recognize if the sentence they were then presented with was from the original set of 26 or not. New sentences that were foils were included in the recognition task by pairing X and Y from the set such as 'the doctor is in the bank'. The results showed that recognition time increased as the

Example sentence	Relation	Recognition time (seconds)
The fireman is in the bank.	$(1X : 1Y)$	(1.11)
The doctor is in the park.	$(1X : 2Y)$	(1.17)
The lawyer is in the church.	$(2X : 1Y)$	(1.17)
The lawyer is in the park.	$(2X : 2Y)$	(1.22)

Figure 3.5   Recognition time increases as the number of facts increase (Anderson 1974)

number of facts about an X and a Y increased. In terms of Anderson's spreading activation theory, this suggests that the amount of activation reaching the proposition is inversely related to the number of relational links from it. Consequently, the amount of activation is assumed to be limited, i.e. increasing the number of links results in less activation along any one link. It seems that interference can slow down the speed at which people can access and retrieve facts from memory. If the fact is only weakly encoded and there are strong interference effects from other information then people will, on occasion, either fail to remember the required fact or recall the incorrect fact.

Consequently, we can now explain the case of using the wrong command to access common functions across applications. The user has built up knowledge in the form of relations between the function and the methods for accessing it (or them). The more methods of access there are, the more relations leading from the memory representation for the function there will be and the less activation there would be for each link to a particular method. In such cases, the designers should not be surprised if users report making errors in recalling the correct function-access method, since it can be predicted as being a potential source of error.

Interference occurs when further information is associated with a given fact, which is misleading, out of context or inappropriate. Facilitation occurs when further information is associated with the fact that is complementary, contextually relevant, coherent and consistent. In the context of user-interface design, this conflict between information that is facilitating and information that is potentially interfering is problematic. The problems arise because what determines if a piece of information is likely to facilitate or interfere with recall depends on the user's associated knowledge-structures within which the fact is encoded. Identifying all the potential associations between items of required knowledge and a person's existing knowledge would be a daunting task. Instead, it is better to make clear to users the meaning of commands etc. and to provide users with protective devises such as 'undo' and querying for operations with serious effects.

Memory is an active store in which information is continuously being activated and restructured. In HCI we should be aware that whenever a person is presented with a piece of information, this will activate other items of information stored in memory and give them a predisposition to those activated items. If, under some contexts, the information that has been activated is inappropriate then we can expect errors or other forms of suboptimum interaction to occur (e.g. slow decision-time). In some cases, it may be possible for the user interface to protect the user from these context interference effects by checking with the user, with reminders of the consequences of user actions, or by making suggestions of what the next appropriate action should be.

Interference through inference errors

A second form of interference, mentioned earlier, was interference due to incorrect inferences being made between facts or units of information stored in memory. For example, a person may know that computers have directories and files, and that each user has a personal directory and filespace. The person may know that this is true for all computers (even if it is not universally true, it may be true for all computers this person has ever met) and may also know that a command for listing files and directories is 'f'. They may then infer that the command for listing files and directories on all computers is 'f'. However, this would be an incorrect inference because there are computers where the command 'f' would not list files and directories.

In the next section, elaborations and inferences in memory (both correct and incorrect ones) are discussed in more detail.

ELABORATED MEMORY STRUCTURES

Information in memory is not isolated. Knowledge is stored alongside other items of knowledge. Propositions and facts are stored within and alongside other facts to form *elaborated structures* of knowledge in memory. Elaborated knowledge structures provide *redundant* retrieval cues and alternative retrieval routes. These alternative retrieval routes make it possible for people to recall information by *inference* rather than directly. Recall through inference is when we infer the fact from remembered associated facts. The difference between redundant information and interfering information is the degree of relevance. Information that is not deemed to be relevant to some aspect of the fact or proposition is likely to interfere with the subsequent retrieval of the original item. As was noted earlier, relevance is something which is difficult to determine. For example, you might be told that the typeface for this text is Times, but will that piece of information in any way help you recall the content of the text?

Elaboration of a memory structure seems to be influenced by the amount of processing that is afforded to the new information. Craik and Lockhart (1972) have shown that the depth of processing afforded to new information can be varied. They suggested a number of different levels of processing that could be undertaken to increase the extent of elaboration of the knowledge structure. For example, suppose the following list of words were presented:

Break
apple
banana
snake
Frog
Run
damage

You might be asked to identify all those in italics, or alternatively to identify all the nouns, or all the fruit. Each of the instructions requires you to perform some form of further processing of the above list. Alternatively, you might be asked to generate vivid visual images to accompany the words or to generate sentences in which the words are included. At school, children are often taught to remember the letters E G B D F in musical notation, by elaborating this into a sentence such as 'every good boy deserves favours'. Bobrow and Bower (1969) had subjects learn simple subject–verb– object sentences. Under one condition, the subjects had to generate a sentence to connect the two nouns (subject and object); in another condition, the experimenter provided the sentences. In a test condition, both groups of subjects were presented with the first (subject) noun and asked to generate the second (object) noun. The results showed far better recall in the self-generated (58 per cent correct) rather than the experimenter-generated condition (29 per cent correct). It seems that requiring the subjects to generate their own sentences caused them to process the material to a far greater degree and hence establish a more elaborated memory structure.

Stein and Bransford (1979) found that generating extensions to facts which are to be memorized can improve the recall of that fact, but that this improvement can be influenced by the quality of the extension. In the experiment, subjects were required to learn 10 sentences such as:

The fat man read the sign.

Under four different conditions subjects were given one of the following:

1 No extension.
2 An instruction to generate an extension to the sentence themselves.
3 An imprecise elaboration (e.g. . . . that was 2 ft tall) by the experimenter.
4 A precise elaboration (e.g. . . . warning about the ice) by the experimenter.

The experimenters interpreted precision as being pertinent and relevant to the intended meaning.

All subjects were then tested by being presented with frames such as

The . . . man read the sign.

and were required to produce the correct adjective. The results were as follows:

No extension	42% correct
Self-generated extension	58% correct
Imprecise experimenter-generated	22% correct
Precise experimenter-generated	78% correct

This shows that a critical factor in improving recall is if the elaboration constrains the memorized material. Clearly, in the above example, the imprecise extension did not constrain the material and may have caused ambiguity to arise (was the man or the sign 2 ft tall?). It further shows that not all subject-generated extensions are better than experimenter- or externally-provided extensions.

In the context of user-interface design, the designer may be able to provide a constraining set of further information that reduces the ambiguity and enables the user to develop an elaborated memory structure for system details. However, the designer should be very careful in selecting what extra information to provide, since, if it leads to further possibilities or ambiguities, the user will be worse off than if no extra information were available.

Without looking back to the list of words presented at the start of the section how many can you now recall? Probably you could remember at least four items from the list. At the time the list was presented, you were not asked to remember or learn its content, but it was necessary to process the list by identifying those items in italics, fruit, etc. The important point to note is that you have learned the content of the list as a function of processing the list. Material is learned not as a function of whether it was *intended* to be learned or not, but as a function of the amount of processing afforded to the material. Thus we must be aware that material may be learned both *intentionally* and *incidentally* and that it is the processing afforded to the material that will determine the outcome, not the intentionality *per se*.

INFERENCE AND MEMORY RECALL

It is not always necessary to be able to retrieve an item directly from memory; instead we may be in a position to retrieve sufficient information to allow us to infer the desired fact. Bransford, Barclay and Franks (1972) demonstrated that people do make inferences from the information they have stored in memory. They presented one group of subjects with the following sentence:

1 Three turtles rested beside a floating log, and a fish swam beneath them.

Another group of subjects were presented with the sentence:

2 Three turtles rested on a floating log, and a fish swam beneath them.

They then asked the first group of subjects if they had seen the following sentence:

3 Three turtles rested beside a floating log, and a fish swam beneath it.

The results showed that almost none of their subjects thought they had seen this sentence.

They then asked the second group of subjects if they had seen the following sentence:

4 Three turtles rested on a floating log and a fish swam beneath it.

Almost all of the subjects in this condition thought they had seen this sentence.

Sentence 4 is implied by sentence 2 but sentence 3 is not implied by sentence 1. Consequently, subjects in the Bransford *et al.* experiment thought they had seen material which they had in reality inferred from the meaning of the material with which they had been presented. They were not able to separate the material from its meaning, and in fact had a better memory for the meaning of the material than the actual sentence.

This can be regarded either as an error or as plausible and acceptable inferences. However, it depends upon the purpose for which the information is required at the time of recall. For example, if the purpose of recalling the above material was to determine the relative whereabouts of the fish and the turtles with respect to the log then either sentence 2 or sentence 4 is adequate. If, however, the purpose of recalling

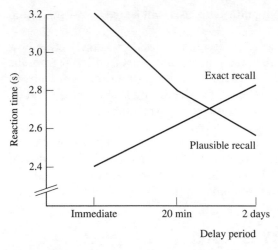

Figure 3.6   Judgements of exact and plausible sentences as a function of delay period (Reder, 1982)

the sentence is to deliver a password or a coded message then only sentence 2 is acceptable.

It appears to be the case that recall in everyday life is more like producing plausible inferences than exact detail. Reder (1982) presented subjects with the following passage:

> The heir to a large hamburger chain was in trouble. He had married a lovely young woman who had seemed to love him. Now he worried that she had been after his money after all. He sensed that she was not attracted to him. Perhaps he consumed too much beer and too many french fries. No, he couldn't give up the fries. Not only were they delicious, he got them for free.

She then tested her subjects by asking them to judge sentences that were:

1 Studied in the text.
2 Not studied in the text but plausible.
3 Not studied in the text and not plausible.

Such as:

1 The heir married a lovely young women who seemed to love him.
2 The heir got his french fries from the family hamburger chain.
3 The heir was very careful to eat only healthy food.

In the test she varied the delay period from immediate to 20 minutes' delay and 2 days' delay before asking them to judge the sentences. Subjects were asked to judge if the sentence was either exact, or in a different condition, if the sentence were plausible.

The results showed that the average judgement time for subjects in the exact condition became slower as the delay period increased from immediate to 2 days. However, subjects in the plausible condition started out slower than the subjects in the exact condition but became faster as the delay period increased (Fig. 3.6).

It appears that the memory for the exact sentences in the passage becomes weaker over the delay period and therefore the exact judgement time takes longer. However, the plausible inferences become faster because the subjects no longer try to use the inefficient memory for the exact sentence and rely more on plausible inferences. One other explanation is that subjects have time to generate for themselves the likely plausible inferences during the delay periods and therefore are more able to recognize a plausible inference.

MEMORY FOR GIST

People are capable of remembering exact facts. However, through processes of elaboration and inferencing, facts become embellished and contextualized in an interpretive knowledge structure. The effect of this elaboration and interpretation is that facts become stored as units of personalized knowledge that represent the individual's interpretation or understanding of the world. Bartlett (1932) in his classic work *Remembering* postulated that memory is not veridical and is biased by the context and understanding of the world that the individual already has. In one of his experiments, Bartlett took stories from one cultural context (Canadian Indians) and presented them without any explanation or contextual information to subjects in his own surroundings (Cambridge, UK). He had his subjects recall the stories after differing time periods ranging from immediately to years later. Subjects omitted parts of the story, changed many facts and brought in new information. He noticed that these distortions were systematic and were the result of subjects distorting the material to fit in with their own cultural, social and personal stereotypes.

To explain this distortion, Bartlett postulated that people have *schemas* or *schemata* for organizing knowledge and providing a structure in which information in memory can be organized. Schema and other forms of knowledge representation such as *frames* will be considered in detail later. However, both schemata and frames are concerned with understanding how our memories are organized. They are less concerned with how we remember words, sentences or lists but focus on higher order and arguably more ecologically valid aspects of memory, such as how we come to understand the world and how we make use of our knowledge to interpret everyday and out-of-the-ordinary events. Consider the following piece of text:

> He was returning from a restaurant in the early hours of the morning with his wife. He had reached the building in which he and his family lived and was almost at the top of the stairs when the tragedy occurred. He was shot. He died instantaneously. The world was shocked.

It is an extract from a newspaper report of the assassination of John Lennon in New York. Readers will elaborate the story with their own knowledge of the normally occurring events that might be part of going out for a meal and returning home in the early hours. We might not have had any personal experiences of assassinations, but we may know about other such events in history or from newsreels, and we may have read novels or seen movies which included similar events. This other information forms part of the knowledge structure by which the facts as they were presented are interpreted.

In developing any theory of memory, it is worth recognizing that memory is not exclusively comprised of unrelated facts. Indeed, it appears that memory for facts cannot be explained simply by looking at how simple facts presented in artificial contexts are remembered. To obtain a more accurate understanding of human memory we need to consider other aspects of memory, such as memory for events, memory for stories and how the contents of our memory provide us with a model of the world. To answer these questions requires us to consider how knowledge is represented, structured and used.

Exercises

1 Produce a propositional network representation for the facts associated with logging into a system where there is a user name and a password. Remember to include facts associated with what happens when an incorrect name or password is given.
2 Consider the different types of remembering, recall or recognition that are required for any program you choose. Identify ways that remembering could be improved by providing more opportunities for recognition.
3 Design suitable elaborative structures for a selection of functions. You might like to run a small experiment to test if your elaborative structures are any better than those users could develop themselves.
4 Write an essay to discuss why memory for gist is better than memory for detail.

4 KNOWLEDGE REPRESENTATION

Summary

- Memory does not solely contain representations of simple facts such as have so far been considered. People also store knowledge of events, actions and images.

- Memory can be thought of as processes operating upon representations. The knowledge people acquire and use is represented in some form of knowledge structure. One form of knowledge structure is propositional networks which represent propositional knowledge. Other forms of propositional knowledge representations include: *semantic features* or *attributes*, and *semantic networks*.

- Evidence from experiments on *mental imagery* suggests that some form of *analogical representation* might exist. The *functional* significance of images suggests some form of representation for *spatial* information. However, it seems that even spatial information can be represented by a propositional format.

- In considering knowledge, attention must also be focused on the knowledge that allows us to act. For example, knowledge of how to ride a bicycle or how to touch-type may not be represented in the same format as our knowledge of what bicycles or typewriters are. This is known as *procedural knowledge*.

REPRESENTATIONS AND KNOWLEDGE

A representation is something which stands for something else. In other words, a representation is a kind of model of something it represents. We must assume that people construct and use models of the world in the form of knowledge representations. We can distinguish between a represented world and a representing world. The represented world is the thing that is being represented, and the representing world is whatever is doing the representing. For example, an architect's plan of a house is a representation of some aspect of the house. The house is what is being represented and the plan is what is doing the representing. Palmer (1978) identified five features for a representational system as follows:

Represented world		Representing world		
Objects	*a*	*A*	15	7
	b	*B*	13	9
Properties	Height	Not directly represented	Numeric	Numeric
Relation	*a* taller than *b*	TALLER THAN (*A*,*B*)	GREATER THAN	LESS THAN

Figure 4.1   Different representations of the property of height

1 What is the represented world.
2 What is the representing world.
3 What aspects of the represented world are being modelled.
4 What aspects of the representing world are doing the modelling.
5 What are the correspondences between the two worlds.

By way of example, consider how in Fig. 4.1 the property of 'height' might be represented in a number of ways. Each form of representation captures some aspect of the relationship between the two objects.

It should be noted that a sixth feature of a representational system is the purpose for which it was constructed. One can distinguish between a person's mental representation of the world and a theory or model of a person's representation of the world (perhaps as would be constructed by a psychologist or an expert system). Psychological theories of knowledge are, in fact, models of people's represented knowledge of the world. Psychological theories of knowledge representation are not concerned with modelling the phenomena in the world. They are concerned with modelling the knowledge people have of the world and how that knowledge is organized and structured. While a person's represented knowledge of the world is not necessarily identical to the objects of that world, their knowledge may reflect much of the structuring of the world and, in many cases, imposes a structure on the world.

THREE REPRESENTATIONAL FAMILIES

Three main families of knowledge representation can be identified from the many theories and models of the structuring of human knowledge that abound.

1 *Propositional representations*   This is the most widely discussed family of knowledge representational formats and includes a wide range of theories and models. These theories have in common the fact that they represent knowledge as a set of discrete symbols or propositions, concepts, objects and features, and relations can all be represented by propositional representations.

2 *Analogical representations*   This form of representation has been postulated to explain phenomena such as mental images. Analogical representations maintain a close correspondence between the representing and represented world. In this form of representation the variable parameters of the representation are assumed to be continuous, in the same way that voltages, maps and pictures all have continuous properties.

3 *Procedural representations* This is perhaps the least well-developed class or family of theories of knowledge representation. Theories within this family are postulated to explain how a person's knowledge of actions are represented. For example, the knowledge a person possesses that enables them to walk, talk, add two numbers together, play chess, ride a bicycle, etc., must be represented in some format. The knowledge used for executing actions is assumed to be represented as procedural knowledge. Procedural knowledge is directly interpretable by an action system. For example, the knowledge one might have of riding a bicycle is assumed to be directly tied up with the activity of riding a bicycle and can only be accessed by carrying out the activity (i.e. riding the bicycle).

It would be wrong to think that people's knowledge can be discretely segmented into different forms of representation or that the types of knowledge considered by each of these three forms of representation were in some way mutually exclusive. For example, the knowledge a person has about a particular computer application would include knowledge of what it could be used for, what particular windows or menus looked like, and what actions were required to position the cursor using the mouse. Moreover, it would be possible to visualize the shape of the cursor to describe how to hold the mouse and to carry out the actions of moving the cursor directly to a target. People's knowledge of the world is rich and polymorphic. The types of knowledge representation referred to above and discussed in further detail below are best thought of as contributing factors to a full understanding of the different functional attributes of knowledge.

Before considering each of these families of knowledge representation in turn, it is worth remembering that representations require processes that can interpret or use the representational structure. Referring back to Fig. 4.1, before any statement or judgement could be made about the property 'height', there would need to be a process for evaluating the expression TALLER THAN (A,B), for comparing the two line lengths or for calculating the difference between the numeric values.

Propositional representations

This form of representation has been given the most attention in cognitive psychology. It assumes that knowledge is represented by a collection of symbols, and includes a wide range of theories that attempt to describe how knowledge is represented for an even wider range of phenomena.

Semantic features or attributes

Concepts can be represented by sets of semantic *features* or *attributes*. This form of representation has borrowed much from set theory and in particular questions the relationships between sets of features. A concept is thought to be represented by a set of weighted features which can then be considered in the following terms:

Disjoint	Non-overlapping attributes
Overlap	Some but not all attributes in common

| *Nested* | All of X are in Y |
| *Identical* | Exact same features in X as in Y |

The attributes or features of a concept can have differing weights to represent the salience and importance of the particular attribute or feature. However, it is particularly contentious as to what constitutes a salient or important feature or attribute of a concept. It is also very difficult to say how importance or salience can be characterized or measured. For example, what are the salient features of a program that allows you to recognize a piece of text is not a program? The language in which a program is written is clearly a feature of the program, but something is not a program because it is written in, say Pascal or Lisp. Many things that are written in programming languages are definitely not programs. Conversely, there are many programs that are not written in conventional programming languages that are indeed programs (e.g., knitting patterns are programmed instructions for a person to knit a garment).

Early experiments carried out to investigate the features of conceptual knowledge and the psychological structure of word-meaning led to the development of initial theories of propositional knowledge being represented in terms of semantic features or attributes. A classic experiment was that of Collins and Quillian (1969) who found that subjects in their experiments took longer to judge a statement such as 'canary eats food' as being true than a statement such as 'canary has feathers', which in turn took longer to judge than 'canary is yellow'. From these results it was suggested that information is stored hierarchically, and that properties specific to the concept 'canary' are stored directly with that concept. However, properties specific to the concept 'bird' would be stored with the 'bird' concept and not the 'canary' concept, and properties specific to the concept 'animal' would be stored with the 'animal' concept not the 'bird' concept (Fig. 4.2). Furthermore, the further up the hierarchy to be searched, the longer time it takes.

Animal (eats food, has offspring, breaths oxygen)
Bird ((is an animal) (has feathers, can fly, lays eggs))
Canary ((is a bird) (has yellow feathers, lives in exotic places))

Figure 4.2   An example hierarchy for the concepts 'animal', 'bird' and 'canary'

However, further experiments by Smith, Shoben and Rips (1974) found some exceptions to the experimental results of Collins and Quillian (op. cit.). In a similar study to that of Collins and Quillian, Smith *et al.* found that subjects were able to judge sentences such as 'a robin is a bird' as being true, faster than they were able to judge sentences such as 'a chicken is a bird'. Results such as these led Smith *et al.* to propose that the more *typical* an instance is of a category, the more quickly it can be verified as belonging to that category. A two-stage process for identifying category membership was proposed as follows:

1 A quick comparison of all features is made:
       if the comparison is relatively good answer yes,
       if poor answer no,
       if undecided then:
2 A more elaborate comparison process is applied to identify the defining features.

Therefore, judgements on the truth value of statements of the sort, 'sparrow is a bird' would be quick, as would be 'door is a bird', but 'bat is a bird' would take longer to judge.

Thus, this type of representation assumes that conceptual knowledge is represented by a set of *features* and that those features include *defining attributes* of the concept being represented as well as attributes that are *characteristic* of the concept. Defining attributes are those which identify the concept as being an instance of a type, for example, the attributes of a 'sparrow' that make it identifiable as being an instance of the 'bird' category. A characteristic attribute is one which the particular instance has but which does not provide sufficient definition for it to be included or excluded from the class.

Semantic representations such as the feature–attribute set are effective models of the class of experimental data produced from studies such as those of Collins and Quillian; however, these models do have the following limitations:

1 All the work is with simple, nominal concepts such as 'animals' or 'fruit'. It is not clear how, for example, to represent simple facts or events such as 'songs are for 'singing' or 'John ran away'.
2 The representations cannot handle distinctions such as, 'sparrow is a bird', 'robin is a bird', but 'sparrow is not a robin'.
3 Quantification is a further problem. For example, the meaning of the sentence, 'everyone kissed someone' is different from the meaning of 'someone was kissed by everyone'.

Semantic Networks

Semantic networks have been, and still are, used to represent the associations that exist between conceptual knowledge in memory (see, for example, Quillian, 1966). Knowledge is represented by a kind of directed labelled graph with nodes interrelated by relations (Fig. 4.3). Nodes represent concepts in memory; relations are associations among nodes; and relations are labelled and directed. The meaning of a concept (or node) is given by the pattern of its relations among which it participates.

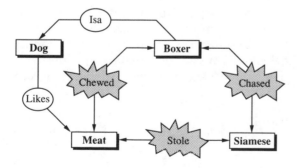

Figure 4.3 A simple semantic network

{Animal}		{Person}	
eats	*food*	**subset**	*animal*
breathes	*air*	**hasaspart**	*legs*
has	*mass*	**hasaspart**	*arms*
hasaspart	*limbs*		

Figure 4.4   Example of the inheritance properties between the two concepts, 'animal' and 'person'

Inheritance properties

One attribute of the semantic network formalism is the convenience with which the property of *inheritance* is formulated. Inheritance is the notion that certain features may be shared between concepts. It is dependent on the existence of categories and the hierarchical structure of those categories. It assumes that child members of the category inherit some of the features from the parent members of the category. For example, the concept 'house' might be categorized as a member of the supracategory 'building'. Buildings might be considered to have features that include 'walls', 'floor', and 'roof'. The concept house might also be expected to have the features of 'walls', 'floor', 'roof'; in which case we might assume that houses inherit these features from the supracategory 'building'. However, is it the case that all members of the category inherit all features from the supracategory?

In Fig. 4.4 the concept 'animal' has an **Isa** relational link from the concept 'person'. One feature of the concept 'animal' is that of **eats** *food*. Where **eats** is a *slot* and *food* is a *filler* of that slot. The concept 'person' inherits all the features of the concept 'animal', but has its own specified slot-filler **hasaspart** *legs* and *arms*. In order for the semantic network to function there must exist a *basic set* of nodes and relations. One important class of relations is the *type* indicating that one node is an *instance* of the *class* pointed to by the relation. Two important type relations are Isa and Subset. Thus, instances and subsets inherit the properties of their types. For example, 'birds' **have** *feathers* and *can fly*: by inheritance this applies to all birds.

However, 'ostriches' are an instance of the class 'bird' but they cannot fly. The solution to this problem has been to add another node to the 'ostrich' definition which specifies that it cannot fly. Thus exceptions to the inherited class properties are important defining features of an instance. This appears to be inconsistent with the view that instances inherit all the properties of the class. Consequently, we cannot assume that concepts are represented in simple class hierarchies with full class inheritance. Process rules for determining and identifying an instance have been formulated as follows:

1 Look first at the node of the concept.
2 If the information is not found, go up one node along the type relation and apply the property of inheritance.
3 Repeat 2 until there is a success or no more nodes.

This will always find the lowest (most specific) level of the relationship that applies. However, it will never notice inconsistencies.

Schemas, frames and scripts

Semantic features and semantic networks focus on basic, elementary units of knowledge. The semantic-features approach focuses on the representation of word meaning. Semantic networks include lexical- and sentential-level knowledge. But neither approach represents higher level knowledge structures (suprasentential level), such as events in stories.

Four strands of theoretical and empirical research have begun to address this type of knowledge representation. These are as follows:

- Frames (Minsky)
- Schema theory (Rumelhart)
- Scripts and episodes (Schank)
- Plans (Abelson)

Both episodes and plans have to some degree been combined in script theory (Schank and Abelson, 1977). These theories try to structure knowledge into higher order representational units. They attempt to add structure to model the higher level relationships between the lower order units (i.e. concept features and attributes).

Schemas

Schemas are data structures for representing the *generic concepts* stored in memory. There are assumed to be schemas for generalized concepts underlying objects, situations, events, sequences of events, actions and sequences of actions. Schemas can be thought of as producing *models* of the world. To process information with the use of a schema is to generate one or more models and then determine which of the generated models best fits the incoming information. A particular configuration of schemas which are used to construct the best-fit model constitutes an *interpretation* of the world. Schemas have a number of characteristics as follows:

- They have variables.
- They can be embedded in other schemas.
- They represent knowledge at all levels of abstraction.
- They represent knowledge rather than definitions.
- They are active recognition devices whose processing is aimed at the evaluation of their goodness of fit to the data being processed.

Variables

Schemas for any concept contain a fixed part for those characteristics which are most true of exemplars of a concept and a variable part. For example:

	Fixed	*Variable*
Dog	has legs	brown
	has tail	30 ins high

Therefore legs and tail are assumed to be fixed or constant while the colour and size are assumed to be variable features of the concept 'dog'. Variables can have *default* values; for example, the default value for the colour of dogs may be brown. Consider the following story extract:

> John saw the balloon man coming down the street. He remembered his brother's birthday and rushed into the house.

To interpret this story there might be schemas for tradesmen passing through a residential community selling toys to children. One schema might be characterized as follows:

> *Fixed*   Relationships between characters of the tradesman–customer drama
> *Variable*   Particular individuals filling specific roles
> Thus: John = Buyer (variable)
> Assume: John is a young boy (although not specified in story)
> Thus: *Default value* of Age, Buyer = Childhood.

In the above example, assumptions about the age of John have been made to make the interpretation of the story fit with an existing schema. However, later in the story we may be informed that John is, in fact, in his twenties and that his brother is in his thirties, and that he is a keen hot-air balloonist. Therefore, the schema that was applied may have been completely wrong, in that the sequence of events was not concerned with tradesmen selling balloons to young children, but instead with hot-air balloonists preparing for a day's flight on the occasion of the birthday of one of their members.

Embedded schemas

A schema consists of a configuration of subschemas. However, some schemas are *primitive*, that is, not decomposable. For example, a schema for recognizing the human body might be made up of the following subschemas:

> HUMANBODY (HEAD, TRUNK, LIMBS)
> HEAD (FACE, EARS, HAIR)
> FACE (2 EYES, NOSE, MOUTH)
> EYE (IRIS, UPPER-LID, LOWER-LID)

Thus schemas propose a hierarchy of levels rather than a single level. In the example above, the components of the embedded HUMANBODY schema have primitive subschemas for IRIS, UPPER-LID and LOWER-LID.

Levels of abstraction

Schemas represent knowledge at all levels of abstraction, for instance, ideological, sentences, words, form of letters, etc. Schema theories assume that the human memory system contains countless 'packets' of knowledge. Each packet specifies a configuration of other packets (or subschemas) and each packet may vary in complexity and level of application.

Knowledge

All our knowledge is assumed to be embedded in schema. Knowledge can be thought of in terms of semantic and episodic components. Semantic components include dictionary knowledge (i.e. the essential aspects of word meaning), and encyclopaedic knowledge (i.e. facts and relationships). Episodic knowledge focuses on experiential components; for example, that you once fed a blackbird with breadcrumbs all winter. Schemas are assumed to exist for both semantic and episodic components of knowledge.

Active processes

Each schema is assumed to have a process. The processing carried out by a schema includes evaluating its goodness of fit to the incoming information, binding its variables and sending messages to other schemas. There are two types of data-sources; bottom-up and top-down:

- *Bottom-up* provides information from subschemas about how well they fit the input.
- *Top-down* provides information from supraschemas about the degree of certainty of their relevance to structuring the input.

Interpretation of meaning consists of top-down and bottom-up processing in repeated loops. The set of schemas that have the best goodness-of-fit constitutes an interpretation.

Frames

Frames are very similar to schemas in that they provide variable *slots* which can take the particular *fillers* for an *instantiated frame*. A frame is instantiated when it is provided with the particular details for a given context. Frames can exist at a number of different levels, with high-level or generalized frame structures and also low-level specific frame structures in the same way that schemas can be embedded. The higher level frames call up the lower level frames which then detail how some component of the higher level frame is to be further interpreted. Unlike schema, frames do not possess active processors which interpret the world; instead, frame theory is restricted to addressing the representation of knowledge and ignores any kind of processing that might be carried out on the knowledge.

Recently, frame-based representations have been used to model the knowledge people possess about a task domain (Keane and Johnson, 1987). In the context of human–computer interaction, Keane and Johnson carried out an empirical analysis of the knowledge people possessed about various tasks such as 'arranging a meeting'. The analysis identified knowledge in terms of *goals, plans, macro-actions (procedures), micro-actions*, and *objects*. The goals were represented as a general goal frame which then became particularized into subgoals at lower level frames. Each frame included either a goal or subgoal depending upon the level of the frame. Within the frame a plan for carrying out the task was detailed. This plan became more specialized as frames were rewritten into lower level frames. The procedures used in the task were represented by the groupings of actions within a particular frame. The individual activities in the task were represented as procedures and actions (or macro- and micro-actions) with procedures being high-level activities and actions being low-level activities. The object sets were then the entities on which the activities

Task: Arrange a project meeting

Plan (meeting (project))
  Consult (information source, information token, project meeting)
    Identify (information source, information token, project meeting)
    Search (information source, information token)
    Retrieve (information token, information source)
    Store (information token, project meeting, working memory)
  Select (media message)
    Identify (long-term memory, constraints, project meeting)
    Choose (media, constraints)
Send message (meeting, (project))
  Consult (information token, information source, letter)
    Identify (information source, information token, letter)
    Search (information source, information token)
    Retrieve (information token, information source)
    Store (information token, letter, working memory)
  Represent (information token, message)
    Write (information token, message, media)
    Compare (message, information token)
    Edit (information token, message)
    Store (message copy, message file, media)
  Execute (transaction requirements, message)
   ⋮

Figure 4.5 An example of a frame-based representation of the knowledge used to create and send a message to arrange a project meeting (from Keane and Johnson, 1987)

were performed or otherwise associated with the activities. Finally, each frame had its procedures and actions related by *enabling* or *causal relations* which determined the dependencies between activities within a frame.

The knowledge represented in Fig. 4.5 was derived from a task analysis of arranging a project meeting (task analysis is addressed in Chapters 11 and 12). The knowledge is assumed to be the knowledge utilized by the people who carried out this task. The purpose of the task analysis and knowledge representation was to assist in the design and evaluation of a messaging system to support a variety of messaging tasks. The terms used in Fig. 4.5 were not technical, but were used to provide a common form of expression for all the different objects and actions that were encountered in the different instances of the task that were studied. Therefore, the model is intended to be a generic model of the knowledge used to carry out the task. For example, an information source could have been an address book, a diary, a note book or an online database. Similarly, an information token could have been a name, a telephone number, an address or a date. The reasons for wanting such a generic model and the methods of producing them are considered in Chapters 11 and 12 on task analysis.

Scripts

Schank and Abelson (1977) developed a framework known as *Scripts* for representing the specific examples of knowledge that people might have stored in memory.

A script is assumed to be a schema for frequently occurring sequences of events. For example, 'visits to a doctor', 'trips on a train' and the most frequently discussed, 'visits to a restaurant'.

Scripts have variables (just as schemas and frames have). There are two categories of variable: *roles* and *props*. Roles are filled by persons and props are filled by objects. In addition to roles and props, scripts include a set of *entry conditions* which must prevail if the script is to be used (these being the context or scope of effect for the given script). Scripts also include *scenes* and *results*. A scene is a particular grouping of activities within a script that can normally occur together and constitute a recognizable subset of the main activity.

Consider the following scenario:

> Mary went to the restaurant. She ordered a quiche. Finally she paid the bill and then left.

Now assume that the following script elements are associated with the above scenario:

Entry conditions	hungry, had money, restaurant open
Roles	diner, waiter, cashier
Props	tables, money, chairs, menu, cutlery, food

The script might then be as follows:

Entry scene	Diner enters restaurant.
	Waiter seats diner at table.
	Waiter places menu on table.
	Diner begins to read menu.
Ordering scene	Diner selects food from menu.
	Diner signals to waiter.
	Waiter approaches table.
	Diner orders food.
	Waiter leaves.
Eating scene	Waiter brings food to table.
	Waiter leaves.
	Diner eats food with cutlery.
	Diner finishes eating food.
Leaving scene	Diner signals to waiter.
	Waiter approaches table.
	Diner asks waiter for bill.
	Waiter writes bill and gives to diner.
	Diner checks bill.
	Diner approaches cashier.
	Diner gives cashier bill and money.
	Cashier checks money.
	Diner leaves restaurant.

The script provides a structure for the temporal order of the elements of the activity and provides sufficient information that can match the script to the instance of the activity of Mary going to a restaurant and having a quiche.

Alongside scripts are *plans*. Plans are more general and more abstract than scripts or schemas. Plans are formulated to satisfy *goals* and, as such, enable further actions to be initiated in an attempt to attain the goal. For example, consider the following scenario:

> John knew that his wife's operation would be very expensive. There was always Uncle Harry. John reached for the area phone-book.

In order to understand this scenario, assume that John wants to borrow money from Uncle Harry and that he is reaching for the phone-book to find Uncle Harry's telephone number and intends to ring his uncle to ask for the money.

There may not be a specific script for this event (unless borrowing money is a frequent activity). Consequently this activity is the result of some problem-solving behaviour.

First we can identify the problem as:

> *Problem = cost of operation*

We then assume a structure of goals, subgoals and plans that might be as follows:

Primary goal	Pay for operation.
Plan	Borrow money from Uncle Harry.
Subgoal	Contact Uncle Harry.
Plan	Call Uncle Harry on telephone.
Subgoal	Discover telephone number.
Plan	Look it up in telephone directory.

There would then be a detailed script for how to go about making a telephone call which would include how to look up numbers in the directory.

Therefore, scripts are one form of knowledge structure for representing high-level aspects of knowledge and are capable of representing the temporal aspects of commonly occurring activities.

Analogical representations

Analogical representations are assumed to be responsible for the representation of *mental images*. The most common form of image is perhaps the visual image. Visualization or visual imagery is assumed, often implicitly, to be partly responsible for the advantages that *icon*-based user interfaces might enjoy over textual user interfaces. The claim often made is that people find it easier to visualize than remember. This is clearly a misguided claim on a number of counts. First, visualization is of course simply another form of remembering. Second, some people find it very hard to visualize anything. Third, most people find it very hard to visualize some things. For example, it is easy to visualize a wastebasket if you have seen lots of examples of wastebaskets, since these are concrete objects which have a visible form. The ranges of wastebasket vary considerably and we would not expect everyone who reported that they could visualize a wastebasket to visualize the same sort. Suppose, though, you were asked to visualize a more abstract or less concrete concept than a wastebasket, such as liberty or a data type. These are two concepts which it would be hard for many people to visualize since they are not things which take a specific form.

Most icon-based interfaces work well for concrete familiar objects and are always supported by a textual name which reinforces the user about the exact nature of the object being represented. Interesting work on icons and imagery has been reported by Rogers (1986) and others. Rogers compared icons for concrete and abstract concepts and also icons with or without verbal labels. She discovered that concrete icons with labels were the most readily understood and recognized form of presentation.

It is worth noting that there is also a relationship between the typicality of the item in the category and its usefulness as an icon. For example, a useful icon for a bird in most western cultures would be a robin or a sparrow, and not a hen or an ostrich, since robins and sparrows are more typical instances of birds than either ostriches or hens. Similarly, an icon for an object should be a typical instance of the class of objects, rather than an obscure, atypical instance.

Imagery and its relation to icon design can be summarized along two dimensions. First, there is the dimension of individual differences, which characterizes the extent to which people are capable of generating and thinking in terms of visual images. Second, there is the dimension of the imagery potential of the concept; this characterizes the degree to which the concept itself has potential for being imagined.

The individual differences between people in terms of their ability to generate mental images has been demonstrated using various types of tests and questionnaires. Two categories of people's ability to generate images have been identified to be *high vivid imagers* and *low vivid imagers*. High vivid imagers report that they can easily generate visual images while low vivid imagers report (and the tests associated with these reports confirm this) that they find it difficult or impossible to generate visual images. The second dimension of imagery is the imagery potential of the concept. Extensive research has shown that, even amongst people who are rated as being high vivid imagers, there are some concepts which they find it difficult to imagine. The results of this research show that concrete concepts can be imagined far more readily than abstract concepts. It appears then that visual imagery is something which is not necessarily universal across all people and not all concepts are capable of being imagined. Consequently, icons rely in part on their association with a concept and the person's image of that concept. Icons, therefore, must be used carefully since not all people can easily form images, and those that can cannot easily imagine abstract concepts. Bell (1989) found that icons without labels are not significantly more effective than labels. Furthermore, for some concepts, labels alone are better than icons alone.

There are of course non-visual images which might include tastes, smells, sounds and perhaps even feelings. However, very little work has yet been carried out in HCI to understand the utility of these kinds of images.

As a demonstration of imagery, imagine the scene described by the following passage:

> It was a hot summer's day. The sky was clear and blue. The sun glistened on the lake and the branches of the trees were reflected in the water. The couple were sat on the grass, under the willow tree, above a small pebble beach. Children were playing in the water nearby. Out on the lake there was a number of sailing boats. One was gliding slowly towards them. It was the most magnificent boat on the lake with a gleaming white hull and a tall mast with three sails. The couple could

hardly believe that just a few hours before they had left the heat and grime of the city. It seemed as if the day had been made for them.

What colour were the sails of the boat?

Most people readily give an answer to this question and often add that it was the colour of the sail in their mental image. Clearly, it was not in the story. This is a rather simple example of imagery. More interesting experimental investigations of mental imagery have suggested that the objects in an image can be subjected to *transformations*. This has been the basis for some researchers (e.g. Shepard, 1978, Paivio, 1978) to suggest that the knowledge underlying images may be analogical rather than propositional.

Shepard and his colleagues have shown in numerous experiments that subjects appear to be mentally rotating or otherwise transforming an object (see, for example, Shepard, 1978). He argues that the process of mentally rotating an object involves a mental analogue of a physical rotation. It is assumed that the representation is being processed in an analogous manner to that which would go on if the subject were actually perceiving an external object physically rotating. Furthermore, it is suggested that the internal representation passes through a certain trajectory of intermediate steps, each of which has a one-to-one correspondence with a physical rotation of the imaged object.

The classic paradigm for Shepard's experiments involves presenting subjects with a complex object and then later presenting them with a set of several objects which includes the original object rotated (in one or more planes). The results of these studies generally show that as the angle of rotation increases, the time it takes for the subject to identify the object as being in the set also increases. From these studies it is assumed that the representation of the imagined object is analogous, in that it preserves some degree of *spatial* structuring of the external object. However, it should be recognized that we could produce a propositional representation of spatial properties (for example, next to, adjoining, above, below, etc.).

Work by Kosslyn (see, for example, Kosslyn, 1980) has lead to the formulation of a theory of image representation which is based on the analogy of a cathode ray tube (CRT) and comprises two layers of representation.

The first layer is a surface representation which has the following properties:

1 Part of the image represents corresponding parts of the object, preserving such properties as distance between parts of the object.
2 There is a limited spatial extent, i.e. images can *overflow* if too large.
3 The surface representation has a *grain size* and detail is lost if the image is too small.
4 There is periodic *refreshing* of the image otherwise fading occurs.

The second layer is a deep representation which generates the image from a propositional representation in long-term memory.

A third component of the theory is a 'mind's eye' which interfaces between the surface image and the deep representation, and which uses parts of the visual system to process or interpret the image. This processor performs functions such as 'generates' the image, 'looks for' parts of the image, 'transforms' the image by 'scan', 'zoom', 'pan' and 'rotate' subprocessors.

It is best not to think of imagery as a separate representational system but as a function of some special-purpose processor. Johnson (1982), in a series of experiments, has shown that subjects can generate images of simple linear arm movements which are functionally equivalent to actual arm movements. The functional equivalence is in terms of the spatial coordinates for the movement and the image. The parameters of the movement and the image are assumed to be one and the same and are abstract representations of spatial properties (such as starting-point, direction, distance, end point).

Procedural representations

We can distinguish between knowledge *about* something (i.e. factual or declarative knowledge) and knowledge about *how to do* something (i.e. procedural knowledge). For example, declarative knowledge of a bicycle would include knowledge of its parts (pedals, saddle, frame, wheels, handlebars, etc.), what it could be used for, and many other items of knowledge, such as examples of good bicycles, where to purchase one, etc. In contrast, procedural knowledge associated with a bicycle might include how to ride and how to repair one.

There is assumed to be a relationship between the type of knowledge (procedural or declarative) and *consciousness*. It is assumed that declarative knowledge is *accessible* to consciousness in that it can be examined and combined, while procedural knowledge is thought to be *inaccessible* to consciousness. It is also generally assumed that the only way to access the procedural knowledge of riding a bicycle is to engage in the activity of riding a bicycle. Note that it is not just physical actions that are represented in procedures. For example, knowledge of how to perform arithmetical calculations will also be represented by procedural knowledge.

Knowledge of this form is assumed to include representations of action procedures, and these procedures are tailored for the performance of specific actions. In contrast, declarative knowledge (represented as propositions) can be used for a variety of purposes. A further distinction between procedural and declarative knowledge is in the context of skilled performance. One characteristic of skilled performance is that the performer has developed highly tuned procedures that support the performance and allow it to be executed with ease and efficiency of effort. In contrast, unskilled performance is assumed to lack the highly developed procedural knowledge that is optimum for the task, and as a consequence the performance is difficult and inefficient.

One concern about procedural representations is how they might be activated. One possibility is that a procedure is activated by *direct invocation*, that is, some other procedure or an interpreter *calls* the required procedure. Alternatively, a *triggering mechanism* might be integrated into the procedure. In this case the procedure would monitor a database for relevant data structures. When a relevant data structure had been identified, the procedure would be *fired*. However, for this triggering mechanism to work there must be some form of *demon* or process which monitors the database.

One solution to the representation of procedures is found in the form of *production rules* and *production systems* (PS). Production rules include a demon or process which monitors and fires the action. A production rule consists of 'if' → 'then'

or

'condition' → 'action'

statements,

IF (*condition for triggering*) THEN (*do these actions*)

Production systems are collections of connected production rules and as such constitute a complete knowledge structure for a given activity. PSs are modular in format but new production rules can be added to existing PSs or alternatively PSs can be replaced by new, more powerful PSs. In this way, learning and improvements in performance can occur. However, that requires us to consider how people acquire skills. Skill and skill acquisition are considered in Chapter 5.

CONCLUSION

Representations can be thought of as notations. Therefore, the problem of identifying the form of knowledge representation can be projected as a set of constraints on a notation. First, any notation for knowledge representation should be rich enough to represent all of the relevant knowledge structures and cognitive processes that might act on them. Second, those processes that are assumed to be easily carried out should in fact be easily carried out through the chosen representation.

Representations consist of two parts, the *data structures* that are stored according to the chosen representational format, and the *processes* that are able to operate on the data structures.

The knowledge that people recruit and use to carry out tasks will include each type of knowledge, procedural, declarative and analogical. There is no reason to believe that each of these types of knowledge is discrete and used exclusively in certain tasks. Instead, we should think of these as functional descriptions of the different types of knowledge that people use. The representational differences that have been postulated in psychological research are less important than the functional differences between the differing types of knowledge. For example, it seems to be less important to consider whether images are generated from an analogue or propositional representation than to consider the functional significance of images in the role of remembering, understanding and thinking.

Our main concerns in the next chapter is how we use our knowledge and how we acquire skill and expertise. The different types of representation discussed here for propositional and procedural knowledge form a part of a theory of skill acquisition that describes how a skill is acquired and how we develop more powerful (appropriate) procedural knowledge.

Exercises

1 Distinguish between represented and representing 'worlds'.
2 Construct a representation of the knowledge you assume a person must possess

to carry out a simple task such as creating a new document file. Remember to represent both the factual and event knowledge.

3 Design and carry out a simple experiment to investigate the use of concrete and abstract icons, with and without labels, for the ease with which people can understand their meaning, and remember their function.

4 Produce a propositional knowledge representation using production rules for the knowledge required to carry out a simple task using any application program you choose.

5 EXPERTISE, SKILL AND SKILL ACQUISITION

Summary

- Skill and expertise are assumed to develop through three stages: the *cognitive stage*, the *associative stage* and the *automatic stage*. At the cognitive stage, knowledge is largely declarative and at the associative and automatic stages, a procedural form of knowledge representation is assumed to have been developed.

- The effects of transfer between tasks are considered. Both *positive* and *negative* transfer may occur.

- Examples of the differences between novices and experts are described from a number of perspectives.

Skill is an important characteristic of human behaviour. People become skilled speakers of one or more languages; they can become skilled at dealing with social relations; they can become skilled drivers, writers and programmers. These are just some of the kinds of skilled behaviour that people can develop during their lifetime. Of course, not all people do develop the same set of skills to the same extent. Skill is concerned with performance and the quality of performance, whether that be a cognitive, perceptual or motor action.

What are the characteristics of skilled behaviour? There are both qualitative and quantitative aspects of skilled behaviour that distinguish the expert from the novice. The expert tennis player appears to have an economy of movement and effortlessness that makes the novice look as if they are somehow physically handicapped. The expert driver is quite capable of talking, changing gear and noticing the direction on the signpost, while the novice driver requires almost all their ability to find the gear, and often stalls the car when releasing the clutch. The expert typist can type at speeds well above 40 words per minute while I have trouble averaging 20 words per minute. The expert typist has at worst about a 5 per cent error rate while I am lucky if I can manage two words at any speed without making a typing error.

The examples of the differences between experts and novices are numerous and often very apparent. Experts and novices differ both in terms of the quality of their respective performances and also in the speed and accuracy of their performance.

STAGES OF SKILL ACQUISITION

The most well-developed theory of skill acquisition is that of Fitts and Posner (1967). While it has been elaborated a little by Anderson (1983), and has been modelled by the use of a production rule system (also by Anderson), the theory remains essentially unchanged. Fitts and Posner postulated three stages of skill acquisition; the *cognitive stage*, the *associative stage* and the *automatic stage*. Each stage is marked by a certain kind of behaviour. Skill is acquired through a progression from the cognitive through the associative to the automatic stage of skill.

Cognitive stage

During the cognitive stage the person learns the *facts* that are associated with the *domain* of the skill. This is in the form of *declarative knowledge* and is thought to be represented as propositions. People engage in *verbal rehearsal* of the facts. In attempting to perform the task the person uses *domain-general* problem-solving procedures, for example

> IF the goal is to achieve state X
> and M is a method of achieving X
> THEN set as a subgoal to apply M

or

> IF the goal is to write a letter on a word processor
> and INSERT TEXT-MODE is one way of creating a textual document using a word processor
> THEN set as subgoal enter INSERT TEXT-MODE

Associative stage

This is the second stage in skill acquisition. First, errors in initial understanding of the domain are eliminated. For example, the novice word-processor user might now learn how to enter insert text-mode directly rather than through having to look at help. Second, the connections between items of knowledge are strengthened. For example, the novice word-processor user might not have to even pause to read the options on the menu before entering text mode—they have learned exactly which option to select and its position on the menu.

The outcome from the associative stage is a successful procedure for performing the skill. This is taken as indicating that the declarative knowledge has been success-fully translated into a *procedural* form of knowledge representation.

The person now possesses, and uses, old and new procedures that are specific to the domain rather than using existing, domain-general procedures. Performance improves in terms of speed and errors; however, it is not just a general speeding-up of the performance by chaining together existing production rules or adding on new production rules. The knowledge is restructured to form new, more powerful production rules.

Automatic stage

The third and final stage of skill acquisition is the automatic stage. In this stage the procedures developed in the associative stage become automated and faster in their execution. However, there is a loss in the ability to verbalize the skill. Speed and accuracy improve and the procedures are more rapidly and more accurately applied. Tuning of procedures occurs to accommodate exceptions and new strategies that have developed.

AN EXAMPLE OF SKILL ACQUISITION

In a comparative study of differing data input devices for parcel sorting, Johnson, Long and Visick (1986) investigated how a group of subjects learned to use three different input devices. One device required the development of skill at using a numeric keypad to enter numeric codes for parcel destinations. A laboratory experiment was devised to identify the different learning requirements of the various devices. The aim was first to focus on the skills required to use the devices effectively, and in a later study to focus on the additional skills required to use the devices actually to sort parcels. Consequently, in the first series of experiments, no actual parcels were sorted. Instead, people were required simply to input destinations of parcels using one of the devices. Basically, the laboratory task for this numeric keypad device was to translate a town name presented on a VDU into a two-digit numeric code and then enter that code into the system using a 0–9 matrix keypad. In the study, subjects were tested at regular intervals over a series of 12 learning sessions.

A proposed model of how the skill developed suggested that, early on (in the cognitive stage), the subjects were operating from a generalized production system that included existing procedures for finding keys on numeric keypads, and had little domain specific knowledge of the town name–numeric code relation except that all the codes were two digits.

As the sessions progressed, subjects were assumed to develop task specific knowledge which included separate procedures for the following activities:

> Read town name.
> Translate town name into a two digit code.
> Find first key on keypad.
> Execute first keystroke.
> Find second key.
> Execute second keystroke.

After further sessions, it appeared that subjects were using a more efficient production system which included procedures for the following activities:

✗ <u>Read town name and translate to two-digit code.</u> ①
Find first key. *q wud·*
Find second key.⌡
Execute first keystroke.
Execute second keystroke.

Two features of this development of skill should be noted. First, the procedures for reading and translating have become one so that the name is automatically translated into a number code. Second, the finding of both keys is carried out completely before any execution is undertaken. Thus procedures that are more closely related in terms of the knowledge they contain are now associated more closely to give a more economical task execution.

After yet further sessions the following procedures were assumed to be in existence:

Read name and translate to two-digit code.   *q expas*
Find keys and execute keystrokes.⌡

Ultimately, the finding and executing of the keystrokes also becomes automated as a single procedure. The optimum automation would be achieved when these remaining procedures were incorporated into a single procedure for reading, translating and keying.

By carrying out various *probes* at every third session where numbers alone were presented to be copy-typed, and by separately analysing the times between keystrokes, the investigators found that subjects acquired the coding component of the skill before they acquired the keying component of the skill. Moreover, at the end of 12 sessions the keying component (i.e. the interkey time) had only just begun to show any sign of reaching an asymptote, which suggests that subjects never achieved optimum automation of the skill (Fig. 5.1). This was confirmed by a further probe carried out after the 12th trial, in which the keyboard was hidden from the subjects'

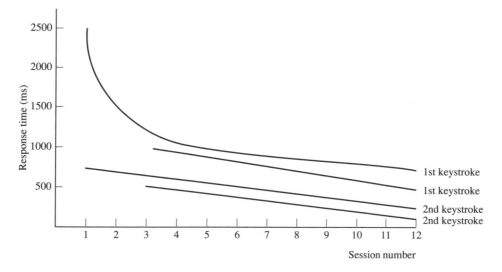

Figure 5.1   The development of coding and keying skill in a simulated parcel-sorting task (from Johnson, Long and Visick, 1986)

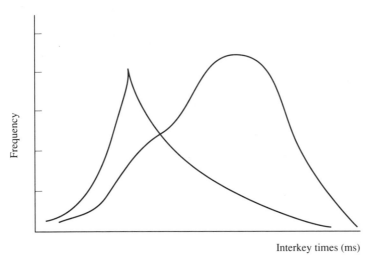

Figure 5.2 Distribution changes as a function of skill (after Long, Nimmo-Smith and Whitefield, 1983)

view so that they were forced to key blind. The results of this probe showed that subjects' performance deteriorated in terms of both errors and speed (considerably more so in the case of the latter) indicating that they had not achieved optimum automaticity.

Further differences between experts and novices

Crossman (1959) studied the skill of cigar-making over a two-year period in a single group of workers. By plotting the number of cigars manufactured per unit time against the number of cigars manufactured, he was able to show that the cycle time for a novice was far greater than that for an expert. Moreover, by looking at the distribution of times for experts and novices, he found that it was not a simple matter of all the times speeding up. Instead, the proportion of short times relative to the long times increased as well as the mean time becoming faster. That is to say, the mean of the distribution shifted to the left and the distribution as a whole became more positively *skewed* as expertise was acquired. Long, Nimmo-Smith and Whitefield (1983) have shown similar distribution changes for the acquisition of typing skills in typists monitored over a two-year period (Fig. 5.2).

PRACTICE EFFECTS

One factor affecting the development of skill is practice. It appears to be true that performance time decreases as a linear function (on a log/log plot) of the amount of practice. This is known as the *power law of practice* and is true for such varied skills as reading, mathematics and geometry proofs, as well as physical skills.

Another feature of skill is that once a skill or level of expertise has been acquired the time taken to achieve the same level of ability after a period of layoff (lack of

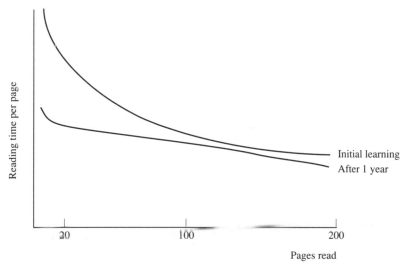

Figure 5.3 Savings score for reading distorted text (from Kolers, 1979)

practice) is far less than the time originally taken to acquire the skill. This is known as *savings*. Kolers (1979) demonstrated the savings effect for reading inverted and otherwise distorted text. After a 200-page practice of reading distorted text, subjects were tested again one year later. He found that on the retest subjects achieved the same rate of reading after only 100 pages (Fig. 5.3). Thus they had a savings score of 100 pages or had remastered the old skill in half the amount of practice.

POSITIVE AND NEGATIVE TRANSFER

A further aspect of skill is the extent to which one skill can affect or influence the learning of another skill. This kind of affect is known as *transfer* and can be either *positive* (helpful) or *negative* (harmful). When the knowledge that was acquired on one skill helps the person perform a new skill 'positive transfer' is said to occur. However, when existing knowledge interferes with the performance of a new skill 'negative transfer' is said to occur.

One aim of the user-interface designer is, of course, to utilize the user's existing knowledge of the domain and task. This enables the user to take advantage of any positive transfer that might occur, and so increase the speed with which the user is able to learn and use the new system to its fullest and most efficient extent.

In a study of post office parcel-sorting on a data entry task (Johnson, Long and Visick, 1986), it was discovered that the keyboard currently in use was almost an exact mapping from a previous technological system in which parcels were thrown into skips by parcel sorters. The designers of the keyboard had mapped the position of skips onto the position of keys. This is a simple example of positive transfer from one version of parcel-sorting to another. However, it should be noted that the keys were not in an optimum position for using a keyboard, since one of the constraints on the previous system was the volume of heavy parcels and the difficulty in throwing these parcels long distances. What was maintained, however, was a rough geographical mapping of the country to make use of the postal workers' knowledge of the locations of towns.

A more extensive study of transfer effects on moving between word-processing applications has been carried out by Pollock (1988). In her studies she showed that word-processor operators experienced both positive (i.e. beneficial) and negative (i.e. harmful) transfer effects when moving from their first to their second word-processing package.

In a different context, Knowles (1989) has shown that both positive and negative transfer effects occur when people attempt to use a new tool to carry out tasks they already know how to perform. In her studies, Knowles looked at the problems that experienced fashion designers had in using a computer-aided design (CAD) program for the tasks of pattern layout.

The issue of transfer of knowledge between tasks is important. Computer-system design involves analysing existing tasks and the design of new or changed tasks which require new knowledge. Wherever it is possible, without constraining innovation and enhancement, the designer should attempt to maximize the amount of opportunity for positive transfer and minimize the occurrence of negative transfer of the user's knowledge and skill.

PROGRAMMING AS A SKILL

Programming has been the subject of much study, as it represents a complex cognitive skill. One feature of expertise in programming is the language-independent nature of the skill. For example, as far as sequence, recursion and iteration are concerned, novices in many cases learn these concepts in terms of a particular mechanism in a specific language such as Pascal. In contrast, experts are capable of thinking about such concepts in the abstract and independent of any language. Consequently, some attempt has been made to teach these concepts in a language-independent manner (Bornat, 1988).

Anderson (1984) and Jeffries et al. (1981), among others, have considered how novice and expert programmers differ in the way they develop programs. Both novices and experts tend to follow a top-down approach, working backwards from the main goal to the subgoal. However, novices take a depth-first approach while experts take a breadth-first approach; that is, novices expand each problem down to its lowest level before starting on the next problem, while experts expand a full plan of all the problems before passing down to the next level. The experts' strategy is better than the novices' because solutions are non-independent, such that lower levels can impact on the higher levels.

Soloway, Bonar and Ehrlich (1983) and others have considered how experts and novices debug a program, and have found that debugging skill is dependent upon the existence of a common template for a solution to a problem. Also, experts have better memories for features of a program than novices. Subjects in a memory experiment were presented with either complete or scrambled programs. The results showed that experts were better at recalling the features of complete programs than were novices, but both experts and novices were equally poor at recalling the features of scrambled programs. It seems then that experts develop templates associated with program goals, and are then able to generate templates for given goals and infer goals from given templates.

CONCLUSION

This chapter concludes the consideration of psychological issues also raised in Chapters 2, 3 and 4. As was pointed out earlier, it is not possible to cover all of the psychological issues that might affect a person's behaviour in using a computer. There are many aspects of psychology concerned with social and emotional/motivational issues that would clearly influence a person's attitude towards, and willingness to use, a particular machine. The reader interested in these aspects is referred to other texts such as Oborne (1985). Similarly, not all aspects of cognitive psychology have been considered in these few chapters. No mention has been made of reasoning, language use, or problem solving, for example. The reader interested in further details on cognitive issues of behaviour is recommended to texts such as Anderson (1985). These aspects of human behaviour also have some bearing on how a person will use a computer system. However, the cognitive issues raised in the previous chapters are considered further in subsequent chapters, when we consider the design of user interfaces.

In these four chapters, some of the fundamental structures, processes and phenomena of human behaviour have been considered from a cognitive psychology perspective. Cognitive psychology underlies HCI as a 'core' discipline. The theories and empirical findings from cognitive psychology must be understood if they are to be applied to HCI. Rather than provide guidelines or so-called principles, it is better that the HCI scholar has a good understanding of the core and contributing disciplines. Psychological theories and data provide the basis from which applicable guidelines and principles can be developed. However, it is much too soon in the history of HCI to have much confidence in the so-called guidelines and principles that have so far been offered. Much greater understanding of the implications of cognitive psychology for HCI design issues needs to be gained. This understanding will only come about through the increased awareness of psychological issues by computer designers.

The kind of statements that currently abound, such as 'never have more than 7 ± 2 items on the screen at any one time' indicate that there is a gross over-generalization of a complex psychological phenomenon. It is clear from what is known about skill and expertise that people can process large amounts of information once they have become experts in that particular domain.

Such statements come about because designers desire guidelines that are simple to apply, and have taken something which appears to be simple without understanding the theoretical and empirical substance behind the generalization.

The implications of skill acquisition for HCI include the changes that occur in patterns of use and level of help required as people progressively become more skilled at using a computer. As people become more knowledgeable about how to use a program, they change the way that they interact with it. For example, in using a program with both a menu-based and command-based interface, novice users make

much use of the menus and little use of the command sets. However, as they become
more knowledgeable, they begin to make greater use of the commands.)A concrete
example is to be found in MacWrite, HyperCard, and many other Macintosh
applications. Such applications have pull-down menus and buttons that allow users
to select the functions they want to use by pointing and 'clicking' with a 'mouse'. For
many functions there is also the option of being selected by typing in a single
'paired-keystroke', such as '#V'. These commands have to be learned and remembered
before they can be used. However, once they have been learned, a selection can be
made quickly. For applications involving text input such as word-processors and
programming environments where the user's predominant mode of interaction is
with a keyboard, having to pull-down a menu and select a function with a 'mouse'
requires the user to take one hand from the keyboard and carry out a perceptual
motor aiming and searching action. This can be more time consuming and more
disruptive than typing in a paired-keystroke, once that command has been learned.
Consequently, it seems that users of such applications start off as novices making
much use of the mouse to select functions and, as they become more skilled, they
make less use of the mouse for selecting functions, using command keystrokes
instead.

A further consideration in HCI is the level and use of help. Inexperienced users
often fail to make use of the help facilities that are available. There are many reasons
for this, including the reluctance of people to invest time in learning new ways of
carrying out something they already know how to do by a different means. However,
there are problems with many forms of help. For example, the help provided in many
typical Unix environments is written for other Unix users, and is often of little use to
people who have no prior familiarity with Unix. In contrast, help is also used on some
occasions by skilled users who, for example, have simply forgotten the syntax of the
command. In some help systems written for novices, it is frustrating for more expert
users to have to search through the help material to find what they want. There are
occasions where different levels of help are advisable so that people with different
levels of skill can make optimum use of the help facility.

Exercises

1 Observe a novice typist and a touch typist at work; try to describe all the features
   of their behaviours. Qualitatively and quantitatively compare the two
   behaviours.
2 Design and carry out a simple experiment to investigate how learning occurs in
   mastering a new application. You might like to record: the time it takes people to
   perform given tasks; the errors they make; and the number of requests for help
   they make. Produce a learning curve showing how their performances change
   over a time. Note the rate of learning and any significant stages in their learning.
3 Investigate how transfer between different application programs affects a user.
   Identify where positive and negative transfer effects have occurred. You might
   like to consider how the negative transfer effects could have been avoided.

6 DEVELOPING INTERFACE DESIGNS

Summary

- Interface design and development is arguably the most labour-intensive and difficult part of the software development process. The reasons for this are that interface design involves making a variety of different design decisions, many of which involve users and tasks where the consequences of these decisions on both users and tasks is unknown.

- Software-engineering approaches to system development are described. Two particular approaches are considered in detail; the *waterfall model*, and the *prototyping* approach. The waterfall approach is essentially a top-down, phased design model, while the prototype approach is an iterative model of design.

Previous chapters have considered some of the psychological issues that arise in HCI. The design of user interfaces and complete systems is now considered from the perspective of software engineering. In Chapters 9 and 10 we will see how the psychology of users and the methods of software engineering can be brought closer together. First, the basic issues of software engineering are considered from an HCI perspective.

The design and development of a user interface is arguably the most demanding part of the complete system to produce, both in terms of the amount of time it takes to develop a good user interface and in terms of the proportion of software that is devoted to that part of the complete system. The reasons why the user interface is seen as being the most difficult and challenging part of the system to design is partly because of the number of different design skills required to develop a good interface. First and foremost, the designers must recognize that they are not just designing a piece of software. Developing the user interface involves designing communication and discourse, graphical and textual material, information and tasks, as well as the software through which the results of all the other design decisions will be reflected.

We will consider some important aspects of the design of the discourse, dialogue and interaction. The subject of graphics is too broad to be adequately considered in this book, but some important issues concerning the design of displays and visual presentations will be mentioned, as will the design of text and information. The main focus of this chapter, however, is the realization of these design decisions in software and, in particular, what kinds of software development processes and tools exist to support this activity.

PERSPECTIVES ON USER-INTERFACE DESIGN

User-interface design is perhaps the most difficult to get right, because the excellence of the design is dependent on so many things that are often thought of as being outside the software designers realm and range of comprehension. However, that should not be and need not be the case. The good interface-designer is, at present, a bit like a master craftsman or craftswoman, in that they have acquired a wide range of abilities. Of course, because of the craft-like nature of user-interface design, the teaching and passing on of interface-design knowledge is through experience and example more often than by books and lectures. However, a number of important advances have been made in recent years that have broadened our understanding of what constitutes good user-interface design methods.

Design of a user interface has to be considered from a number of different perspectives, each of which interacts to affect the quality of the overall design. Three perspectives to consider are as follows:

1 The functional perspective
2 The aesthetic perspective
3 The structural perspective

The *functional perspective* is concerned with whether or not the design is serviceable for its intended purpose. This perspective is largely concerned with issues of usability and the thoroughness of the support for user tasks. There is a trend to ignore function sometimes and design systems that can be used for anything. This is misguided, and usually results in systems that can be used by very few people to do not very much. The functional view of the design is at least as important as the other two. Achieving a good functional design is difficult, because in the first instance it needs the designer to define for what purposes the design is intended to be used. This is difficult for designers to do, largely for reasons of pride, because in stating what the design can be used for there is at least an implicit statement of what it cannot be used for. Somehow, software designers like to feel that their designs can be used for many if not all things. This assumption is incorrect inasmuch as no design, whether it is software or otherwise, can be used for any- and everything. However, there is some foundation for this assumption, in that designers can never fully predict all the things that their software might be used for, and would not want to restrict people from using their system for purposes that the designer had failed to consider. In fact, there is a tendency for designers to try to produce systems that users can then tailor, adapt or extend, so that they can be used to do more and more things. It is clear that designing a new system will have unpredictable and unknown effects on the tasks that people can perform. There is a cyclical relation between designing computer systems for known tasks, which systems, in turn, allow people to do new tasks.

This tension between defining the purpose of a design and wanting to allow users to use their software for anything the user chooses is costly, both in terms of the time taken to design software and in the final usability of the software. The answers seem to lie in having a good understanding of what the tasks users want or need to be able to perform through using a task analysis. The design of the system should then be approached in such a way that it can be clearly and easily seen to support those tasks for which it is intended, and at the same time allow for new uses and hence new tasks to be performed, following Carroll's (1990) design–artefact cycle.

The *aesthetic perspective* is concerned with whether or not the design is pleasing in its appearance and conforms to any accepted notions of artistic design. This aspect of the design is directly concerned with the design of the visual appearance of the interface. The designing of the graphical and textual figures and characters, as well as their layout on the screen, are of concern. For example, the design of textual information that might appear as prompts to the user, requests in dialogue boxes or labels for icons all mean that the designer has to be aware of the different fonts that are possible and their effect on the overall appearance of the interface. Large font sizes, in particular styles such as Geneva, can appear childish or patronizing for simple messages, while the same printer message in a different font would appear helpful and informative. For example, the message **Print now–yes/no?** in Helvetica 12-point bold, may be more or less attractive than the same message printed in the same size, etc., but a different font. Here it is in 12-point Rockwell Print now-yes/no?. Marcus (1990) has shown how the design of font styles, colour and the general grid-layout of the screen can ease confusion and be more aesthetically pleasing.

The aesthetic aspects of design do not stop at the screen. The size and shape of the input devices, and the position, shape, colour of buttons and keys all influence the aesthetic quality of the design. It is becoming more common to involve industrial and graphic designers as members of user-interface design teams to enable their contribution to this important aspect of design to be made more effectively. As time progresses and such things as interactive video and animation are more widely used, we may even need to include film designers and producers in design teams.

The *structural perspective* is concerned with whether or not the design has been built in a manner that will make it reliable and efficient to use and can be easily maintained and extended. This is perhaps the area of design with which the software developer is most at ease. There are many different approaches to providing a good structural perspective to the overall quality of the design. The essence of the problem is that the design of the interface should be structured in a way that produces efficient use of software, provides for easy construction, is executable in a reliable and efficient manner and allows for the reuse of software components and the construction of new components out of existing components. One solution to the problem has been found in the use of object-oriented programming languages that support the construction of class hierarchies and have inheritance mechanisms for sharing properties between members of a class. Through these properties, object-oriented languages have enabled user-interface design to be based around sets of primitive objects that each have their own behaviours and connections to other objects. From these primitive objects (often known as user-interface objects) the designer can construct newer objects as composites of the primitives (these are often known as composite-interface objects).

SOFTWARE-ENGINEERING METHODS AND HCI DESIGN

Howden (1982) estimated at that time that there were over 400 commercially available software development tools. This number is likely to have increased in recent years and will probably continue to do so as a result of research initiatives in this area. The number of different approaches to software development may well approach this number; however, we can categorize them into a smaller number of classes of software development processes. It is interesting to examine these different approaches to see how they relate, if at all, to the special needs of user-interface design, which is, after all, part of the system which is under design. This section does not try to provide a comprehensive view of software engineering; the interested reader is referred to more complete texts such as Pressman (1987), or Sommerville (1989).

An early definition of software engineering by Bauer in Naur and Randall (1969, page 19) was as follows:

> The establishment and use of sound engineering principles in order to obtain economical software that is reliable and works efficiently on real machines.

A better definition is as follows:

> The development and use of principles, methods and tools to design and develop, economically and optimally, software systems that are aesthetically pleasing, efficient, reliable and usable for the purposes for which they were designed.

Software engineering encompasses principles, methods and tools that enable design by providing a foundation for the development of software systems which allows the quality and production of the software to be managed and controlled when necessary.

Principles include principles of usability, design and construction. They should lead to the formulation of criteria by which the quality of the design can be tested. Examples of HCI principles are found in Thimbleby (1990) and Bellotti (1990)

Methods provide the process model for software development. The methods of software engineering cover such tasks as project planning, estimation of cost, time and scope; system and software requirements analysis; user requirements analysis, task analysis; design of data structures; program architecture; algorithm and procedure design; coding, testing and evaluations; and software maintenance/support.

Tools commonly include, but are not restricted to, languages, notations, semi-automated and automated support tools for the various methods, editors, browsers, libraries and toolkits. Special classes of tool are CASE (computer-aided software engineering) and IPSE (integrated project support environment). These offer some form of integration between tools, so that information from one can be used by another.

In Howden's (1982) review of software-engineering tools, a software lifecycle is described that includes requirements, design, programming, verification and maintenance to focus the different tools and methods of software engineering that were then available (a further category of tools and methods was project management). Using this model of the software lifecycle, he developed a classification with four different

Requirements	Informal charts and diagrams; informal prose specifications; formal charts and diagrams; informal requirements test plans.
Design	Informal functional design specifications; informal design test plans; automated data dictionary.
Programming	Text manager; automated source-code manager; program cross-reference tool; informal program test plans.
Verification	File comparator.
Management	Systematic manual methods (e.g. milestones).

Figure 6.1 Typical software development products from SEE type I (after Howden, 1982)

groupings of tools that were provided by particular software-engineering environments. Software-engineering environment (SEE) type I was the minimum set of tools and techniques that might have been expected to be used for a medium-sized project (e.g. a data-processing application with a 16 person-year development time). While at the other extreme SEE type IV included the set of tools that a large project might be expected to use (e.g. a real-time defence system with a 385 person-year development time).

In a type I environment, no automated requirements tools are provided but certain systematic methods were assumed. For design, an automated data dictionary was available. During coding a simple source-code control tool would be provided. For verification, an automated file comparator would be available, but no management tools would be provided. The support provided (both automated tools and methods) in an SEE of type I are shown in Fig. 6.1.

Comparing the two extremes of Howden's classification (type I and type IV), the characteristics of a type IV SEE were as shown in Fig. 6.2. Each classification shows the methods and tools that are used in software development. The type I classification provides some support for all activities but no automated support for requirements definition or project management, yet does provide some automated support for design, programming and verification. In contrast, a type IV SEE provides automated support for all aspects of this software lifecycle. Requirements definition is supported by various tools including machine-readable specifications, automated archives and cross-referencing. The design is supported by tools including machine-readable design specifications, module interface checker, automated archiving of design specifications and an automated simulator tool (such as a user-interface simulation tool). Programming is supported by tools including automated configuration managers, source-code formatters, flow charter and debugging and archiving tools. Verification support includes a test harness and test generator, various checkers and performance monitors. Project management receives support from automated project control systems and status report generators.

However, even in a type IV SEE, the support for HCI and user-interface design-related activities such as user or task requirements, dialogue design, presentation design, user-interface programming and verification, is minimal. In discussing type IV SEE's, Howden suggested that, during the requirements definition and design stages, experiments may be necessary where the requirements are actually tested by simulating aspects of the system so that feedback from users could then be used to

Requirements	Informal charts and diagrams; informal prose specifications; formal charts and diagrams; informal requirements test plans; machine-readable specification; machine-readable test plans; automated archive for requirements specification; specifications cross-reference tool; incremental requirements specification method; formal requirements specification reviews.
Design	Informal functional design specifications; informal design test plans; automated data dictionary; formal design specification methods; machine-readable design specifications; machine-readable design test plans; module interface checker; module cross-reference tools; automated archive for design specifications; formal design reviews; incremental design and review methods; design build plans; automated simulator tools.
Programming	Text manager; automated source-code manager; program cross-reference tool; informal program test plans; machine-readable program test plans; automated configuration manager; source-code formatter; flow charter; source-code debugging tool; program archive tool.
Verification	File comparator; test coverage analyser; test harness; units checker; test data generator; performance monitor; control flow analyser; data flow analyser; test plan archive tool.
Management	Systematic manual methods (e.g. milestones); automated project control system; projects status report generator; build plans tool.

Figure 6.2   Typical software development products from SEE type IV (after Howden, 1982)

determine if the proposed specification was acceptable. To this end some form of prototyping or simulation tools would be required. From the point of view of design methods, an ordering or sequential dependence between activities might be undesirable; however, all the toolsets described and reviewed by Howden would have been difficult to use in a truly unconstrained and unordered manner. Finally, Howden recognized that any SEE would be relatively useless if its own interface was poorly engineered from a human factors point of view and that simply to postulate that an SEE would produce more usable systems at less cost is unacceptable unless those claims can be supported with evidence. At that time there was little or no data on the effectiveness of any SEE in improving the quality, performance or usability of developed systems or the cost of development.

FORMAL METHODS

An important issue in both software engineering and HCI is the use of formal methods. Formal methods are included in Chapters 9, 10 and 12 in the context of particular approaches to user-interface design. However, the general belief is that using formal methods provides the designer with a clear and precise description of the requirements and/or the design, which can then be reasoned about using the precision of logic and mathematics. The problem is not with the power and use of formal methods, since that is generally accepted as being advantageous, but in the case of HCI, there is great uncertainty about what exactly it is that should be captured in a specification. Most specification languages were developed to specify machines or

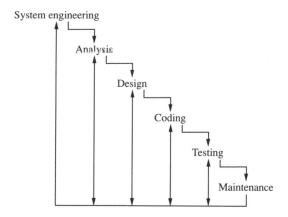

Figure 6.3 The classic lifecycle or waterfall model

programs. This presents a further problem when applying formal methods to HCI, since we must also consider how we would specify *user* behaviour. In subsequent chapters, the use of grammars, notations, temporal logic and algebraic specifications are considered with respect to modelling users, machine and task interactions. Harrison and Thimbleby (1989) and Dix (1991), include a variety of approaches to the use of formal methods in HCI.

THREE SOFTWARE-ENGINEERING PARADIGMS

The classic lifecycle or waterfall model

This model of software development requires a systematic, sequential approach to system development, that begins at the system level and progressing through analysis, design, coding, testing and maintenance (Fig. 6.3).

System engineering

This involves the following activities:

- Analysis of tasks, domain, users, hardware, software, all at a general level.
- Establishing user requirements.
- Establishing system requirements.
- Allocation of requirements to software.

The purpose of this phase of the lifecycle model is to identify the scope of the system and the general design area. The output from this phase produces a general requirements document that addresses each of the areas mentioned above.

Analysis

This involves detailed analysis of the following:

- Tasks
- Users

- Domain
- Software

The purpose of this phase is to understand the information exchanges, the domain entities, the required function of the system, the required performance characteristics and the interface characteristics and to establish the criteria for evaluating the resultant design. It produces as an output a specific requirements document.

Design

This includes design of the following:

- Data structures
- Software architecture
- Procedural detail
- User interface

The purpose of this phase of the lifecycle model is to translate the requirements specification into a model for the software. It produces a software design specification.

Coding

The *coding phase* of the lifecycle model involves the following activity:

- Translation of design specification into machine-runnable form.

The purpose of this phase is to produce a runnable version of the design and the final implementation of the design specification.

Testing

The *testing phase* of the lifecycle model involves testing the design in its implemented form in terms of the various requirement documents that were produced at the earlier stages of design. It includes the following:

- Logical testing of the software.
- Testing of the functionality.
- Testing of the usability.
- Testing of the efficiency of the design and the implementation.

The purpose of the testing phase of the lifecycle model is to assess the quality of the design and the coding. It produces a report on the design quality and a set of recommendations for any redesign that is required.

Maintenance

This is the final phase of the lifecycle model; it is said to involve the following:

- Repairing any errors or faults in the design or the coding.
- Updating the design because of changes in the requirements.

- Updating of the design because of changes in the environment in which the design will be used.

The purpose of this phase is to allow the software and the design to be adapted to the changes that *will* occur. It produces a revised set of requirements, a revised design and revised software.

Some observations about the lifecycle/waterfall model

There are a number of points that can be made about the lifecycle model of system design and development as follows:

1 Real projects are not sequential in the rigid way that this model assumes. Each phase may occur in a different order with iteration between phases or within a single phase. Thus it makes it difficult for any software design/development team to follow the sequential structure of the model.
2 It is often difficult to elicit or identify all the requirements at the start of the project because of the uncertainty that may exist in the users' and the designers' minds about the purpose of the project. This is particularly true about the requirements for the user interface.
3 The late production—in terms of the overall design/development lifecycle—of a runnable version of the design means that any errors in the earlier stages of the design may go undetected until the system is built.
4 Testing occurs late in the design/development lifecycle and fails to assess the design before the effort of coding has been spent. Thus errors in the design could have been detected earlier and rectified before coding took place.

However, there are some advantages to the lifecycle model. These are as follows:

1 It provides a comprehensive template in which many important aspects of design and development can be placed.
2 The steps which the model contains are in some way generic steps that are found in most software-engineering paradigms.
3 It is claimed to be the most widely used model of software design and development, at least among large software projects.
4 It is arguably better than a haphazard approach to design and development, at least from the point of view of being able to manage the production of the software.

An alternative framework, in which the process of software design and development can be considered, is one that has commonly come to be known as the prototyping approach. This approach is considered next.

PROTOTYPING

When the requirements are general or not well defined, as, for example, when the efficiency of an algorithm, the adaptability of an operating system, or the form of the user interface is not defined, a prototyping approach is often used. Prototyping

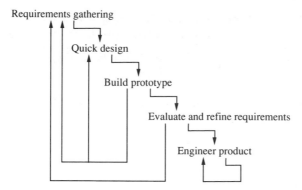

Figure 6.4   The prototyping model of software design and development

enables a designer to create an examinable model of the design. Prototypes can be runnable or not runnable and can be simulations or evolutionary:

- *Runnable prototypes*   can be either simulations of all or part of the overall design or early versions of the implementation. The difference between a simulation and an early version of the design is that a simulation cannot be evolved into the final system; it must be recoded, often on a different machine and in a different language. In contrast, an early version of the implementation can be evolved in the same environment and language into the final system.
- *Non-runnable prototypes*   can be paper based or computer based. Examples of non-runnable protyping are often found in interface design when drawing tools are used to produce sketches of what the interface could look like. One version of this is known as storyboarding, in which a number or sequence of screens are sketched and the sequence of an interaction can be illustrated by showing how each screen may change as some input is received or some process completed.

Each of the phases of the prototyping model of the software design and development process is shown in Fig. 6.4 and would involve the following:

- *Requirements gathering*   In this phase the system designer and the customer define the overall objectives of the system, any *known* requirements are identified and areas where further definition of the requirements are needed are also identified.
- *Quick design*   Focuses on the design of the user interface, especially those aspects of the user interaction that will be visible to the user.
- *Building the prototype*   This can be in any of the forms described above, and is a more detailed version of the quick design.
- *Evaluation*   At this stage an evaluation is carried out involving the designer, the customer and the user. The results of the evaluation are used to refine the requirements and add more detail to those areas of the requirements that were omitted during the initial requirements-gathering exercise.
- *Iteration*   Occurs at the stage where the prototype is tuned, modified or rebuilt until the results of the evaluations show that it satisfies the user and customer requirements and no new requirements are identified.
- *Engineering of product*   From the designed prototype the final product is

engineered. This may involve completely recoding the design in a different language and environment, or it may be a case of evolving the design from the prototype. During this phase there will occur further evaluations to ensure that the design is being developed in line with the requirements.

Some observations about the prototyping approach to design and development

There are a number of points about the approach to design that should be considered as follows:

1 The customer may not be prepared to let the designer modify or throw away the prototype because they see that it is a system that could be used, even if it is not the best system as far as the requirements are concerned.
2 The designer may have used quick and perhaps inefficient solutions to build the prototype quickly and then be reluctant or simply forget to change these if the design is then evolved into the final product.
3 It is essentially a trial and error approach to design.

However, prototyping has strong and important advantages in that:

1 It enables the user and customer to see and evaluate the user interface before the final system has been constructed.
2 It enables the prototype to be used to elicit further and more fuller requirements.
3 It enables evaluations of running designs.

A third class of system development approaches are those which embody some form of fourth-generation languages or tools.

Fourth-generation approaches to system development

A fourth-generation tool allows the software design to be specified at a high level of abstraction and then the tool or set of tools automatically generate the source code from the specification. Fourth-generation tools include non-procedural languages for database queries, report generation tools, data manipulation tools, screen interaction and definition tools, code generation tools, high-level graphics tools and libraries, type checkers and so on. These tools are developed for highly specific application areas and are rarely general purpose. Furthermore, there may be little or no integration between the various tools such that the output of one tool might be used as the input for another.

Figure 6.5 depicts Pressman's (1987) view of what a system development approach involving the use of fourth-generation languages and tools would be like. Each phase of the process would involve the following:

- *Requirements gathering* phase; this would involve gathering requirements, as in the prototyping approach, from the user and the customer. Ideally, the requirements would be specified in a form that could be interpreted by a specification tool.
- *Design strategy* phase; enables the approach to design using the fourth-generation tools to be defined. This might involve deciding how to address

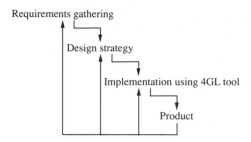

Figure 6.5   A development process involving the use of fourth-generation tools/languages

quality assurance, evaluation maintenance and design rationale, to mention but a few, within the production plan leading to the developed system.

- *Implementatation* phase; involves the designer in describing the required design in terms of the fourth-generation language used by the tool. This design is then translated by the fourth-generation tool into runnable source-code.
- *Product* phase; involves testing and evaluation of the developed system. Also documentation and maintenance are addressed during this phase.

Some observations about a fourth-generation tool approach to design

If we are to take Pressman's view as a true reflection of design using a fourth-generation toolset then the following points can be raised:

1 The application domain of many fourth-generation tools is very limited and few tools are widely applicable to all domains.
2 Even with a fourth-generation tool the need for analysis, design and testing is still present and these are not supported by any tools.
3 One positive point is that the time it takes to produce the software for the developed system is reduced, but there is nothing to ensure that the software that is produced constitutes a good design.

Each of the three approaches considered above have some good feature which could be utilized in a combined design model.

PRESSMAN'S MODEL OF SYSTEM DEVELOPMENT

Pressman suggests that instead of viewing the three approaches (i.e. the lifecycle model, prototyping and fourth-generation tool model) as being alternative choices for the design team, they can be combined such that the approaches complement one another.

In the approach shown in Fig. 6.6, the design and development begins with a requirements-gathering phase in which the designer, user and customer (if they are different people) must communicate with one another to establish and agree a set of requirements, and to identify where requirements are unknown and need to be defined during the subsequent phases of the project.

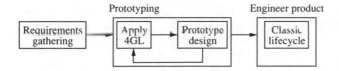

Figure 6.6 A combined view of the software development process (from Pressman, 1987)

Having defined the user requirements, a prototyping phase can be embarked upon in which early designs of the user interface and the visible parts of the system are developed and iteratively evaluated until no more requirements remain undefined or unsatisfied. This prototyping should make use of fourth-generation tools and other rapid prototyping environments that allow designs to be developed into a runnable form quickly and easily.

The transition from prototype to product requires a more conventional approach to design, since the issues of maintenance and quality assurance of the final software have to be managed.

GENERIC PHASES IN SOFTWARE DEVELOPMENT

Having considered a number of different approaches to software development, it can be seen that there are a number of generic activities that must or do exist. There are three generic activities: *definition*, *development* and *maintenance* (Fig. 6.7).

Definition is concerned with identifying what information is to be processsed; what functions and performance are required; what interface is required; what tasks the system must support; what are the characteristics of the user group; what design constraints there are; and what criteria can be established by which the design can be evaluated. System defintion seems to involve three subactivities:

1 *System analysis* To define the role of each element in the system and to define the scope of the system.
2 *Software project planning* To define the approach to design and cost/resources required and to allocate tasks to the members of the design team.
3 *Requirements analysis* To define the user, task and domain and to identify criteria which the design should meet.

The second generic activity is development, and this is concerned with: how data structures and the software architectures of the system are to be designed; how procedural details are to be implemented; how the user interface is to be developed;

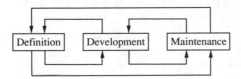

Figure 6.7 Three generic activities in software development

how the design will be translated into a programming language; and how testing and evaluation will be performed. This activity can be divided into four subactivities, namely:

1 *Software design*   The requirements are translated into a set of representations describing the data structures, architectures and algorithmic procedures and the user interface is designed in terms of its style of presentation, the form of the dialogue and its linking to the application.
2 *Coding*   The design ideas are translated into an implementable language.
3 *Testing*   The design is evaluated in terms of the different types of requirements and criteria identified in the definition activities.
4 *Redesign*   The requirements and the design are reconsidered in the light of the results of the evaluations.

The third activity is maintenance, in which the changes, corrections and adaptations of the system to meet new demands are made.

CONCLUSION

Software engineering is concerned with developing principles, methods and tools to assist in the production and management of software. The focus of software engineering is on the complete system and its lifecycle. However, it is often the case that no specific principles, methods or tools are provided for a most crucial part of the system—the user interface.

The different models of the software-engineering process that abound are largely idealized and tend to be diluted and deviated from in many design contexts. It seems that the type of project, the type of design team, and the organization in which the design team work can all influence the particular form of design process that occurs.

However, we need to understand something of the process of design if we are to apply HCI methods and tools to design. There have been a number of interesting surveys of designers and design processes, in particular, Bellotti (1989, 1990) has carried out detailed surveys of designers working in small- and medium-sized design teams. From her surveys of designers and her investigations of HCI methods, she was able to generate a framework for applying HCI methods to design and to provide a basis for identifying the requirements for HCI methods.

The particular software-engineering processes discussed in this chapter have evolved over time to accommodate the changing needs of software designers and developers. As was discussed in Chapter 1, HCI requires a detailed understanding of the user and tasks that form part of the task–artefact design cycle. Interface design requires an understanding of the users' tasks and it results in changes to users' tasks. The old tasks influence the design of new artefacts, and the new artefacts influence the nature of tasks by allowing people to carry out more and different tasks than were previously possible. Consequently, design methods must recognize that analysis of tasks is required before, during and after the design is produced.

In a different project, Maclean, Bellotti amd Young (1990), have investigated how designers rationalize their designs. This interesting but early work may well lead us to a better understanding of the psychology of user-interface design. In the meantime, it seems that merely making designers document the reasons behind their design decisions is itself a useful process, since it provides a record which can be returned to at a future date when the design is being evaluated or reconsidered.

Exercises

1 If you have access to any software designers, you might like to ask them to tell you the stages and activities of design that were gone through on a recent design project. From this account, can you see any place where the design process might have been improved?
2 Produce a requirements specification for a cash dispenser by consulting potential end-users.
3 Produce a design specification from the requirements specification.
4 Produce a 'storyboard' design prototype user interface from your design specification.

7   Evaluations of Interactive Systems

Summary

- Evaluations of interactive systems can occur at various stages in the design process and can assess different aspects of design.

- Those aspects of design which are of interest from a human factors perspective are *usability*, *learnability*, *efficiency* and *acceptability*. These four aspects of design are defined in general terms.

- The problem for the designer is to know what aspects of design are likely to affect what kind of outcome in any of these four areas. This requires each of the four areas to be *operationalized* in some way that makes them readily assessable. One solution is to provide *metrics* as part of the design specification, which can be used to assess the resultant design.

- Evaluation methods vary in their sophistication and in their applicability. The least sophisticated approaches require little preparation and are the least time-consuming but are the least diagnostic with respect to the cause of the design problem. The more sophisticated evaluation methods are often time consuming and require technical knowledge of experimental methods, but in turn are the most diagnostic with respect to identifying design problems.

- Experiments to evaluate a design have to be carefully constructed and are themselves a form of design. The experimenter must identify the *dependent* and *independent variables*, the *control* and *experimental conditions*, the *subjects*, the experimental *method*, and the form of *data analysis*.

In this chapter, the concept of evaluation is considered in some detail. The aim is to make the reader aware of the need for, and the complexities and methods of evaluation in system design. The aim of human factors evaluations is to identify inadequacies in design and to provide the design team with a sufficient understanding of how the design is inadequate, so that it can be redesigned without the same inadequacies being present. Of course nobody likes to be told their design is inadequate, or wrong in some way, especially if no constructive suggestions are being made about how it can be improved. The discomfort that is felt from receiving criticism is a feature of human nature and is true of all aspects of human endeavour. However, evaluation should not be seen as a form of criticism, but as a part of the design process that is as crucial and fundamental to that process as writing the code. Furthermore, there is no need for the evaluation to be carried out by a third party who is outside the design team. The role of evaluation in the design process is to help develop a system that has been *designed* rather than one that has been 'thrown together'. Design is about taking care and striving for perfection. Evaluation methods are one of the tools that can help the designers achieve a closer match to perfection in their designs.

EVALUATION AND DESIGN PROCEDURES

The first point to recognize is that there is no one design procedure. There are many different views about what is the best or right way to design a software system, all of which are more or less equally wrong (or right depending upon your point of view). The point is that these methods are the ones that work for the particular design team project, and as such they are right for that team and project. At some level, these different design methods will have particular consequences for the appropriateness of a particular evaluation method, and it may require the design team to 'fine tune' one or other of the design or evaluation methods. However, at a more general level, it is possible to separate the design process into two stages at which evaluation may occur. The order of these stages is not fixed. They are of interest because they have consequences for what is available for evaluation. The first stage considered here is referred to as the *design-specification stage*. It is presumed that at some stage in all design procedures a specification of the system is produced. This specification may take a variety of forms and may be at one or more levels of abstraction. The second stage is referred to as the *implementation stage*. At the implementation stage there is some form of runnable program implemented on a particular machine.

In their survey of design-and-development practice in IBM, Rosson, Mass and Kellogg (1989) found that very few designers carried out a 'formal' evaluation of the design. Most evaluations were of a very informal and subjective nature. This seemed to be true regardless of the project size or the type of design project it was (i.e. what was being designed). However, they did discover that evaluations were more often iterative than once and for all. Thus, evaluation would occur at various stages in the lifecycle of the development project. It is not known from Rosson *et al.*'s study if the evaluations were always on implemented/runnable versions of the system or if they included some evaluation of the design as a specification rather than an implementation.

Evaluation at the design-specification stage

There is little to be said about evaluation at the specification stage because it is still the subject of much research and speculation. However, the concept of evaluating a specification is of much interest, since it offers the designer a method of evaluating the design before committing resources to program writing and implementation. At present, there are no well-worked-out methods for evaluating a design from a specification. Some of the modelling techniques considered later in Chapters 9 and 10 can be used to predict some degree of usability and learnability of the design. For instance, Reisner's (1981) task action language (see Chapter 9) can be used to predict the difficulties a user might face in using a system. Task action language (TAL) allows the command language to be evaluated for its consistency and learnability. TAL does not predict performance times; Reisner claims it can predict the relative consistency and usability difficulties of two alternative interfaces to the same underlying functionality. This can be done by counting and comparing the number of rules in the grammar required to describe each of the two command languages to achieve the same task using the particular interface. In a similar vein, the technique of modelling developed by Payne and Green (1986) known as task action grammars (TAG) also allows the consistency of command language to be evaluated (see Chapter 10). Like TAL, TAG does not predict performance times. Both TAL and TAG use the idea of defining a grammar of the interaction which can then be used to describe which rules of a given grammar wall be invoked for some user task to be performed. The grammars of TAL and TAG attempt to capture some property of usability and learnability that arises through inconsistencies in the user interface. The evaluation in each case is performed by counting properties and features of the rules (e.g. number and complexity) that in turn reflect some feature of usability. The premise is that inconsistent interfaces are difficult to learn and use. The two ways of modelling used by TAL and TAG are reviewed in more detail in Chapters 9 and 10 respectively.

Performance evaluations from specifications are provided by the GOMS (see Chapter 9) approach of Card, Moran and Newell (1983). This approach provides time-based predictions of the different tasks a user might want to perform with a designed system. Furthermore, these predictions can be made at different levels of detail depending upon the grain of analysis chosen. More recently, Kieras and Polson (1986) have extended GOMS into cognitive complexity theory (CCT). CCT uses production rules to predict the learnability and complexity of a user interface (see Chapter 10). The evaluator is required to count the number of productions required for any task and each production represents an item of knowledge which it is assumed that the user would have to acquire or possess already. This approach offers the designer an evaluation of the user interface from a specification. Both GOMS and CCT predict performance, although CCT is similar to TAL and TAG in its reliance on counting rules.

While there are a growing number of approaches to the evaluation of designs at the specification stage, none of the above-mentioned techniques have been applied with sufficient success to be able to make any recommendations at this stage. The current focus seems to be on the use of approaches such as cognitive complexity theory. However, they have yet to be used as an evaluation technique in a 'real' design-and-development project, as opposed to being used in a research project to develop the method further. Many of the modelling approaches considered in Chapters 9 and 10 have some potential for supporting evaluations from design specifications. One common feature of all approaches to evaluation is that they require models of the user, the task and the design. Two further dimensions which must be considered are the domain and the organization. Each of these five dimensions provides a set of constraints which are used in the evaluation.

Evaluation at the implementation stage

The conventional approach to evaluations is to evaluate the design once there is a runnable program that can be used. There are a number of different approaches to evaluating an implemented design. Each approach varies in both the amount of information it can disclose and the amount of time it takes to perform the evaluation. Evaluations also vary in their diagnostic ability. The easiest and least diagnostic form of evaluations is an 'expert walk-through'. In this approach, an expert in interface design is asked to go through the designed system and identify any point at which they feel a user may have problems. This is heavily reliant upon the judgement of the expert. It may be strengthened by having independent experts 'walk-through' the system. It does provide a quick-and-easy way to perform evaluation and it may lead to an improved design.

Another technique for assessing an implementation is to use questionnaires to identify what features of the system users themselves find difficult to use and/or to assess the user's attitudes to the new design. The main criticism of questionnaires of this sort is they are often good at identifying the acceptability of a system but not good at identifying its usability or reasons why it may be unusable.

A further technique is to use an observational approach in which the designer simply observes without intervening in the user's attempts to use the system. Through taking video recordings of the user's attempts to use the system, the designer can quickly and convincingly see where the design causes problems and what the problems are. However, a more detailed analysis or further evaluation may be necessary to diagnose correctly the real nature of the user's problems by an experimental method.

EXPERIMENTAL METHODS

Experiments are frequently used in HCI to evaluate implemented designs. An experiment has to be planned and requires some knowledge of experimental design and analysis. The power of experiments are that they enable the experimenter to *control* and *manipulate* particular *variables* in the environment. A definition of terms in experimental design follows:

Dependent variable	That which is measured (e.g. time to task completion).
Independent variable	The features which are manipulated (e.g. style of icons or order of items on a menu).
Experimental control	Those features of the experiment (variables) that are held constant and not allowed to vary at all in the experiment (e.g. time of day, machine on which the program is running).
Experimental factor	The dimensions along which the independent variables are being manipulated (e.g. interface style might be one factor and level of expertise of users might be another factor).

Levels within a factor	The particular manipulations within a single dimension (e.g. interface style might have two levels—icons and menus, while level of expertise might have three levels—novice, partial expert, expert).
Between groups design	Different groups of subjects used in each condition of the experiment. (enables asymmetric transfer effects to be controlled.)
Within-groups design	The same group of subjects are used in all conditions of the experiment (where repeated measures on different variables or levels are obtained from each subject).
Mixed-groups design	Some conditions of the experiment are given to the same subjects, but other conditions require different groups of subjects (i.e. a mix of between- and within-group designs).
Longitudinal study	Same group of subjects are measured repeatedly over time. (e.g. as in a learning study where the same group are observed over a period of time).
Cross-sectional study	Different subjects are measured at different stages of the study (e.g. sampling different people at each stage of learning).

A useful reference on experimental design for the behavioural sciences is Meyers and Grossen (1972).

EXPERIMENTAL METHODOLOGY

What is an experiment?

Much of the research in psychology relies on empirical evidence, normally attained through carrying out an experiment. One of the most powerful ways of evaluating a software design is to use a controlled experiment. Normally, experiments are designed to test some predictions arising from an explicit hypothesis that arises out of an underlying theory. For example, the theory of working memory hypothesizes that there is a limited capacity for maintaining information in an active state without that information being lost from working memory. From this hypothesis, it might be predicted that a computer interface which required the user to maintain a list of command names in working memory while moving between different modes of the application would produce more errors and slower performance due to the user forgetting items in the list, than a design which made visible all the different command options and did not have occasions where the user was required to move between different modes.

An experiment must satisfy the following three criteria:

1 The experimenter must systematically manipulate one or more independent variables in the domain under investigation.

2 The manipulation must be made under controlled conditions, such that all variables which could affect the outcome of the experiment are controlled (the problem of control in experiments is addressed shortly).

3 The experimenter must measure some unmanipulated feature that changes (the dependent variable), or is assumed to change, as a function of the manipulated independent variable.

Thus experiments are concerned with the systematic manipulation of one or more independent variables under controlled conditions, and involve careful planned measurement of the effects of those variables on relevant dependent variables.

A variable is some general property or characteristic that may be present, absent or take on a range of values. A variable must meet the following two conditions:

1 There must be some property or characteristic that can be manipulated.

2 The value of that property or characteristic must be measurable. It is normal to specify the way that the variable can be measured.

As we have already seen a variable can be an independent or a dependent variable.

Independent variables

In an experiment, independent variables are those factors that are systematically varied by the experimenter. On some occasions the independent variable is also called the experimental treatment or manipulation. For example, if an experimenter wishes to determine whether different rates of learning exist for three different types of interface, (direct manipulation, form based and command based), then each of these types of interface would be a level of the independent variable 'type of interface'. We would also say that in this case there were three *levels* of the independent variable; a level is a particular value that the independent variable can take in the experiment. The experimenter will design the experiment so as to manipulate which level of the independent variable is used in which *condition* of the experiment. In an experiment there may be more than one independent variable. For example, suppose it was felt that learning rate would be influenced not only by the type of interface, but also by whether or not help was provided. In this case, there would be two independent variables: type of interface and provision of help. There are three levels to the type of interface (command line, form filling and command line) and two levels to the provision of help (help provided and no help provided). This experiment would be a 'two-factor experiment' or a 'two-treatments experiment' because there would be two different independent variables—type of interface and provision of help. The difference between a factor and a level is that if two or more independent variables constitute different types of independent variable then they are different factors, while a level would be the same type of independent variable but with a different value associated with it.

Dependent variables

These are the particular dimensions by which the effect of the independent variable is measured. For example, we might decide to measure the rate at which people learned to use one of the three types of interface described above (direct manipulation, form based, command based) in terms of the number of trials they had on some preset tasks, before they finally managed to perform the tasks three times in succession without making any errors. Thus, the number of trials required before three correct performances of the task had been achieved would be the dependent variable. It would, of course, also be necessary to define what was meant by an error-free performance and hence what was meant by an error. This same dependent variable (the number of trials to correct performance of the task) could be applied to all the levels of the type of interface factor and also to the second factor of the experiment, the provision of help. The results would be interpreted in terms of how many trials were required with a given interface type when help was either provided or not. The interface type that had the lowest number of trials in any condition would be the one that had the fastest learning rate as measured by that particular dependent variable. It would always be possible to choose a different dependent variable, such as the quickest time to complete the task correctly. In this case, it would be necessary to define how to measure time. The results of the experiment when measured by this dependent variable would show a better interface to be the one that had the lowest learning rate in terms of producing the fastest time to complete the task. This could mean that one interface provided the quickest way to learn to perform the task correctly, but a different interface produced the fastest correct task-performance time. We would then have to explain this difference, perhaps by performing a further experiment to test if the explanation was valid.

The particular dependent variable chosen must always depend upon the theory and hypotheses which led to the design of the experiment. Dependent variables must have the following properties:

1 They must be readily observable.
2 They must be stable and reliable so that they do not vary under constant experimental conditions.
3 They must be sensitive to the effects of the independent variables.
4 They must be readily related to some scale of measurement.

The purpose of undertaking an experiment is to gain more knowledge or to test some prediction about any given factor(s) (variable(s)) that are of interest. Normally experiments are carried out to test a set of predictions from some hypotheses that have arisen out of a particular theory. Occasionally, experiments may be performed, not to test any particular prediction, but to simply gain more information about the problem space and to identify factors to be considered in the development of any theory.

In HCI investigations, the researcher often needs to gain more knowledge about the user or the use of design artefacts with the least cost in terms of time and effort to the system development process. For example, before developing an interface, the designer may want to investigate whether or not icons with labels are better than icons without labels, or labels alone. Instead of the designer/developer making an intuitive or personal choice it would be very easy to design and run an experiment to test these ideas.

The purpose of an experiment can be thought of as a means of identifying a functional relationship between an independent and dependent variable. This means that there is some correspondence between the values of the independent variable and the values of the dependent variable. Through this correspondence it is then possible to infer some form of cause–effect relationship between the independent variable and the dependent variable.

Examples of commonly used dependent variables in HCI experiments are as follows:

- Number of errors made
- Where (at what point in the task) were the errors made
- Time taken to complete a given task
- Time taken to recover from an error
- Quality of the resultant task output
- Preference ratings
- Attitude scores
- Latency time before initiating a response
- Event times (e.g. inter-key times)

These dependent variables differ in their scales of measurement in that they produce different kinds of data. Some produce *qualitative* data while others produce *quantitative* data. For example, the quality of the resultant task output is clearly a qualitative dependent variable, while others such as time taken to complete a task are clearly quantitative. Many experiments will use more than one dependent variable and different types of dependent variable. For example, it is common to measure both the time to complete a task and the number of errors made. Also, the experimenter may include a questionnaire to record the subjects' preferences or attitudes to the different levels of a given independent variable, such as the type of interface. The first two are quantitative measures while attitudes are more often qualitative measures. The dependent variable can be classified according to a scale of measurement.

Scales of measurement

Generally, measurement consists of assigning numbers to behaviours according to some rules. There are four different types of measurements. These are known as scales of measurement and are as follows:

1 Nominal Scale
2 Ordinal Scale
3 Interval Scale
4 Ratio Scale

Nominal scale This is simply a naming or classification scale. The differences between categories on a nominal scale are qualitative differences. In a nominal scale of measurement, the numbers or labels serve no other function and provide no further information other than to differentiate the two categories of behaviour. Furthermore, within a nominal scale, those entities which are similarly classified receive the same label. For example, we might label two groups of users, experts and partial experts respectively. We cannot apply any operations such as greater than, less than, add, subtract, divide or multiply to a nominal scale. So, for example, we cannot say that a menu selection is more or less than mouse movement. They are simply different categories of behaviour.

Ordinal scale   This scale is a little more sophisticated than the nominal scale in that it has the following properties:

1 Different points or values on the scale represent different things.
2 The things that are measured on this scale may be ordered or ranked along a given dimension.

With the ordinal scale, the differences along the scale are quantitative because they are all differences along a single dimension. Ordering along an ordinal scale is by the application of the mathematical operators, greater than or less than. To order things is to say that one point on the scale has more or less than another point on the scale of the particular characteristic that is being measured. However, the scale does not indicate how much more or less of that characteristic any individual datum possesses. For example, we might have rated the quality of five interface designs in terms of their appearance to the user and given the value 1 to the lowest rating and 5 to the highest. We cannot say that a design with the rating 1 is five times worse than a design with the rating 5. The concept of how much more cannot be given by ordinal data; only the concepts of more or less are given by the scale. Another example of ordinal data are attitude scales and preference ratings. Thus the scale might have points such as strongly agree, agree, weakly agree, neither agree nor disagree, weakly disagree, disagree, strongly disagree. Such a scale would allow us to rank subjects' responses but we could not tell how far apart the responses on the scale were, we could only say that strongly agree represents more agreement than weakly agree. Thus the points on the scale cannot be assumed to be equidistant from each other and therefore the arithmetic operators of add, subtract, divide and multiply cannot be applied to measurements on this scale.

Interval scale   This is more sophisticated than the ordinal scale and has the following three properties:

1 Different points or values on the scale represent different things.
2 The things that are measured on this scale may be ordered or ranked along a given dimension.
3 The intervals between adjacent points on the scale are of equivalent value.

An interval scale sets points equidistant from one another. The Fahrenheit temperature scale is a good example of an interval scale because each number represents a different temperature. The numbers are ranked (60 degrees is cooler than 70 degrees), and the difference between the intervals is equidistant (the interval between 60 and 65 degrees is equal to the interval between 55 and 60 degrees). But we cannot say that 40 degrees is twice as cool as 80 degrees because this is not a ratio scale.

Ratio scale   This is more sophisticated than the interval scale. It has the following properties:

1 Different points or values on the scale represent different things.
2 The things that are measured on this scale may be ordered or ranked along a given dimension.
3 The intervals between adjacent points on the scale are of equivalent value.
4 There is an absolute or fixed zero point.

By including a fixed zero point in the definition of the scale, we can now make ratio judgements of differences. (Examples of ratio scales are time, distance, mass, etc., for instance, 20 seconds is twice as long as 10 seconds).

The use of different scales has important consequences for the kind of statistics that can be carried out on the data because of the different arithmetic operators involved in computing the statistic and the properties of the scale of measurement. One important point is that it is inappropriate to calculate the average of nominal and ordinal scales because they will not allow the arithmetical operator of add to be applied in any meaningful way.

EXPERIMENTAL DESIGN

Experimental design is concerned with the general plan for conducting an experiment. An experiment is the primary means by which we are able to establish cause–effect relationships between certain events in the environment and the occurrence of particular forms of behaviour.

An experiment is carried out to:

1 Provide empirical support/evidence for a theory.
2 Test hypotheses which arise from the theory.
3 Validate results from previous experiences and experiments.

A simple notion is that two or more groups of subjects (people) are treated exactly alike in all ways except one—the experimental treatment. Any differences observed in the behaviour of the two or more groups of subjects is then attributed to, or said to be caused by, the difference in the specific treatment conditions.

Hypotheses

The research hypothesis is a succinct statement of the purpose of the experiment. The experiment is set up to manipulate independent variables and observe their effect(s) on the dependent variable(s) which will either confirm or reject the experimental hypotheses. An example of a research hypothesis might be that users learn quicker with a structured rather than an unstructured interface. The independent variable in this example will be the type of interface and the dependent variable(s) could be the number of errors made, the length of time to complete the task and users' preference rating for the two interfaces.

Differences in experimental designs

Experimental designs may differ in the following ways:

1 In the type of, and how many, subjects participate in the experiment.
2 In the number of independent variables to be manipulated, and the number of levels of those variables.
3 In the method of assigning subjects to different treatment conditions, resulting in independent groups (between), a repeated measure (within), or mixed (an element of both) design.

The simplest experiment that can be carried out involves two conditions, the experimental condition and the control condition. One meaning of the term 'control', used in connection with experimental design, is where the control condition is used as a baseline against which the effects of the experimental manipulation may be evaluated. A control condition is identical to the experimental condition in all but the manipulation of the experimental treatment. Another meaning of control, in the context of experiments, is concerned with the need to control confounding variables so that they do not affect or bias the results of the experimental manipulation.

Subject selection

A subject is the person who participates in the experiment. It is not advisable for the designers themselves to act as subjects for a number of reasons. First, if there is to be generalization of the experimental results to a target population then a random, representative sample of that population must act as subjects. Therefore, if computer users are the population of interest then it is advisable to test a random sample of those users. Second, potential users of the proposed system (users who are not designers) are likely to carry out their tasks in a different manner to the way in which the designer carries out the same task; for instance, they may use a different vocabulary or they may have a different conceptualization of the task, resulting in different plans and sequencing of the task. For example, in designing a system to aid architects in designing room layouts, a random sample of subjects from the architect community is appropriate and will provide the best possible information for the designer of the proposed system with which to work. Third, there are differences between computer-users (e.g. novices versus experts), and the appropriate population should be sampled so that the proposed system is suitably targeted. Novice computer-users have different expectancies and consequently different patterns of behaviour from expert users. In evaluating a system, HCI researchers are usually interested in ease of use and learning. Ease of learning is often measured in terms of the time required to achieve some asymptotic (plateau) level of performance. Ease of use is then measured in terms of how high that asymptote is and the rate of change in the learning curve to the asymptote. However, it is not always the case that speed to complete a task is important and therefore the subject's subjective impressions of the system might also be recorded (although it is interesting that there is often no correlation between subjective preference ratings and performance).

The factors to consider in subject selection include the following:

1 The subject's previous experiences.
2 The level of skill.
3 The number of subjects needed.

Other subject factors often taken into account or controlled are age, experience (of computers and of the task), intelligence, sex, handedness, motivation and anxiety. If these factors are not systematically manipulated, i.e. treated as independent variables, then they often must be controlled.

The availability of subjects is often an important constraining factor. The number of subjects is a matter of choice, but there are general rules. You need enough subjects to provide a relatively sensitive test of the research hypothesis. 'Sensitivity' is concerned with the ability to detect differences when they are present. One way to increase sensitivity is to increase the number of subjects. However, significant statistical results rely on the treatment variance being greater than expected by chance. Generally, the minimum number of subjects in a controlled experiment should be no less than six but the increase in sensitivity with ten subjects or more is considerable.

Single case studies (where $n = 1$) might consist of a single subject keeping a diary of interaction events at the interface, or alternatively, could consist of observation by the experimenter and then subsequent questioning of the subject, and the use of protocols. Single case studies are undertaken when time is limited, when subjects of a particular type are in short supply, when in-depth knowledge about a number of factors affecting behaviour are of interest, and also when generalization is not a major issue.

In HCI, as in other disciplines, single case studies tend to provide initial information for the researcher/designer on an array of topics. The results can then provide the basis for research hypotheses and controlled experiments about a factor of particular interest or concern to the experimenter. The method or approach adopted for collecting data, whether a single case study adopting one or more data collection methods, or controlled experiments utilizing ten or more subjects, depends on the purpose of obtaining such data and how it fits in the overall framework of computer-system design.

There is no one correct experimental design or approach, but there are principles of experimental design, which ought to be adhered to.

Designing experiments

Designing HCI experiments involves at least the following:

1 Formulating the hypotheses.
2 Developing predictions from the hypotheses.
3 Choosing a means to test the predictions.
4 Identifying all the variables that might affect the results of the experiment.
5 Deciding which are the independent variables (and levels of the independent variable), dependent variables and which variables need to be controlled by some means.
6 Designing the experimental task and method.
7 Subject selection.
8 Deciding the experimental design, data collection method and controlling confounding variables.
9 Deciding on the appropriate statistical or other analysis.
10 Carrying out a pilot study (i.e. prototype the experimental design).

Confounding

The strength of the experimental method depends on the experimenter's ability to guarantee that only the manipulated variables are permitted to vary systematically from condition to condition. When a second or other variable is unwittingly permitted to vary along with the intended one, we say that the variables are *confounded*. There are a number of ways of controlling confounding or nuisance variables if they are not being treated as independent variables. The two main ways are by holding them constant, achieved by applying them equally to all the treatment conditions, and by randomizing (a weaker version is counterbalancing) the sequence from subject to subject.

Assigning subjects to different treatment conditions (independent groups, repeated measures and mixed designs)

In this section, we will consider experimental procedure. In the between-groups design (also known as the independent-group design), the subject contributes just one score to the data analysis thereby avoiding all the problems of asymmetric transfer effects (i.e. order or practice effects) from one condition or trial to the next. However, it is costly in terms of subjects, and if there are large individual differences within the groups, from one individual to another, then there is the possibility that the within-groups differences will be greater than the between-groups differences, resulting in non-significant differences between the control and experimental conditions because the subjects were highly variable. To reduce subject variation, the subjects can be matched on whatever factors might be thought to affect performance, including skill, age, IQ, etc.

Between-groups design—an example   **Within-groups design—an example**

| Group 1 | Group 2 | Group 1 | Group 2 |
Interface A	Interface B	Interface A	Interface B
S1	S6	S1	S1
S2	S7	S2	S2
S3	S8	S3	S3
S4	S9	S4	S4
S5	S10	S5	S5

Within-group designs are more efficient in that more information is obtained from each subject; this is important where time is limited and the availability of subjects is scarce. Within-groups designs (or repeated measures) are also appropriate where training is required. For example, in learning experiments or where complicated instructions are required before any specific treatment is introduced. In within-groups designs, the same subjects receive all treatment conditions. The subject acts as their own control. Consequently, the subject variance is less and the design is more powerful. Within-group designs usually require fewer total observations than the between-group design to achieve the same degree of sensitivity or statistical power.

However, the major problem with within-groups designs is the *carry-over effects*. Carry-over, practice and range effects all affect subsequent user behaviour. Performance of the last task can be influenced due to having experienced the earlier conditions. Alternatively, there is the possibility that fatigue might result in the later tasks being performed less well than the earlier tasks. These effects have to be taken into account in the experimental design. Some of these effects can be diminished by having half the subjects in a group perform under condition A first and then condition B second, etc., while for the other half of the subjects the order is reversed, i.e. B then A.

A popular type of design is the mixed factorial, where the carry-over effects are not so great and where subjects' performance can be measured over a number of trials on one of the independent variables. Mixed-factorial designs involve one or more independent variables being treated as within groups and also one other, or more, independent variables being treated as between groups.

Mixed factorial design—an example

Group 1	Group 2
Interface style—pictures	Interface style—text
Trials, 1. 2. 3. 4.	Trials, 1. 2. 3. 4.
S1	S7
S2	S8
S3	S9
S4	S10
S5	S11
S6	S12

In this example, the independent variables are interface style (2 levels) and trials (4 levels). The design is a 2×4 mixed factorial design. Interface style is between groups, while trials are repeated measures. Mixed-factorial designs are particularly useful where learning (as in this example) is being manipulated along with another variable. Learning variables are best treated as repeated measures.

STATISTICAL TREATMENT OF THE DATA

To test whether the differences between the means of the groups of data observed are statistically significant, we set up a null hypothesis. The null hypothesis states that the two (or more) groups come from the same population, i.e. that there is no difference between the two groups, or more succinctly, there is no effect of the experimental manipulation. Testing the null hypothesis involves computing the probability that the result could have arisen by chance. Obviously, the researcher wishes to reject the null hypothesis and accept the alternative hypothesis that there is an effect of the experimental manipulation. Having computed the probability of obtaining a given result, the next step is to decide whether that probability of that result having occurred by chance alone is small enough to safely reject the null hypothesis.

Arbitrary critical levels are set for this purpose; if the probability is less than this, the result is said to be significant beyond that level. The critical levels are known as *significance levels*. Three significance levels are commonly used in HCI: 0.001, 0.01 and 0.05. The interpretation of the 0.05 significance level is that it is believed that the probability of this result occurring by chance is five in one hundred.

Significant results mean nothing if the experimental design is poor and the research hypothesis and, in turn the theory, are uninteresting.

Parametric and nonparametric statistics

Statistical designs are divided into two crude categories: parametric and nonparametric. The proper use of parametric statistics includes not only measurements but also a variety of assumptions regarding certain characteristics of both the collected data and the population from which the sample has been drawn.

Assumptions of parametric tests

There are three general assumptions as follows:

1 The selection of subjects from the population was random and independent, i.e. every subject in the sample has an equal chance of being chosen from the population and the selection of one subject in no way influenced the sampling of any other subject.
2 The observations were drawn from normally distributed populations. The experimental data, when plotted in terms of their frequency of occurrence, should have the shape of a normal distribution, that is, the scores would be normally distributed within the population.
3 The variance of each set of scores or group of scores must be comparable; this is known as homogeneity of variance.

In addition to these assumptions, parametric tests also assume that the data are either interval or more commonly ratio scale. If the data are not, i.e. are either nominal or ordinal scale, or do not meet the assumptions of parametric tests, then nonparametric tests must be used. Parametric tests tend to be used for 'hard' dependent variables while nonparametric tests tend to be applied when the data are more subjective or 'soft'.

Assumptions of nonparametric tests

The assumptions are as follows:

1 The selection of subjects from the population was random and independent.
2 If the scale of measurement is ordinal or higher then homogeneity of variance must also be assumed.

When all the assumptions underlying the interpretation of parametric tests are satisfied, then use parametric in preference to nonparametric tests, since they are more likely to reveal a significant difference between the conditions when one actually exists.

CONCLUSION

Evaluations in HCI are a widely discussed but seldom-practised event. The time taken to design and carry out an evaluation is often considered to be too great. The idea of having an evaluation as part of the design cycle must include some form of iteration of the design. The output from an evaluation should provide a set of recommendations for the redesign of the system as well as some performance indicators that would suggest how the design was likely to perform in everyday usage. Design recommendations and redesign can be fed into the design/development lifecycle. There are many solutions to a design problem, and these should be laid out as recommendations arising from the results, together with some considerations of the likely costs involved in implementing or not implementing each option. The ability to generalize the results of an evaluation to the everyday usage of the design is a difficult problem. The evaluation may have been on a small group of users and on a constrained set of tasks in a laboratory setting. However, it is safer to assume that the evaluation failed to identify all the problems with the design rather than that it identified unreal problems. The designer is best advised to treat the evaluation results as being over conservative about the quality of the design rather than as being over critical. (Recently, Bellotti (1989, 1990) has shown that design contexts and evaluation techniques vary on many dimensions and that matching a particular HCI evaluation method with a given design context is often difficult, or impossible.)

Exercises

If you have never designed an experiment before you might like to try the following exercises; learning to design experiments is a bit like learning to program—you really have to try it out to appreciate the subtleties.

1 Design an experiment to test if icons with labels, labels alone or icons alone produce the best types of interface. What dependent variables would you use? What controls would you need to introduce? What other factors might also affect the outcome of this experiment that you could easily manipulate?

2 Give examples of nominal, ordinal, interval and ratio scales of measurement.

3 What are the differences between within-, mixed- and between-groups experimental designs and when would you use each of them?

4 What are the following:
   a   independent variable
   b   dependent variable
   c   controlled variable
   d   nominal scale
   e   ordinal scale
   f   internal scale
   g   ratio scale
   h   asymmetric transfer
   i   confidence level

5 What is the difference between a theory, a hypothesis and a prediction?

8 USER-INTERFACE DESIGN: ENVIRONMENTS, MANAGEMENT SYSTEMS AND TOOLKITS

Summary

- Architectures, frameworks and models of user-interface development are considered in an area of human–computer interaction concerned with user-interface management systems. Some examples of user-interface management systems are presented and discussed.

- Arising from the needs and problems of developing user-interface designs, a number of approaches have been taken which include the development of toolkits, prototyping environments and user-interface design environments. Some examples of these are considered.

Myers (1991) argues that the design and development of user interfaces is the most demanding and difficult part of the design and development of an interactive system. In recognition of this fact, a number of research groups have been developing both frameworks in which the components of a user interface can be considered, and architectures within which user interfaces can be developed. A distinction between a framework and an architecture is that a framework provides a way of thinking about and modelling the structure of an interface; in contrast, an architecture can be used to produce a runnable system and attempts to convey some information about how the parts of the implemented interface will be developed and related to each other. Both frameworks and architectures are often discussed in what have been called *user-interface management systems* (UIMS) with confusion as to whether a particular model is part of a framework or an architecture. Johnson, Drake and Wilson (1991) have reviewed some of the literature in this area and have made a clear distinction between the two. A brief summary of their review, highlighting the most important and well-known frameworks and architectures follows.

The recognition that large proportions of software systems are devoted to managing the interaction between user and application, coupled with the desire to produce quality user interfaces, has provided the impetus for the emergence of new system architectures. Recently, there has been a proliferation of different tools and environments providing support for user-interface design and management of the interaction. This gives rise to the question of what exactly is meant by a UIMS. Myers (1989) offers a useful categorization of these systems by dividing them into user-interface toolkits and user-interface development systems or environments (UIDE). Toolkits provide libraries of interaction techniques such as windows, menus and buttons for the interface designer but provide little support for the design of dialogue. UIDE's are integrated sets of tools for the creation and management of user interfaces. UIDE's help the interface designer to combine and sequence interaction techniques: they handle all aspects of the user interface. Myers uses the term UIDE rather than UIMS because he views the UIDE as providing design support as well as the run-time management functions of the early UIMSs. Within the class of systems that he calls UIDE, Myers makes the following further subdivisions:

- *Language based* The designer describes the user interface in a special language.
- *Graphical specification* Visual programming techniques are used to create the interface.
- *Automatic generation* The UIDE generates an interface automatically from a specification of the semantics of the system.

A number of criteria are of particular relevance: language or dialogue control notation, presentation, linkage between the user interface and the application functionality, concurrency, styles of interface supported, environment and tools offered to the designer, support for the overall design process, and extensibility. In the following section, some of the more commonly known UIDE's are described.

USER-INTERFACE DESIGN ENVIRONMENTS

A selection of UIDE's are reviewed below. The selection is made on the basis of those that have been most influential in the development of user-interface design environments.

Sassafras

Sassafras (Hill, 1986) falls into Myers' category of a language-based UIDE. It is based on an event response language (ERL). A typical interactive system built in the Sassafras environment would consist of a control module written in ERL forming the dialogue control component, several interaction modules forming the presentation component and an application. These components all run as separate asynchronous processes and are event-generated by any process that is broadcast to all other processes which are waiting for that event. The environment provides a local event broadcast mechanism (LEBM) to support this. The emphasis is on providing support for multithreaded dialogues (i.e. dialogues with multiple paths and concurrent events) and, in particular, user interfaces where multiple input devices are active concurrently. It also aims to support a mixed-control model where the user and the application can in turn take control of the dialogue.

TUBE

TUBE (Hill and Hermman, 1989) is based on an object-oriented paradigm and uses the notion of building user interfaces by composing objects. An interactive system built with TUBE consists of an application and a user interface constructed from user-interface objects (UIOs). UIOs can be combined to form composite UIO's providing higher levels of abstraction. Each UIO contains both display (presentation) and behaviour (dialogue). The behaviours of objects are described in a rule-based language which is a variation of the ERL language designed for Sassafras (Hill, 1986). All objects are implemented as very lightweight processes, providing concurrency and multithreading. They communicate via an asynchronous message-passing mechanism based on the LEBM from Sassafras. The UIOs are constrained to be composed in a tree-structured fashion and may communicate only with their neighbours. Finally, TUBE incorporates an attribute system and an attribute grammar, on which objects may have associated attributes. The attribute grammar can be used to specify relationships between objects and to describe the display properties of objects, thus providing constraints and dependencies between objects. The system automatically maintains any such constraints. It is also possible to incorporate some of the semantics of the application in the user interface via the attribute grammar—simplifying the problem of providing immediate semantic feedback from the application to the interface display. TUBE is implemented in a common Lisp environment.

GARNET

Myers (1991) has developed a very sophisticated UIDE known as GARNET that provides an object-oriented approach to user-interface construction. GARNET has

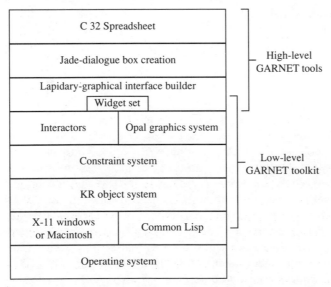

Figure 8.1: GARNET'S architecture (Myers 1991)

evolved out of earlier toolkits and less complete UIDEs also developed by Myers. The architecture of GARNET includes two major classes of tool; high-level tools for fast and easy construction of graphical interfaces and dialogues, and lower level tools that translate the high-level designs into one form runnable on standardized operating systems. The complete architecture of GARNET is shown in Fig. 8.1.

Some of the main features of GARNET, in contrast to other UIDEs described earlier, are as follows. The Jade dialogue box creation tool allows dialogue structures to be defined by providing interconnections between different states of a dialogue. The graphical structure of the interface is designed using the Lapidary tool which allows user-interface presentation objects to be designed, and includes an extensible library of interface objects for the designer to use. Whereas TUBE used an attribute system to detail how each interface object should behave and relate to other UIDs, GARNET has a constraint system which fulfils the same function.

GARNET is one of the most complete UIDEs in that it both provides high-level tools and has a sound implementation basis. With GARNET it is claimed (Myers, 1991) that direct-manipulation interfaces with fine-grained semantic feedback and good graphical interaction can be created quickly and easily.

IDL

Recent work has focused on describing an interactive system at a higher level of abstraction than is supported by traditional UIDE. These are the systems that Myers terms 'UIDE involving automatic creation'. The aim is to create an interface automatically from a specification of the semantics of the system. Foley (1987) and Foley *et al.* (1989) use the idea of specifying the user interface at the semantic and conceptual level. At the heart of their UIDE is a knowledge base containing the specification written in terms of objects, actions, relations, attributes, and pre- and post-conditions associated with the actions. Foley has built an interactive system using a frame-based expert-system shell to help the designer create the specification for an intended interface. The specification does not describe the syntactic (i.e. structure of commands) or lexical (i.e. physical form of the command, name, label, icon, etc.) aspects of the user interface so, for example, a number of user interfaces with different syntactical and lexical forms may be created to meet any given specification. Having constructed a formal specification of this sort, it is possible to check it for completeness and consistency, to evaluate the interface, to transform it into functionally equivalent specifications, each of which has a slightly different user interface, and to run it.

Summary of selected UIDEs

There are a variety of UIDEs available, all with a slightly different emphasis and underlying philosophy. Quite apart from any limitations arising from their architecture, builders of UIDEs have discovered that their systems are not always easy to use. The language-based nature of many UIDEs is largely oriented towards programmers rather than human factors experts and the environments do not directly support other aspects of the design process such as analysis of the user and tasks or scenario modelling, and evaluation tools are non-existent. Consequently, these are far from being complete design environments.

Furthermore, UIDEs provide support for only a limited part of the interface design process. The original goal was to assist a designer who has formulated a design to produce a prototype or working system, and UIDE research has tended to focus on the architectures and methodologies for implementing user interfaces. As Rhyne *et al.* (1987) point out, they fail to support other phases of design such as requirements analysis, conceptual design or evaluation. There is no way of ensuring that the delivered system embodies any task or requirements analysis that may have been carried out. Work such as Foley's IDL is of interest as it signals a move away from concerns with the architecture of run-time systems towards a more complete view of supporting user-interface design. However, even in IDL, the designer is still writing only a specification of the user interface. There is no notion of including a model of the user or the user's tasks in the specification, and no way of ascertaining whether the specified interface meets the requirements of the users' tasks, how it will change those tasks or enable new tasks to be performed.

USER-INTERFACE MANAGEMENT SYSTEMS

The Seeheim model for a user interface management system (UIMS) is given in Fig. 8.2. It is based on the concept of the separability of the user interface and the functionality of an interactive system. A UIMS is a software module that manages the communication between various components of the designed interactive system. A UIMS is considered to be comprised of three major components: a presentation component, a dialogue-control or manager component and an application-interface component. These three components manage the interface and link it to the application functionality. These components communicate via tokens. This is sometimes referred to as the 'linguistic model' of a UIMS. Drawing on traditional programming language and compiler terminology, the presentation component is the lexical layer of a linguistic model; the dialogue represents the syntactic level; and the application is considered to embody the semantics of the system functions.

Many early UIMSs were based on this model, e.g. Viz (Van Harmelen and Wilson, 1987) and RAPID (Wasserman and Shewmake, 1982). Such UIMSs differ in the nature of their dialogue control language (BNF, transition diagrams, event languages, etc.), their model of control (internal, external, or mixed) and their ability to handle multiple threads of interaction.

The appeal of such a model lies in the complete separation of the interface from the application. However, there are drawbacks with this arrangement which provides for only a narrow channel of communication between the user interface and the application. Most notably, the goal of separability conflicts with the need to support

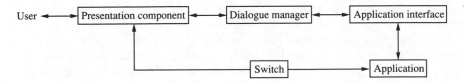

Figure 8.2   The Seeheim model

Dialogue manager

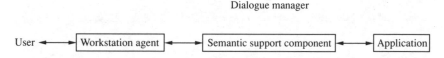

Figure 8.3   Dance's framework for UIMS

semantic feedback as Dance (Dance *et al.*, 1987) and others have indicated. Sophisticated direct-manipulation interfaces must provide the user with fine-grained semantic
feedback (Hudson, 1987).

User-interface management systems that have attempted to address the semantic
feedback problem are not easily represented by the Seeheim model. A number of
alternative frameworks have been proposed. Dance *et al.* (1987) discuss a framework
which provides for tighter coupling of the application and the dialogue manager
through what they term the 'semantic support component' (Fig. 8.3).

The semantic support component is a subcomponent of the dialogue manager. It is
similar to the application interface component of the Seeheim model, but is now an
active part of the dialogue manager. It defines not only the interface to the application, but also how the semantics of the application are incorporated in the user
interface; it contains information that is of concern to both the dialogue manager and
the application.

Hudson (1987) is particularly concerned with architectures for supporting direct-
manipulation interfaces. Schneiderman (1983) argues that lexical command arguments should be minimized and replaced by more physical actions such as pointing
and dragging. For this reason, Hudson presents a framework without any explicit
dialogue control component. The application interface component is replaced by the
shared application data model (Fig. 8.4).

This component consists of a set of shared data objects. As in Dance's framework,
these are active objects rather than passive data: they react to changes in ways that
reflect the semantics of the application, and through this are able to facilitate a
greater degree of fine-grained semantic feedback.

PAC

PAC stands for presentation, abstraction control (Coutaz, 1987) and is based on an
object-oriented paradigm. The PAC model of an interactive system structures it into
three modules: *presentation*, *abstraction* and *control*. The presentation module displays information to and receives input from the user; the abstraction module
contains application functionality; and the control maintains consistency between
the presentation and the abstraction. The presentation is itself composed of a set of
PAC objects (called 'interactors') such as buttons, menus and sliders, each of which
may be built up from a further set of PACs. Thus, the whole of an interactive system

Figure 8.4 Hudson's framework for UIMS

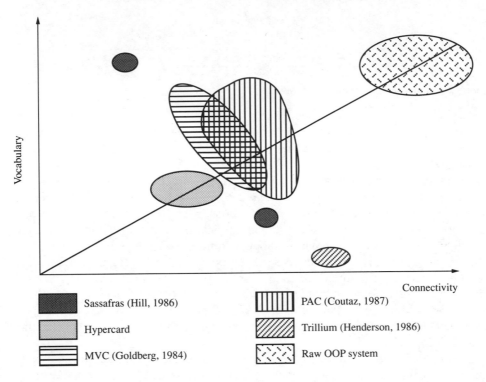

Figure 8.5   UIDE and tools in terms of the vocabulary and connectivity (after Cook *et al.*, 1988)

may be built up recursively as a set of PAC objects. PAC provides the user with the ability to switch between interactions: the control part of each PAC object retains the state of the interaction at a local level to facilitate this. This gives some degree of multithreading of interactions, though not concurrency. PAC has an external model of control with some 'hooks' for mixed control. PAC is not really a UIMS but it has provided a basis for the design of UIDEs such as TUBE.

One problem with Hudson's framework is that it is not much use for controlling or predicting user interface behaviour nor for deciding which portions of the application semantics need to be known by the UIMS components. The framework is still too general and does not allow for useful characterization of UIMSs. To mitigate this problem, Cook *et al.* (1988) propose that some sort of constraint must be enforced upon the object pool. They suggest a framework for characterizing all of the UIMSs that can be represented by such a shared object model, based on two independent criteria: *vocabulary* and *connectivity*. Vocabulary refers to the set of messages that given objects need to understand. Such messages may originate from within the object pool or be external to it. Connectivity refers to which objects can send or receive messages to or from other objects within the pool and to or from the presentation component and the application. Particular paradigms may impose constraints upon the connectivity (e.g. MVC (Goldberg, 1984), PAC (Coutaz, 1987) and TUBE (Hill and Hermman, 1989). A given UIMS model may be characterized in these terms as a point in 2D space. Figure 8.5 shows an overview of this characteri-

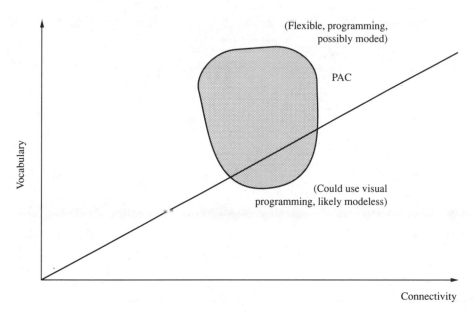

Figure 8.6   Characterization of PAC (from Johnson *et al.*, 1990)

zation for a number of better known tools, paradigms and environments for user-interface design.

This framework for characterizing UIDEs and tools in terms of vocabulary and connectivity allows more to be said about the systems than was possible with Hudson's framework. It seems to capture at least some of the properties that are relevant in determining the suitability of a given UIDE or tool for constructing various systems.

For example, consider PAC once more in terms of these characteristics: PAC organizes objects into triplets of presentation, abstraction and control. The overall system is then recursively composed from these triplets. The set of messages sent between the control and the other two components of a triplet can be large. Thus the characterization in terms of vocabulary spans a vertical range from medium to high in Fig. 8.6. The level of connectivity is fairly constrained by the organization as a hierarchy of triplets, although the resulting tree can be as large as desired.

If the vocabulary chosen is at the low end, then visual programming techniques—with their present relatively limited expressive power—might be appropriate. If the maximum expressive power is required, then the limits on the final system are fewer but a textual programming language is probably required.

TOOLKITS

Having considered how UIMS frameworks and UIDEs can be used to characterize the design of user interfaces, we will now examine some particular user interface design tools.

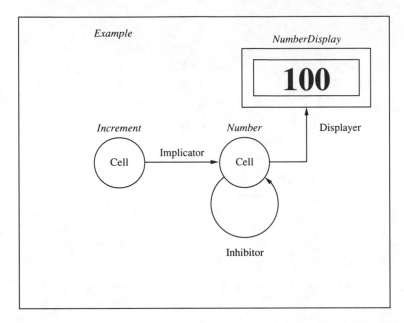

Figure 8.7   An example of the cell network of CHOICE (from Hyde, 1989)

CHOICE

CHOICE is a user-interface rapid prototyping tool. It was designed as part of the research and development work of the London HCI Centre at QMW by Chris Hyde (Hyde, 1989). A version of the system has been implemented in PostScript using the Sun Microsystems Network/extensible Window System (NeWS).

The strategy behind CHOICE was to produce a prototyping system for direct-manipulation user interfaces that has, itself, a direct-manipulation user interface. These types of programming environment are often called visual programming systems. CHOICE consists of a library of component items from which user interfaces may be constructed using a prototype–copy–customize paradigm.

CHOICE can be split into three simpler models as follows:

1 A *state model* in the form of cell networks.
2 An *interaction model* in the form of windows and events.
3 A *structuring model* in the form of environments.

Cell networks: state model

These are similar to the cell networks used by the Trillium (Henderson, 1986) user-interface design tool. The idea, however, has been extended to cope with the hierarchical structure of CHOICE interfaces. Cells are shared values (data) and may thus be used to implement a shared data model user interface as in Hudson's (1987) framework for UIMS.

Figure 8.7 shows an example of a simple cell network implemented using CHOICE. The network has the following behaviour. Changing the value of the cell

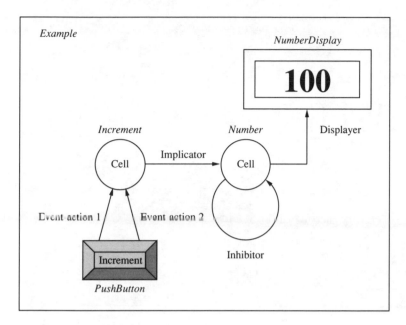

Figure 8.8 An example of windows and events in CHOICE (from Hyde, 1989)

named *increment* fires the implicator. The implicator checks the value of *increment*; if it equals true then the implicator gets the value of the cell named *number*, adds 1 to it and then attempts to change the value of *number* to it. This triggers the inhibitor connected to *number*. This inhibitor checks to see if the new value is greater than 100. If it is the inhibitor returns true to indicate not to modify the cell *number*, otherwise the inhibitor returns false. If the inhibitor returns false then the cell is modified (incremented) and the displayer *numberDisplay* is updated to display the new value of the cell *number*.

Windows and events: interaction model

Windows and events are the means by which the CHOICE system inputs and outputs data to the user interface. The windows present visual information to the user, and the events are the interactive input from the user.

The example in Fig. 8.7 could be used in a situation where a window acting as a pushbutton would be connected (via an event action) to the cell *increment* (Fig. 8.8). The value of the cell would be set to true when the button was depressed, and set to false when the button was released. The pushbutton (called *pushButton*) would be a child window of *example*, the window containing the above-mentioned cell network. As *pushButton* is a child window of *example*, its environment contains the naming context belonging to *example*; thus it has direct access to the cell *increment* in the window *example*. *PushButton* would have the following two event-actions associated with it:

1 Set *increment* to true when a mouse button goes down in it.
2 Set *increment* to false when a mouse button goes up in it.

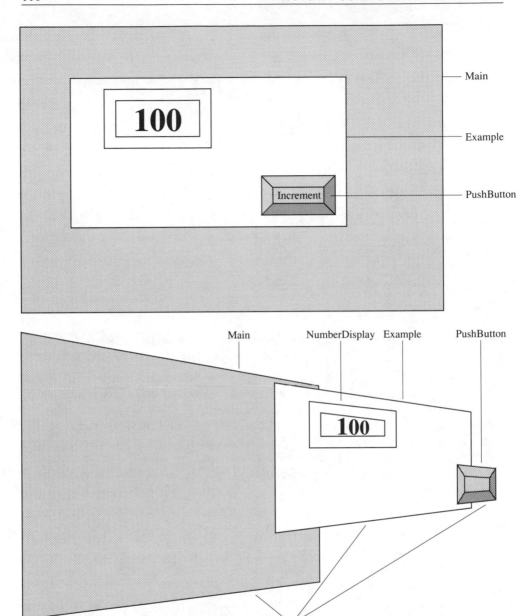

Figure 8.9   The finished design and the hierarchical structure of the finished design in CHOICE (from Hyde, 1989)

The window *pushButton* would also have an 'artwork' which is its visual aspect. The cell *increment* would be initialized to false, and *number* to 0. Henceforth, for the next 100 mouse clicks above the window *pushButton*, the displayer *numberDisplay* would show the number of mouse clicks.

Environments: a structuring model

The environments paradigm is actually an extension of the windows and events idea. It extends the use of windows from being visually enclosing objects and user-interaction objects to also being enclosing environments for programming purposes (like procedures in Pascal).

To continue with the example from Figs 8.7 and 8.8, it may be visually more pleasing if the pushbutton were to be visually different while it was in a depressed state (giving visual feedback). To achieve this it is necessary to use a 'displayer' as its graphic instead of the artwork currently being used. This displayer needs to be connected to a cell, the value of which will change when the button is depressed to provide this feedback. The obvious candidate for this cell is the cell called *increment*. However, this cell belongs to the window *example*, so any displayers connected to it would also be updated to this window. The way to overcome this problem is to make the cell *increment* common between the windows *example* and *pushButton*. After this, it is possible to have a displayer that belongs to the window *pushButton*, and is updated to this window, but is also connected to the cell *increment*. This displayer is a boolean displayer; it draws itself one way when its cell value is true, and another way when its cell value is false.

Figure 8.9 shows the user view of the finished design constructed with CHOICE and the hierarchical structure of the example. CHOICE was implemented by Chris Hyde at QMW in 1987. It runs under UNIX running NeWS.

Intouch

The last design tool we shall consider is called Intouch and was also developed at QMW by Chris Hyde, Peter Rosner, Mark Magennis and Anna Newman. This interface design tool was developed to support the easy and quick design and development of user interfaces that did not require direct manipulation. The kinds of interface catered for by Intouch are widespread and growing. They are largely used to provide public information systems and services. Examples of systems with these kinds of interfaces are automatic telling-machines or cash dispensers, route finding and planning machines and tourist information machines giving details of accommodation, restaurants and entertainments available in a given town or region. Intouch has been developed on an Apple Macintosh and runs on any Macintosh II or above. Intouch allows the interface designer to work from a high-level abstract definition of the interaction dialogue that can be obtained from an analysis of the various tasks in the domain and the goal structure of carrying out those tasks (see Chapters 11, 12 and 13). This high-level dialogue is represented in terms of states and events and has a visual programming interface to it. To give the dialogue specification an actual screen representation and behaviour, a scripting language (known as ScreenScript) has been developed by Chris Hyde, which allows the designer easily to program and edit the physical and spatial characteristics of the display screens with which the user of the designed system would interact. This scripting language is similar to HyperCard in that it uses scripts and is object oriented, but is much more powerful in that it is portable to other machines and environments and has far greater sophistication in terms of the screens that can be designed because it is based upon PostScript.

Thus the two main representations of Intouch are the statechart formalism and the ScreenScript language. Both are briefly described next.

ScreenScript

ScreenScript is a PostScript-like language designed to produce presentation-quality screen graphics. It is written in C and both its development and execution environments are currently on the Apple Macintosh. It forms an intersecting set with the PostScript language, differing from it in several respects, to make it more compact, efficient and appropriate for the class of user interfaces Intouch is targeted at.

Statecharts

Statecharts were introduced by Harel (1988) as an application of his HiGraph formalism to state transition representations. A set of mutually exclusive (XOR) states in a diagram can be enclosed by a superstate. If a transition is drawn from the superstate to another state or superstate, whichever child state was active is exited and the transition is traversed. This allows us to represent the following type of statement more easily in diagrammatic form: 'whichever screen is currently being displayed, if the user does x, it will be exited, and event y will occur'. For example, the user of a cash dispenser might type in an incorrect PIN number for the third time, in which case the screen will be exited and the user's card will automatically be retained by the machine. Superstates can be nested to any level.

As with normal state-transition formalisms, Harel's notation incorporates procedures to be associated with transitions and conditions to be attached to a transition enabling or inhibiting its traversal. Harel's statechart notation also enables the representation of parallel states or superstates. An event-causing exit from one of several parallel (AND) states causes exit from them all. The formalism also allows events to be generated synthetically.

CONCLUSION

User-interface design can be assisted by common architectures for implementing user interfaces and frameworks for conceptualizing the functional components of the user interface. Through such architectures and frameworks, it is possible for the designer to attain some form of consistency across designs, in terms of each one being based on the same architecture or framework. In attempts to provide tools to assist in the design and implementation of user interfaces, user interface design environments have been developed.

There seems to be some general properties for UIDEs. First, a common approach to UIDEs is to use an object-oriented paradigm. It seems to be that the focus of designing user interfaces is on designing objects: interface objects, application objects, etc. A second common property of UIDEs is that the degree of separability between the application and the interface is a central issue. A third feature of UIDEs is the form of communication between the objects and the connectivity between them.

There has been a steady progression in the design of UIDEs to provide environments that can produce applications rather than just user interfaces, and that can be ported from the development machine to other machines.

Finally, the user interface for a UIDE is difficult to design. It seems to be that visual programming, direct manipulation and structured (textual) editors are all needed.

Exercises

1 Consider a simple slider mechanism that can move up and down a gauge. As the slider moves the values on the gauge are highlighted. When the gauge is positioned on a value on the gauge, the same value is displayed in an output window.

   (a)   How would you decompose this design in terms of a PAC model?

   (b)   How would you structure the design in terms of the Seeheim model?

2 Discuss the claim that separability between user interface and application is impossible and undesirable.

3 What are the distinctions between TUBE and GARNET?

4 Object-oriented approaches to user-interface construction are prevalent—why is this so?

9

EARLY ATTEMPTS AT MODELLING HUMAN–COMPUTER INTERACTION

Summary

- A variety of models are used in human–computer interaction for many purposes. These include models of users, interactions and interfaces. The purposes of modelling include predicting user behaviour, communicating designs, providing consistency between levels of design, and evaluating aspects of a design. It is useful to be able to classify the differences between these various models and to consider how they might be used in a design process.

- One particular form of modelling human–computer interaction is known as command language grammar (CLG). This form of modelling is particularly aimed at software engineers/designers to help them develop a detailed design description of the user interface and the intended user interactions. It provides a method for describing a user-interface design at six levels of abstraction. It is intended to maintain consistency between each level of abstraction. CLG could also provide a means of communicating designs between designers and could possibly be extended to provide an evaluation of certain aspects of a design.

- One approach to modelling the user's knowledge of the interface is provided by a task action language. This form of modelling uses a Backus–Naur Form (BNF) notation to represent an assumed model of the person's knowledge of the interface. The main purpose of TAL is to attempt to evaluate designs by predicting how difficult a system will be to use, and how consistent the interface is.

- Perhaps the most ambitious approach to modelling in HCI has been the goals, operators, methods and selection rules family of models. These models start with a simplified model of a user, in the form of a human-information processor known as the model human processor (MHP). The MHP is used in conjunction with a model of how a user would use the system. The purpose of using the GOMS modelling approach is to predict how much time it would take an expert user to carry out a given task using the system and thereby evaluate alternative design solutions.

114

- These three examples of modelling in HCI have given rise to more refined models which attempt to formalize different aspects of HCI. They are in sharp contrast to the mathematically based formalisms that are predominently used in software engineering.

A CLASSIFICATION OF EARLY MODELS IN HCI

The use of models in HCI proliferated in the years 1981–1983. This proliferation led to much confusion about what exactly was being modelled, who was supposed to use or do the modelling, and what purpose the model was intended to serve. In a now-classic paper, Young (1983) pointed out that there were important differences between the designer's model of the system, the person's model of the computer system and the researcher's model of the user. A further category arises when the computer system's model of the user is considered. This last case is now more prevalent than previously, largely because of the advent of knowledge-based systems (KBS) and intelligent tutoring systems (ITS), in particular where there is an attempt to write programs that construct models of users, and adapt to suit the user according to the modelled features.

Thus, from Young we have the following possible models:

- Models of users
- Models of computer systems

being modelled by:

- Designers
- Researchers
- Computer systems
- Users

Clearly, not all possible combinations of the above two dimensions are likely to occur. Perhaps the one to be excluded for the present is the computer system's model of itself. This kind of introspective power has yet to be fully realized. However, it is possible that such a model could be required, for example, to provide explanation facilities that would help the user understand why a particular system event had occurred. This is perhaps most obvious in the case of an expert system, but to some degree programming-language compilers provide an explanation of why the program could not be compiled. A further example of a computer system's model of itself can occur in user interface management systems, where a program is written to manage the interface between what is often called the application software and the user interface hardware and software. Figure 9.1 summarizes the possible models arising from Young's position.

More recently, Whitefield (1987) has provided a more extensive framework for classifying models in HCI by distinguishing between the system and the program. For Whitefield the program is assumed to be all or some of the software that runs on a particular machine, in other words, the program could be the application package being used to draw a diagram. In contrast, the system includes the software, the hardware, the user and the support services such as documentation. Thus the

		Model of	
		computer	user
modelled by	designer	×	×
	researcher	×	×
	computer	×	×
	user	×	

Figure 9.1   Some possible classes of models in HCI (from Young, 1983)

program excludes the user while the system includes the user (among other things). Whitefield also considers two dimensions of 'model of' and 'modelled by'. Figure 9.2 presents Whitefield's extended classification of models in HCI. This classification is interesting because it highlights the areas where the user of the model and the content of the model can be distinguished.

In Whitefield's classification, more combinations are permitted; however, it is even more obvious that certain combinations possible within the framework would hardly ever be realized. For example, the program is unlikely to have a model of the researcher. The types of model likely to be useful and to occur are indicated by an × in Fig. 9.2.

The program's model of the user, as we have already seen, is most likely to be found in applications such as tutoring systems, some types of knowledge-based systems. The user's model of the system and the program are both highly plausible models. However, in the strictest sense, these models are possessed by the user and are therefore not open to inspection or analysis. However, taking a weaker position, there may be a model of the program or system which is assumed to be isomorphic to the model possessed by the user. In essence, such a model is a psychological theory of the user's model of the system.

The researcher's model of the system and the program are often described by a more formal model that allows the researcher to predict some aspect of either the program or the user–program interaction (i.e. the system). The researcher's model of the user is, in fact, the correct dimension under which psychological theories would be classified. The researcher's model of the designer is, in reality, often found to be a model of the design process or how designers design. The designer's model of the system is often some form of general system model including the various rules and

Model of	System	Program	User	Researcher	Designer
Modelled by					
Program			×		
User	×	×			
Researcher	×	×	×		×
Designer	×	×	×		

Figure 9.2   An extended classification of models in HCI (from Whitefield, 1987)

functions connected with the system. The designer's model of the program is often some form of abstract and possibly formal specification of the system. The designer's model of the user may be a simplified version of the researcher's model of the user, which can be likened to an engineer's model of the terrain or traffic flows in the design of bridges in that it is approximate but robust and does not require a detailed understanding of users.

In the next section, some of the more common approaches to modelling are considered. It will become obvious that the models and methods described were not designed with either of the above classification systems in mind. The classifications were developed to enable the different types of model to be compared and contrasted and to identify more clearly what kind of models are being used. Two points are worth mentioning. First, the classification of particular techniques into the above frameworks is made on the basis of current or potential uses of the models. This may at times contradict what the original authors intended or claimed when they published their method. Second, some models may fall into more than one category because the model can be used in more than one way (for example, it might be used either by the researcher or the designer). Alternatively, the model may be used to describe more than one item (for example, a model may be used to describe either the complete system or just the program).

COMMAND LANGUAGE GRAMMAR

Command language grammar (CLG), developed at Xerox Parc by Moran (1981) can be considered as a designer's model of the interaction described from the perspective of the inputs to, and outputs of, the computer system. Although Moran claims that CLG is also a user's model of the system, this is clearly not the case since it does not include any characteristics of the user. CLG assumes a particular style of design and is structured in terms of a top-down design approach. This is one of the few modelling approaches in HCI that has attempted to address how it might relate to a design process. However, CLG only concerns itself with the design of the user interface and not with a complete application. Furthermore, it does not address the implementation aspects of design or any of the software-engineering considerations such as testing and verification.

CLG assumes a decompositional or top-down design approach where the interface design is evolved from a high level of abstraction to a low level of detail. The purpose of the CLG is to show how the *conceptual* components of the interface design can be separated from the particular *command language* and to show how the two are related. A command language is assumed to be the specific details by which the user interacts with the application. In this sense, a command language includes textual-command-style interfaces and also graphical interaction with direct manipulation (e.g. using windows, menus, icons and pointing devices).

CLG is made up of a number of *components* and *levels* of description. There are three components with two levels to each component (Fig. 9.3). The first component is the *conceptual component* which includes the task level and semantic level of description. The second is the *communication component* which includes the syntactic and interaction levels of description. The lowest levels are included in the *physical*

Conceptual component	Task level
	Semantic level
Communication component	Syntactic level
	Interaction level
Physical component	Spatial level
	Device level

Figure 9.3   The three components and six levels of CLG

component and are the spatial layout and device level. The details of the grammar have only ever been worked out for the first four levels of description.

The task level describes the tasks users can accomplish, structured according to the system. Thus the task level describes only those tasks that can be carried out with the system; in addition, the tasks are structured according to the features of the computer system. The task level describes the design in terms of preconceived tasks. It does not constitute an analysis of tasks and it does not describe tasks in terms of the user.

Moran uses two forms of notation to describe the task level, a hierarchical tree diagram and a pseudocode language. The remaining levels of all components are described in the form of pseudocode. Each level is described in as much detail as is possible without assuming the properties of the next level down. This rather rough rule proves to be difficult to follow. To illustrate the task level, suppose we have a graphics system called DOODLE which is designed to support a drawing task such as drawing a clock face. (DOODLE is not a real system, it is purely an example that is used to illustrate the features of CLG.) Using CLG we would attempt to describe how the task would be achieved using DOODLE.

Task level

The task level defines what the computer system is supposed to do without being specific about the components of the computer system or its interface. It is claimed to be a description of the conceptual entities in the task domain. The model in Fig. 9.4 shows what a user would be able to do with the proposed system but not what the user does. It assumes that some form of analysis and design synthesis has been carried out which has enabled the designer to understand what a user would want to find in a

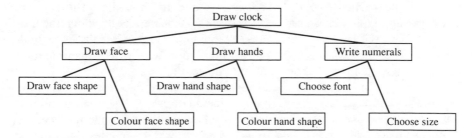

Figure 9.4   A CLG task hierarchy for drawing a clock using DOODLE

computer system. The model is in the form of a structured hierarchy of *tasks* and *subtasks*. CLG defines a task by giving an informal definition of the *goal* of the task and a *procedure* for achieving the goal in terms of subtasks. The sequence in which the subtasks are assumed to be carried out is also determined and represented in the model by the order along the vertical and horizontal axis of the task hierarchy. The diagram is thus read in a top-down, left-to-right order. For example, 'draw clock' requires first 'draw face' then 'draw hands' then 'write numerals', and 'draw face' requires first 'draw face shape' then 'colour face shape'.

Semantic level

The semantic level of CLG defines the computer system objects or entities (or data structures) and the permissible manipulations/actions/operations (procedures). These objects and actions are known as *conceptual entities* and *conceptual operations*. The sequencing or proceduralization of the operations is described by *methods*. The semantic level describes the entities, operations and methods that are required to accomplish the tasks defined at the task level. This description is in terms of the computer system and not in terms of the user, so it does not say what behaviours, knowledge or other cognitive requirements are placed on, or expected of, the user.

Figure 9.5 shows how DOODLE might be described by CLG at the semantic level in terms of conceptual entities. The grammar uses a Lisp-like pseudocode and is a symbolic notation in the spirit of FRAMES, SCHEMA and semantic nets.

Figure 9.5 can be interpreted as follows: the computer system DOODLE has the name DOODLE; it represents the entities SHAPE TEXT LINES POINTS and COLOURS, and allows operations of DRAW PAINT WRITE POSITION and DELETE to be carried out. SHAPE is one of the conceptual entities and that has a name which is shape and the SHAPE entity represents any drawn shape. Similarly, TEXT is a conceptual entity which has the name text and can take on, at any time, one of the values of numbers, letters or specified characters.

The conceptual operations define both the behaviour of the conceptual entities and the operations that these can be involved in. The objects defined as conceptual entities are now used as parameters which the conceptual operations act upon.

```
DOODLE    = (A SYSTEM
              NAME = "DOODLE"
              ENTITIES = (SET : SHAPE TEXT LINES POINTS COLOURS)
              OPERATIONS = (SET : DRAW PAINT WRITE POSITION DELETE) )
SHAPE     = (AN ENTITY
              REPRESENTS (DRAWN_SHAPE)
              NAME = "shape")
TEXT      = (AN ENTITY
              NAME = "text"
              VALUE = (ONE-OF : NUMBERS LETTERS SPECIFIED_CHARACTERS))
```

Figure 9.5 CLG extract of semantic-level description of DOODLE: conceptual entities

```
DRAW      = (A SYSTEM OPERATION
               OBJECT = (A PARAMETER
                          VALUE = (AN ENTITY))
               IN (A PARAMETER
                          VALUE = (A PLACE ON SCREEN)
                          DEFAULT-VALUE = (UNKNOWN))))
PAINT     = (A SYSTEM OPERATION
               OBJECT = (A PARAMETER
                          VALUE = (A SHAPE)))
```

Figure 9.6 CLG extract of semantic level description of DOODLE: conceptual operations

The extract of conceptual operations described in Fig. 9.6 are designed to be used to accomplish the tasks defined at the task level. It can be interpreted as follows: DRAW is a system operation which must be associated with a conceptual entity and is executed in a place on the screen; PAINT is another system operation which has to be associated with a particular conceptual entity—a SHAPE.

The way that the conceptual operations can be used is described by the conceptual methods. A method is described for each subtask defined at the lowest level of the task-level description. A method spells out a procedure by its DO component of the subtask with which it is associated by its FOR component. The conceptual operations are the primitive actions of a conceptual method. CLG uses conventional programming control constructs including Sequence (SEQ), Conditionals (IF...THEN...ELSE), Iteration (REPEAT). Other control structures are FAILURE, OPT (optional), START and STOP.

Figure 9.7 shows an extract of the conceptual methods that would be defined in CLG for the example system DOODLE. This description can be interpreted as follows: SEM__M1 is one of the semantic methods associated with the DOODLE computer system. This method is the method to be used to draw a face shape, and involves doing the sequence of operations: first start doodle system, then draw a shape, then stop doodle system. This is a description of the logical temporal dependencies between the conceptual operations when associated with conceptual entities. It does not describe the user behaviour or any other aspect of the user. This completes the semantic level description of CLG and exemplifies its features in terms of DOODLE.

```
SEM__M1   = (A SEMANTIC__METHOD
               FOR DRAW__FACE__SHAPE
               DO (SEQ : (START DOODLE__SYSTEM)
                        (DRAW SHAPE)
                        (STOP DOODLE__SYSTEM)))
```

Figure 9.7 Extract of a CLG semantic level description of DOODLE: conceptual methods

```
DOODLE_CONTEXT = (A COMMAND CONTEXT
                     STATE_VARIABLES = (SET : CURRENT_SHAPE
                                               CURRENT_COLOUR
                                               CURRENT_TEXT)
                     DESCRIPTORS = (SET : SHAPE_TYPE
                                          COLOUR_TYPE
                                          TEXT_TYPE)
                     DISPLAY_AREAS = (SET : DRAWING_AREA
                                            TEXT_AREA
                                            PAINT_AREA)
                     COMMANDS = (SET : DRAW_SHAPE
                                       DRAW_LINE
                                       DRAW_POINT
                                       INSERT_TEXT
                                       PAINT_COLOUR
                                       SELECT_COLOUR
                                       DELETE_SHAPE
                                       DELETE_TEXT
                                       DELETE_LINE
                                       DELETE_POINT
                                       SAVE_SHAPE
                                       QUIT_DOODLE)
                     ENTRY_COMMANDS = (SET : START_DOODLE))
CURRENT_SHAPE     = (A STATE_VARIABLE
                     CONTEXT = DOODLE_CONTEXT
                     VALUE = (A SHAPE)
                     NAME = "current shape")
```

Figure 9.8   CLG syntactic-level description of DOODLE: entities

Syntactic level

The syntactic level of the CLG describes the structure of the language through which the users must communicate their commands to the system. The basic syntactic primitives of the command language are *commands* which are imperative statements issued by the user to the system. Commands contain *arguments* which refer to the conceptual entities involved in the commands. Arguments denote entities by using *descriptors*. Commands are issued within *command contexts* or *conversational contexts*. Contexts limit the commands that the user can use at any given time and define the scope of other command-language entities.

Some of the entities of our fictitious drawing system DOODLE are described in Fig. 9.8. It includes *state variables*, which define the state of information remembered by the system between commands. This state information can be used as implicit or default arguments in commands. A state variable is only active in the context in which it is defined. *Descriptors* are used to designate the conceptual entities to the system. The user designates the entities (shapes) to be operated on. The syntactic level also gives a rough description of what information is displayed to the user at any given time. This is done by defining *display areas*. In Fig. 9.8, CURRENT_SHAPE,

```
DRAW__SHAPE     = (A DOODLE__COMMAND
                      NAME = "shape"
                      OBJECT = (AN ARGUMENT
                                     FORM = (A SHAPE__TYPE))
                      DOES (SET : (DRAW (SHAPE__TYPE)
                                   IN DRAWING__AREA))
                      SIDE__EFFECT = (BIND CURRENT__SHAPE TO (SHAPETYPE)))
```

Figure 9.9 CLG Syntactic level description of DOODLE: commands

CURRENT__COLOUR and CURRENT__TEXT are all state variables that exist between commands when DOODLE is in use. SHAPE__TYPE, COLOUR__TYPE and TEXT__TYPE must all be defined by the user as the particular form of the conceptual entities (shape, colour, text) that are being used at any given time. DOODLE has three display areas for displaying text, drawings and painted areas (painted areas are only displayed within enclosed drawings). The complete command set of DOODLE is specified, but the syntactic structure of the command arguments are not defined in the syntactic-level description of entities. There is one special class of command(s) and that is the command(s) required to gain access to DOODLE in the first case. These are termed *entry commands*.

Each of the commands listed in the description of syntactic entities is further defined in the CLG syntactic-level description of commands. The commands within the DOODLE__CONTEXT are described at the syntactic level, an example of the DRAW__SHAPE command is shown in Fig. 9.9. Commands are imperative statements by the user to the system. Each command is defined by enumerating its arguments and by spelling out as a semantic procedure how the system will interpret it. The example in Fig. 9.9 can be interpreted as follows: DRAW__SHAPE is a legal command of the DOODLE system; its command name is 'shape'. It must have an argument passed with it which is the type of shape (SHAPE__TYPE) to be drawn. The command with its argument then enables the user to draw a shape of the defined type in the drawing area of the DOODLE display. A consequence of issuing the shape command is that the defined shape-type becomes the current shape-type.

The methods at the semantic level are translated into syntactic methods. This is done by translating the conceptual operations in the procedure into the commands that evoke them. The result is that syntactic methods as shown in Fig. 9.10 are

```
SYN__M1      = (A SYNTACTIC__METHOD
                   FOR DRAW__FACE__SHAPE
                   DO (SEQ : (START__DOODLE)
                             (LOOK IN SHAPE__AREA AT SHAPES
                                  FOR (A SHAPE__TYPE))
                             (DRAW__SHAPE TYPE (THE RESULT OF LOOK)
                                      IN (A LOCATION (IN (DRAWING__AREA)))
                             (QUIT__DOODLE)))
```

Figure 9.10 CLG syntactic-level description of DOODLE: methods

defined. Where there is more than one method for carrying out a particular task, CLG shows these as two alternative methods. However, it does not state how a method is selected. Furthermore, it does not provide any precise details as to how to choose appropriate command names or command strings. Thus, CLG does not provide any assistance from a human factors perspective about the choice or structure of command languages. Later, in Chapter 10, other models (for example TAG) are considered which address this issue of the design of command languages. This completes the description of CLG at the syntactic level.

Interaction level

The interaction level describes the system at the level of physical actions both by the system and by the user. It also describes the structure of the dialogue in terms of who (the system or the user) initiates and who responds at each moment. The interaction level starts with a *syntactic hierarchy* which enumerates the syntactic elements of the system. It is a canonical ordering of the syntactic elements, related to the sequence in which they occur during the interaction. For example:

- An entry command leads to the command context it enters.
- A command leads to the command context it enters.
- A command leads to its arguments.
- An argument leads to its descriptors.

The interaction level adds interaction elements to each syntactic element. The *interaction constituents* are a fixed set of functional parts out of which all interactions between the user and the system can be described. The specific constituent types include nonterminal and terminal constituents (Fig. 9.11). The interaction level also includes 'input devices' (e.g. keys, buttons, pointing devices), 'primitive' system and user actions (e.g. press a key, press a button, give an audio signal) and 'dialogue control rules' which spell out the relationships between when the user specifies syntactic elements and when the system interprets them. Further properties of the

---

Nonterminal interaction constitutents
- S = specification
- B = body of a specification
- D = designation of/in the command (i.e. the name of the command)
- F = form of/in which describes the value of the argument
- T = termination of specification by user (i.e. finished)
- I = interpretation of the specification (S) by the system.

Terminal interaction constituents
- W = when is (e.g. when interpretation takes place (immediate or delayed) or when an element in a command should occur)
- P = prompt for (i.e. by system to user)
- A = action for/in (a primitive user constituent such as typing a name)
- R = response to user by system

Figure 9.11 The terminal and nonterminal interaction constituents

interaction level are as follows: ordering rules, which determine the temporal order (this is done by using a tree structure); user-action rules, which associate user actions with the 'action constituents'; system action rules, which associate primitive system actions with the 'prompt' and 'response' constituents; 'interaction procedures', which are programs composed of primitive actions and user operations; and 'interaction methods', which associate interaction procedures with tasks.

The rules of the interaction level describe both the interactions that can take place and the consistency between the differing forms of interaction for a given system. For example, a rule for DOODLE might be as follows:

R1. = (RULE FOR (W.S. OF A DOODLE-COMMAND)
→(ANYTIME IN DOODLE-CONTEXT))

This would be translated as a specification of a DOODLE command that can be given at anytime while the user is in the DOODLE system.

This completes the description of the interaction level of CLG. As no other levels have been defined, no details can be given about the form of CLG at the spatial and device levels. The interaction level provides the rule structure and command set for the user interaction. At this level, CLG is similar to TAL (Reisner, 1981 (see this chapter)) and TAG (Payne and Green, 1986 (see Chapter 10)), in that it describes the detailed structure of the command language as the user might be expected to perceive it. CLG is very different to both TAL and TAG, as we shall see. It does not attempt to predict user behaviour or the amount of learning/training required by the user. However, it is possible that by describing an interface at the level of detail required by CLG, inconsistencies or bad design choices may be identified in the user-interface design. Attempts to verify these and other claims about CLG are rare. A study by Sharratt (1987) showed that designers using CLG did not produce better designs than a control group who did not use CLG, nor did they find CLG an easy to use approach to user-interface design.

Some Observations about CLG

The intention of CLG is first and foremost to provide a method of describing the user interaction or more precisely the user interface, without defining the complete application. It attempts to separate the conceptual design of the system from the structure of the user interface and to describe both of these. This idea of separating the user-interface design from the application is discussed in Chapter 8 from the perspective of interface development and on UIMS. CLG enables a user-interface design to be described independent of the complete application with some degree of success. With respect to contributing to the design of a system, its main advantages seem to be that it enables the designer to think about the user interface and the conceptual components of the system, without having to consider how the various operations will be carried out by the application program. It also encourages the designer to think about how the system might be used to carry out user tasks. The methods of the various levels of CLG are one useful way in which the details of how a user might be able to accomplish specified tasks can be described.

The limitations of CLG are obvious. It would be a very large task to describe any real system in a given application-domain using CLG. Having written the details of the design at each level not much can be done with them. No evaluations can be performed on the design, since there are no metrics or criteria associated with CLG. It is not possible for the user to read and understand easily the CLG description and so get a feel for the interface design and thereby provide feedback about the quality of the design. It is not possible to run the system since the design still has to be coded. A further point is that, in using CLG, the designer is given no help in determining how to map one level on to the next lower level of CLG. Furthermore, the initial assumption that design can be carried out in a completely top-down fashion appears to be untrue in some (and possibly in the majority of) cases. Few empirical studies of the use of CLG have been carried out. Sharratt (1987) studied a group of 'designers' using CLG to describe interface designs. His results show that CLG is difficult to use and that his designers made many errors in specifying the interface at the appropriate levels of CLG. Furthermore, there was no evidence that the designs specified in CLG were in any way better or less free of 'bugs' through using CLG.

Once a decision has been made about what tasks the system should support, CLG can be used. It assumes that some form of task analysis has already been performed to provide an adequate representation of the extant task-domain. In addition, some principles or guidelines are required to help the designer to determine for what parts of a task to provide online (computerized) support. Alternatively, the designer uses only intuition to decide what support can be provided.

In the next section we will consider a different approach to modelling HCI. The approach of Reisner (1981) is less ambitious than that of CLG. Task action language was developed by Reisner to provide a form of modelling that could be used to predict user errors and learning difficulties for an interface design, without having to observe or otherwise monitor actual users interacting with a runnable version of the design. As such, it constitutes a specification-based approach to the predictive modelling of user behaviour and evaluation of user-interface designs.

TASK ACTION LANGUAGE

Reisner (1981) introduced the idea that a form of notation or grammar could be used to evaluate the design of a user interface employing metrics to assess various aspects of the usability of the design. Reisner suggests that by using a common grammar to describe alternative designs, metrics can then be applied to assess the usability of the system before it has been implemented or even prototyped. Thus the intention behind TAL is to provide a formal grammatical description of human–computer interaction that can be used as a predictive tool to assesss individual or compare alternative interface designs for their respective ease of use.

Formal grammars are often used to describe languages precisely. The TAL is specifically an action language for interactive systems. It describes the sequences of button presses, mouse movements, typing actions, etc., performed by a user inter-acting with a program. Using the grammar it is possible to compare alternative designs in terms of simplicity and consistency. The grammar of TAL is assumed to provide a formal description of the cognitive factors of a user's behaviour, that is, what a user has to learn and remember.

Task action language uses a production-rule grammar or Backus–Naur form

(BNF). It describes a language as a set of rules for describing correct strings in the language. Any particular string can then be described by the particular rules involved in producing it. The structure of the string can then be shown by a tree diagram based on the rules. TAL includes the following:

- A set of terminal symbols (the 'words' in the language).
- A set of nonterminal symbols (invented constructs used to show the structure of the language).
- A starting symbol.
- The meta-symbols × (and) | (or) ::= (is composed of).
- Rules constructed from the above.

Reisner claims that a grammar constructed from the above can then be evaluated in terms of the following:

1 The number of different terminal symbols.
2 The lengths of the terminal strings for particular tasks.
3 The number of rules necessary to describe the structure of some set of terminal strings.

The first represents the total number of different action steps in the language. The second represents the number of steps the user has to perform for some given subtask. The third represents the consistency (or lack of it) in the steps required for a set of related subtasks. These last two are often referred to as *string simplicity* and *structural consistency*, respectively.

Reisner argues that good design involves minimizing, in the following order of importance, the number or forms of rules, the lengths of terminal symbols and the number of terminal symbols.

BNF was chosen for TAL because it is relatively compact, is easy to manipulate automatically, and can describe an infinite language with a finite set of rules. However, a much better notational scheme is needed to reveal both the structure and the legal strings of the language.

Task action language offers the possibility of carrying out a 'pencil-and-paper' evaluation of a system rather than waiting for a working model of the system to experiment with. As such, it does not replace the need for evaluations with runnable prototype designs and actual end-users, but it may give rise to an earlier and less costly evaluation of some design decisions. Furthermore, as with CLG, simply using a formal grammar to describe the user's interactions forces the designer to be more aware of and more precise about the user-interface design decisions they are making.

Reisner demonstrates the grammar by describing an early graphics system with two different user-interfaces. Figure 9.12 is an extract from the grammar Reisner developed for one of the two user-interfaces to the graphics system. Terminal symbols are indicated in upper-case letters, nonterminal symbols in lower case. The rules are numbered.

In her original study Reisner (1981) compared the predictions derived from comparisons of two interfaces described by the grammar with the results of an empirical study of actual end-user behaviour on the two working prototype systems. From the analyses of the two grammars it was first predicted that learning and/or remembering how to select shapes in system 1 would vary in difficulty. The shapes

---

1   picture ::= coloured shape | picture + coloured shape
2   coloured shape ::= colour + shape | colour + shape
3   colour ::= new colour | old colour | starting default colour
4   new colour ::= CURSOR IN RED | CURSOR IN BLUE | CURSOR IN GREEN
5   old colour ::= NULL
6   starting default colour ::= NULL
7   shape ::= discrete shape | continuous shape | text shape
8   discrete shape ::= separate discrete shape | connected discrete shape

---

Figure 9.12   Grammar for user-interface to graphics system

described by the shorter strings would be easier to *select* than the longer ones (in particular line and rectangle would be easier to select than continuous circle). Other predictions were as follows: second, that learning and/or remembering how to select shapes would not vary in difficulty with system 2; third, that learning and/or remembering how to select any shape in system 2 should be easier than selecting the corresponding shapes with system 1. These predictions were derived by Reisner from her analysis of the grammars for the two systems. The results of her empirical assessment of the working systems by-and-large supported the above predictions.

The advantages of TAL as a modelling approach in HCI are that it attempts to describe the user interface by using a more formal notation than CLG and that it has metrics applied to it. These metrics, in turn, allow interface designs to be compared and evaluated at an earlier stage in the design than would otherwise be possible if a working system were required for the evaluation.

However, the design must be specified to some considerable degree of detail to enable the TAL grammar to be constructed. Also, there needs to be a model of the tasks which the user will want to perform, and which the system should support in some way. Finally, there needs to be a model of the user from which the predictions about what is easy or difficult to learn, remember and/or perform can be derived. This last requirement is in fact a serious constraint, since it implies that without such a model there is no principle or rationale for assuming that the rules and terminal symbols etc. of the grammar in any way represent cognitive aspects of behaviour.

It is clear that the approach adopted by TAL is an important contribution to a developing methodology for the evaluation of user interfaces during the design process, and at possibly an earlier and less costly stage in that process, than with a running prototype. This should encourage others to produce better and more well-worked approaches following the early work of Reisner. In Chapter 10 a different approach is considered that follows from the ideas developed by Reisner about using grammars to predict user behaviour. This approach is known as task action grammar and owes much to her earlier work.

GOALS, OPERATORS, METHODS AND SELECTION RULES

A main weakness of TAL is that it attempts to make predictions of usability without any reference to any theory of human behaviour. This means that there is no rationale or principled way of determining what the terminal symbols or rules of the grammar should include. TAL could be criticized for producing a formalism without first coming to terms with what the formalism is attempting to describe. With this weakness in mind the next approach to be considered also attempts to provide a form of modelling that can be used to predict user behaviour and so assess the usability of the system. However, unlike TAL, this approach has an explicit model of the user upon which predictions of user behaviour are based.

In the GOMS approach (goals, operators, methods and selection rules), Card, Moran and Newell (1983) make use of a model of human behaviour in the form of a human information processing model referred to as a *model human processor* (MHP). The MHP is an approximation of the assumed information processing capacities of a person. Card *et al.* liken the MHP to an engineering model of an information processor described at the systems level (as opposed to the component level). Thus, in the same spirit, the MHP suppresses details about how the information-processing components of the model might function or what their structure might be, and describes human behaviour in terms of memories, processors, their parameters and interconnections. The MHP in this form is then used to make approximate predictions of gross behaviour. In summary, the MHP is a simplified view of psychological theories and empirical data which is intended to be used by nonpsychologists to predict user behaviour in human–computer interaction. The MHP therefore comprises a set of memories and processors together with a set of principles of operation.

The MHP is divided into three interacting subsystems (Fig. 9.13): the *perceptual system*, the *motor system* and the *cognitive system*, each subsystem having its own memories and processors. The perceptual system comprises an *auditory image store* and a *visual image store* to hold the output of the sensory system while it is being symbolically encoded. The cognitive system receives symbolically coded information from the sensory image stores in its *working memory* and uses previously stored information in *long-term memory* to make decisions about how to respond. The motor system then executes the responses. For each subsystem there is assumed to be a separate processor: a perceptual processor, a cognitive processor and a motor processor. The processors are assumed to be capable of both serial and parallel processing.

The parameters of the memory system are the storage capacity in items (μ), the decay time of an item (λ) and the main code type (κ) (i.e.. physical, acoustic, visual, semantic). The main parameter of the processors is the cycle time (π). Card *et al.* then provide approximate values for the various parameters they have identified. These approximations are determined by a synthesis of relevant research in psychology. The model is limited to account for skilled or errorless performance only and predicts only the time it takes to produce a response or series of responses. The intention is that a user task is analysed and the MHP is used to provide the performance predictions for the behaviour associated with that task.

The GOMS approach considers that users act rationally to attain their goals and therefore that a user's behaviour can be predicted by determining the user's *goals*, *methods* and *operators* and the constraints of the task. They assume that underlying the detailed behaviour of a particular user there are a small number of information- processing operators, that the user's behaviour is describable as a sequence of these, and that the time the user requires to act is the sum of the time of these individual operators.

A user's cognitive structure is assumed to consist of four components: a set of

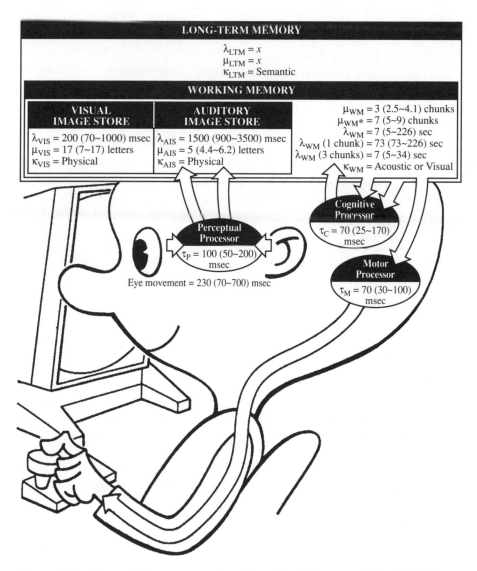

Figure 9.13   The model human processor (from Card, Moran and Newell, 1983)

goals, a set of operators, a set of methods for achieving the goals, and a set of selection rules for choosing among competing methods for goals. A model specified by these components is then a *GOMS model*.

Goals

Goals are symbolic structures that define a state of affairs to be achieved and determine a set of possible methods by which it may be accomplished. The function of a goal is assumed to be to provide a memory point to which the (human) system can return on failure or error, and from which information can be obtained concerning what is intended, what methods are appropriate, and what has already been achieved. An example of goals in an editing task taken from Card *et al.* are as follows:

GOAL: EDIT-MANUSCRIPT
    GOAL: EDIT-UNIT-TASK
        GOAL: ACQUIRE-UNIT-TASK
            GOAL: EXECUTE-UNIT-TASK
                GOAL: LOCATE-LINE
                    GOAL: MODIFY-TEXT.

The user's top level goal is therefore to edit the manuscript. A user segments a task into a sequence of smaller discrete subtasks. The goal–subgoal hierarchy is reflected by the levels of indentation used in the above notation. The term 'unit task' denotes these user-defined subtasks. In the example above, the GOAL: EDIT-UNIT-TASK is a subgoal of the main goal, GOAL: EDIT-MANUSCRIPT. In order to edit a unit task, the user must first acquire the instructions from the manuscript and then do what is necessary to accomplish them. This leads to the further subgoals of EXECUTE-UNIT-TASK, LOCATE-LINE and MODIFY-TEXT.

Operators

These are elementary perceptual, motor or cognitive acts whose execution is necessary to change any aspect of the user's mental state or to affect the task environment. The behaviour of a user is ultimately recorded as a sequence of these operators. The GOMS model does not allow for concurrent behaviour; it assumes that behaviour is a sequence of the serial execution of operators. An operator is defined by a specific effect and a specific duration. It is the operators that define the grain of analysis of the task. The finer the grain of analysis, the more the operators are assumed to reflect basic psychological mechanisms. The coarser the grain of analysis, the more the operators reflect the specifics of the task environment. An example of a coarse grained analysis of operators from Card *et al.* is as follows:

GET-NEXT-PAGE
GET-NEXT-TASK
USE-QS-METHOD
USE-LF-METHOD
USE-S-COMMAND
USE-M-COMMAND
VERIFY-EDIT

Later we will see how these operators fit within the previous goal structure but first let us consider the methods and selection rules.

Methods

Methods are descriptions of procedures for achieving goals. These are assumed to be one of the ways that the user stores knowledge of the task. In GOMS, the methods are conditional sequences of goals and operators, with conditional tests on the contents of the user's immediate memory and on the state of the task environment. For example:

GOAL: ACQUIRE-UNIT-TASK
    GET-NEXT-PAGE *if at end of manuscript*
    GET-NEXT-TASK

The method above is associated with the GOAL: ACQUIRE-UNIT-TASK. It will give rise to either the operator sequence GET-NEXT-PAGE or the single operator GET-NEXT-TASK depending on the results of the test for end of page in the task environment. Methods are assumed to be learned procedures that the user already has. They are not plans that are created during a task performance. These methods are assumed to be stored in long-term memory and are part of the user's knowledge structure of the task built up from past experience, instruction, etc. They are assumed to reflect the knowledge of the exact sequence of steps required to achieve the goal.

Selection rules

There may be more than one method for achieving a given goal. In a GOMS model, the selection rules handle the process of choosing between methods. A selection rule is of the form, if X is true then use method M. For example, the selection rules for GOAL: LOCATE-LINE could be as follows: if the number of lines to the next modification is less than three, then use the line-feed method (LF-METHOD); else use the quick-search method (QS-METHOD).

Thus a task model for editing a manuscript produced in the GOMS framework might be as follows:

GOAL: EDIT-MANUSCRIPT
    GOAL: EDIT-UNIT-TASK *repeat until no more unit tasks*
        GOAL: ACQUIRE-UNIT-TASK
            GET-NEXT-PAGE *if at end of manuscript*
            GET-NEXT-TASK
        GOAL: EXECUTE-UNIT-TASK
            GOAL: LOCATE-LINE
                [select: USE-QS-METHOD
                    USE-LF-METHOD]
            GOAL: MODIFY-TEXT
                [select: USE-S-METHOD
                    USE-M-METHOD]
            VERIFY-EDIT

It should be noted that the GOMS framework only allows for models of error-free behaviour with no problem solving involved. (This results from the fact that all users are assumed already to possess the knowledge of the appropriate methods.) Furthermore, the concept of a unit task is vague since this is a user-defined subtask, but it is clear, from what is known about the way that people develop skill, that what constitutes a unit task will vary with the level of skill of a user. Another feature of the GOMS framework is that it is capable of producing a family of models at varying grains of analysis. The level of analysis is determined by the operators. For example, the analyst may decide to choose just one operator at the level of the unit task (e.g.

EDIT-UNIT-TASK): this would result in predictions of time on task at that level. Alternatively, at a much lower grain of detail, the analyst may choose to describe operators at the level of basic perceptual, cognitive and motor actions such as LOOK-AT-HOME-KEY, TURN-PAGE, TYPE, MOVE-HANDS, in which case the analysis would produce predictions of time for each of these components.

To use the GOMS framework in analysing and evaluating a system design, it is assumed that the designer will be able to analyse how the user will approach the task using the proposed system. The analysis would be in terms of the GOMS approach and at a chosen grain of detail. Having produced the task analysis, the designer is then required to fit the time predictions to the model to come up with a quantitative assessment of the time it would take a skilled user to carry out a task or part thereof using the proposed system.

Fitting time parameters at the keystroke level would be as follows:

- The execution of a task can be described in terms of four physical-motor operators, k (keying), p (pointing), h (homing) and d (drawing) together with one mental operator (m) and a system response operator (r). Thus execution time would be described as the sum of the times spent executing the different operators:

$$\text{Texecute} = \text{Tk} + \text{Tp} + \text{Th} + \text{Td} + \text{Tm} + \text{Tr}$$

- The time values for these different operators are then calculated from existing empirical evidence. Thus we might expect for a very good typist the following:

$$\text{Texecute} = 0.08\,\text{s} + 1.1\,\text{s} + 0.4\,\text{s} + 1.06\,\text{s} + 1.35\,\text{s} + 0.65\,\text{s}$$

Clearly, there are a number of problems with the GOMS approach which limit its usefulness. The first limitation is the restriction to skilled task performers with no problem-solving behaviour required by the task. A second limitation is the diffculty of using the various aspects of the approach. For instance, asking a designer to construct a task model for a system which does not yet exist requires a formal method of task analysis and a task model of how the user would approach the task based on extant technological systems (i.e. how they do it at present). Once the task model has been constructed, the designer must then make decisions about how the tasks will be affected by the system and what new tasks are likely to be introduced. A further problem in using GOMS is that choosing the grain for the analysis may crucially affect the usefulness of the results. A further difficulty seems to be in having an adequate database of empirical evidence from which to select the appropriate time parameters.

All these problems impact on the usability of the GOMS approach. A more fundamental problem is the way that the MHP simplifies the whole of psychological theory to four stores and three processors. This is far too simplistic and is a gross over-approximation. A final problem is the way in which the predictions are derived from an additive model. This is again too simplistic since it ignores the possibility that the user will be able to do two or more things at once (such as type and read).

The advantages of the GOMS approach are that it provides more insight to modelling in human–computer interaction than had previously been possible. It makes explicit a theory of human behaviour on which predictions can be based. It also identifies the importance of task analysis, and at least attempts to produce a theory of task knowledge in terms of the different components of the GOMS framework.

SUMMARY OF EARLY MODELS IN HCI

This chapter has introduced the notion of modelling different aspects of HCI. The three modelling approaches considered were CLG, TAL and GOMS. These three approaches are interesting from a number of perspectives. First all the models are meant to be application oriented, that is to say, they are not offering a new theory of HCI, psychology or computing. Instead, the models are meant to be applied in the process of system and interface design in particular. The models differ in their intended purposes or uses in the process of interface design. CLG is aimed at the generation of design ideas. It provides a top-down approach for the design of user interfaces preceding a consideration of the tasks in the domain. In contrast to this TAL and GOMS are intended to be used to evaluate the usability of the interface design by predicting user behaviour without having to test actual users employing a runnable version of the designed system and its interface.

Each of the three approaches considered in this chapter uses some form of notation to express the contents of the modelled interaction. Both CLG and GOMS use a psuedo-functional notation, while TAL uses BNF and production rules. In each case no attempt is made to justify the choice of the notation or its suitability to the task in hand (i.e. characterizing aspects of HCI). In all cases there is little or no documentation about the notations or how to use them to construct the resultant model. This brings us to the question of the usability of the approaches. Only CLG has been evaluated for use by designers (other than by the developers of the modelling approaches), and this has proved to be difficult to use and unclear.

On a more positive note, this early work on modelling has highlighted the complexity of the problem of developing applicable models of HCI. Each approach has considered the user, the tasks and the interface. It is clear that these are three central elements in developing good HCI. In subsequent chapters we will examine in more detail the nature of tasks and interfaces. In Chapter 10 we will consider some more recent approaches to modelling HCI.

Exercises

1 What is the distinction between a user's model of a computer system, and a model of a user?
2 Describe the four components and six levels of CLG.
3 Describe the interface for a cash dispenser using CLG.
4 TAL can be used to assess the structural consistency, string simplicity and the number of different actions steps in a given task. Write a description of a user interface (perhaps you would like to try describing the interface to a video-recorder) using TAL and assess it in terms of the above three features.
5 Analyse a task in terms of GOMS (you might like to analyse the tasks involved in programming a video recorder).

10 INTERACTION AND USER MODELLING IN HUMAN–COMPUTER INTERACTION

Summary

- By modelling the user's mental representation of the interaction language, task action grammar extends the work of Reisner (discussed in Chapter 9). The approach taken by TAG is to develop a competence model of an ideal user's representation of the interaction language. This model can be used to assess the consistency of the interaction.

- The complexity of an interaction is modelled by *cognitive complexity theory*. CCT has been developed from the GOMS approach (see Chapter 9). The aim of CCT is to model the rules that an ideal user would have to acquire to use successfully the interactive system to perform a given task. By comparing the number of rules that are required, an assessment of the complexity of the interface can be made, and by focusing on the number of new rules that are required, some estimate of the amount of learning needed is obtained.

- There are a number of approaches to modelling the characteristics of users in HCI in this chapter. We focus on two approaches that model the psychological structure of the user. First an approach known as *interacting cognitive subsystems* (ICS) is considered. This approach provides a framework for modelling the particular psychological structures that are involved when a user carries out a task using an interface design. The intention of this approach is that by constructing a model of the different structures that are invoked to perform the task, the designer can identify how difficult it will be for a user to use the interface. A second approach is known as *programmable user models* (PUMs). The aim of PUMs is to provide an environment in which the designer is able to assess the usability of the design through a series of constraints. The constraints reflect the user's cognitive processing limitations. The design environment reflects the constraints of user's cognitive processing. Through this design environment, the designer is directly made aware of the user's cognitive processing limitations.

INTRODUCTION

In the previous chapter we considered some of the earlier approaches to modelling users, tasks and interfaces in HCI. In this chapter some of those forms of modelling are developed further. Task action grammar, developed by Payne and Green (1986), models the user's understanding of the interaction language. The interaction language is the set of user inputs and computer outputs that the user must understand. These inputs and outputs can be thought of as forming a language just like any other computer language such as Pascal or Lisp. An interaction language more closely resembles a computer language than a natural language. Some interaction languages resemble a restricted subset of a natural language. In a growing number of applications, the dominant paradigm for interaction is one of direct manipulation. In the direct-manipulation paradigm, the computer provides a display of the available objects and operations which may be represented to the user by icons. The user is able to interact with the application by selecting and moving/positioning these visible objects, often using a mouse or some other pointing device. Direct manipulation can also be thought of as forming a language with a finite set of rules (a grammar) about what objects can be used in particular contexts and what the correct sequence of selecting particular objects is.

In HCI some form of language is required for the dialogue between the user and the computer. To understand what makes for well-designed human–computer interaction requires us to investigate the structure of the interaction language, the ease with which the language can be used and the ease with which it can be learned. Questions such as these are addressed in part, and in different ways, by each of the following modelling approaches: task action grammar, cognitive complexity theory and interacting cognitive subsystems. The first considers the structure of the language and its consistency; the second considers the amount of learning required to use the interaction language to perform tasks and the likely performance on those tasks; while the third addresses the amount of cognitive processing required to use the interaction language.

TASK ACTION GRAMMAR

Task action grammar (Payne and Green, 1986) is a method of modelling user interactions which has much in common with the approach taken by Reisner (1981) in producing a task-action language. However, the work of Payne and Green gives much more attention to the cognitive basis for their grammar of user interaction. The intention of TAG is to provide a formalism for modelling the mental representation of an interaction language, and so to allow a formal specification of that language as perceived by the user. Thus TAG attempts to identify the salient features of an interaction language that will affect the usability of the language. To this end (of determining the usability of a language), TAG attempts to capture the regularity or consistency of the language. Several forms of consistency have been considered: syntactic and lexical consistency, semantic–syntactic alignment and semantic consistency.

Syntactic consistency The consistent use of one expression as a common element in other expressions, for example, the arithmetic expression might be an element common to rules for assignment statements, array bounds, Boolean expressions and FOR-statements. Similarly, with an interaction language it might be that every command has a common form, perhaps a string followed by a return, or pointing followed by a button click with a mouse. Payne and Green (1986) refer to this as common structure. They also identify family resemblances as a form of syntactic consistency when, for example, different sequences all exhibit a clear similarity. Payne and Green give the following as an example of family resemblance in a programming language:

⟨declaration sequence⟩   ::−⟨declaration⟩
                                | ⟨declaration sequence⟩ + ⟨declaration⟩
⟨statement sequence⟩   ::−⟨statement⟩
                                | ⟨statement sequence⟩ + ⟨statement⟩
⟨letter sequence⟩   ::−⟨letter⟩
                                | ⟨letter sequence⟩ + ⟨letter⟩

This latter kind of syntactic consistency is not detected by BNF but is clearly detectable to the user of the language. TAG captures both common structure and family resemblance forms of syntactic consistency.

Lexical consistency   Refers to the relationship between lexemes, symbols (words, icons, etc.) and their meaning, which is assumed to be non-arbitrary. If the word or icon matches the semantics of the entity it represents then there is said to be congruence of the lexical and semantic relations of the interaction language. For example, if the icon for an entity that is a container in which files can be placed has the perceptual appearance of a folder as opposed to an abstract shape, then the folder icon has a more congruent relationship than the abstract shape to the semantics of the entity container.

Semantic–syntactic alignment   This is where the semantic relations are mirrored in the lexical/symbolic relations and the structure of the commands. For example, in a command language delete file, delete folder, delete word, etc., should have the same ordered structure so that they all take the form command followed by the object name (e.g. d ⟨file-name⟩, d ⟨folder-name⟩, etc.).

Semantic consistency   The principle of completeness gives rise to semantic consistency. If an interaction language allows, for example, the undo command to be applied to text deletion then we should expect it also to be applied to text insertion. Thus there is some consistency in terms of the semantics of the application with respect to the function undo, in that it can be applied to all operations of the application. This form of consistency is not concerned with either the syntactic or lexical/symbolic form of the command.

TAG builds on the notion of *set grammars* in which the rewrite rules of the grammar operate on sets of grammatical objects rather than individual terminal or nonterminal symbols. Payne and Green (1986) argue that consistent languages can be expressed by a small number of set grammar rules while inconsistent languages require a larger number of set grammar rules. Through this notion of set grammars TAG expresses the concept of family resemblance. However, set grammars provide no mechanism for relating the syntax of the language to its semantics and many of the most important aspects of consistency rely upon semantic properties. TAG extends the idea of set grammars by attempting to represent the semantics of tasks. The resultant grammar tries to map the semantics of tasks on to sequences of actions. This aspect of TAG is the most interesting and best developed, however it neither makes reference to nor develops any theory of tasks, and has no principles for mapping tasks on to actions.

TAG as a competence model

Task action grammer is claimed to model competence rather than performance. Therefore, TAG will not necessarily predict a given user's actual performance on a particular task in a defined context. Instead, it will predict what an ideal user would be expected to know of the language. This distinction between competence and performance has important consequences for the utility of TAG. A competence model cannot be expected to have its predictions validated by empirical data since it does not claim to model how knowledge is translated into behaviour. This distinction between competence and performance has been common in linguistic models of knowledge (see, for example, Chomsky, 1965).

Simple-task dictionary

Task action grammer includes the notion of a dictionary of 'simple tasks'. A simple task is defined by Payne and Green (1986, page 121) to be those tasks that can be performed without any problem-solving or iteration. In other words, these simple-tasks are any task that a user can 'routinely' perform with no demand for 'control structure, such as branching or iteration, that requires monitoring of plan progress'. Simple tasks can be seen as being equivalent to operators in the Newell and Simon (1972) view of problem-solving. Simple tasks are not static but dynamic in that they can be 'chunked' together to form new simple tasks as expertise is acquired. In this way, it is claimed that simple tasks are a form of conceptual knowledge structure that users possess (see Chapters 11 and 12 for a theory of task knowledge structures).

   In constructing a TAG model of an interaction language, the modeller has to identify the simple tasks, and then produce a dictionary of those simple tasks. Payne and Green (1986) state that to identify simple tasks requires the modeller to rely on intuition. The simple-task dictionary is nothing more than a list of the identified, intuited simple tasks and their semantic components. For example, the simple-task dictionary for moving a cursor might be as follows:

> *List of commands*
> Move cursor one character forward   ⟩
> Move cursor one character backward   ⟨
> Move cursor one word forward   ⟩⟩
> Move cursor one word backward   ⟨⟨
>
> *Dictionary of simple tasks*
> move-cursor-one-character-forward {Direction = forward, Unit = character}
> move-cursor-one-character-backward   {Direction = backward,   Unit = character}
> move-cursor-one-word-forward {Direction = forward, Unit = word}
> move-cursor-one-word-backward {Direction = backward, Unit = word}

In this example there is an implicit list of features and their possible values for the simple-task dictionary, namely, 'Direction' and 'Unit'. These are features of the simple tasks and their possible values are 'forward/backward' and 'character/word' respectively.

Rule schemas

The rule schemas in TAG are used to generate action specifications from simple tasks. Each rule is expanded by assigning the values to all the features in the rule, such that a feature is assigned with the same value wherever it appears in that rule. For example, from the simple-task dictionary above we might generate the following TAG rule schemas:

TAG rule schemas
1.1   Task [Direction, Unit] → symbol + length [Unit]
1.2   Symbol [Direction = forward] → "⟩"|"⟩⟩"
1.3   Symbol [Direction = backward] → "⟨"|"⟨⟨"
1.4   Length [Unit = word] → "⟨⟨"|"⟩⟩"
1.5   Length [Unit = character] → "⟨"|"⟩"

Taking the above example, the rule 1.1 is expanded by assigning values to all the features in the square brackets. The symbol and length objects are given in rules 1.2, 1.3, 1.4 and 1.5 and the simple-task object is given by the simple-task dictionary, for example:

move-cursor-one-character-backward → "⟨"

This simple example gives the essence of a TAG definition of an interaction language.

Some observations regarding TAG

Interaction languages are often designed in an ad hoc and piecemeal manner. It is often inevitable that when design proceeds in such a manner there will be 'bugs' in the resultant language. These bugs are not always evident to the designer and may only come to light when users begin to make use of the application. TAG aims to enable the designer to identify these errors in the design of the interaction language. The ability of TAG to identify the previously described form of inconsistencies in interaction language design is well demonstrated by Payne and Green (1986) for a number of relatively small extracts of interaction languages and relatively small parts of real tasks. It is clearly a problem for TAG that it is based on a set of primitives (simple tasks) whose identity is vague and intuitive. Consequently, it is possible to produce a variety of different grammars for the same interaction language when using TAG. Such variability may be of little or no consequence to the overall utility of TAG if the variability does not lead to differences in the predicted consistency of a language. However, since the variability is likely to arrive at a fundamental level (the identification of simple tasks), it is likely that such variations will lead to widely different grammars being developed. Applying TAG to a full interactive language raises a number of further problems in addition to the variability of the grammars produced. First, the user of TAG must be able to analyse tasks and subtasks to the vaguely defined level of simple tasks. Second, it is impossible to identify all the tasks that any design might be used for, therefore the user of TAG will never be sure that a complete grammar of the interaction language has been produced. Third, there is no method or principle for selecting representative tasks to be modelled by TAG. Fourth, the view of a task implied by TAG is relatively low level, and as such it is difficult to see how it would be applied to evaluate a complete interaction language in terms of higher level tasks, such as using a document processor to write a book with all the concomitant subparts such as page layout, font selection, inclusion of graphics, etc. A fifth concern for the user of TAG must be the amount of detail and development of the interaction language that is needed before TAG can be applied. It is clear that there must be at least a full and detailed specification of the interaction language and it may even be necessary to have an implemented version of the language in order to produce a full TAG model. TAG does not prescribe a design of an interactive language; it is a descriptive and, to some degree, an evaluative tool.

COGNITIVE COMPLEXITY THEORY

Cognitive complexity theory CCT is an extension of the GOMS (Card, Moran and Newell, 1983) approach to modelling user interactions. Kieras and Polson (1986) developed cognitive complexity theory to predict the difficulties a person is expected to encounter in learning and using an interactive computer system. The main feature of CCT is that it uses production rules and production systems (i.e. collections of production rules) to model the knowledge a person (user) is assumed to require to use a particular interactive computer system.

Cognitive complexity theory attempts to predict the complexity of a device from the point of view of the user. Kieras and Polson define complexity to mean, 'the amount and structure of knowledge required to operate the device successfully'. CCT attempts to provide a quantitative measure of the learning time and performance difficulties that users might expect when using a designed interface to perform a prescribed task. The approach taken by CCT is to specify the assumed knowledge required to use the interface and to identify which items of knowledge have to be learned as opposed to those already known by the user. The learning time is then computed from the sum of all items to be learned and the performance time is computed from the sum of all the required knowledge to use the interface. CCT is also a task-based approach to evaluating a user-interface design. It decomposes the interaction tasks into components of required user-knowledge.

Cognitive complexity theory identifies a number of different types of knowledge that are assumed to make up the users required knowledge for using a piece of interactive software to carry out prescribed tasks. Fundamental to the objectives of CCT is an attempt to model aspects of knowledge in terms of the user's existing knowledge and the required knowledge of the software (called 'device' by Kieras and Polson) in a notation that would allow direct comparisons between the two. The model of the software (device) is intended to allow the designer to identify what knowledge a user would need to use the software efficiently and without error. The model of the user models the knowledge possessed by the user of the tasks to be performed.

The required knowledge of the software (device) is represented using a generalized transition network (GTN) with the properties of an augmented, recursive transition network. The nodes in the GTN are assumed to be states in which the software can legitimately be at any time during the interaction. Moving from one node to another is achieved by fulfilling specific conditions (pre-conditions) about the states of the nodes that must be satisfied before the target node can be accessed. The states of the network are considered to form a goal structure.

The user's knowledge of the task is represented by a goal structure. An intention of CCT is that the GTN and the goal structure representations of the device and task respectively could be compared to identify which aspects of the user's knowledge of the task can be mapped on to the required knowledge of the software. Kieras and Polson also distinguish between device-dependent and device-independent knowledge. Device-independent knowledge is the knowledge the user has about a task that is independent of any particular software system. For example, in mailing tasks, users have knowledge of how to greet others that is independent of any type of mailing system, electronic or otherwise. In contrast, device-dependent knowledge is concerned with the knowledge that is special to a particular aspect of the task when it is carried out using a given system or class of systems. For example, in the mailing task, the form of the address will vary depending upon the mail system being used and will vary within classes of both electronic and conventional mailing systems.

Knowles (1988) has considered the contrast between device-dependent and device-independent knowledge for using CAD systems to accomplish different tasks involved in fashion design. In her research, Knowles has been able to identify the knowledge that fashion designers have of pattern-design tasks. Pattern design is the process of transforming a fashion design for a garment into a cutting pattern that can be used to make the garment. Knowles studied fashion designers using conventional pattern-design tools involving pencil and paper, and using computer systems for 2D and 2½D design. She was then able to identify where the device-independent knowledge would readily support transfer of knowledge across devices and also where device-dependent knowledge would lead to errors and hence where learning was required.

Cognitive complexity theory employs the notion of the user's knowledge of the software system to model what Kieras and Polson term 'how-it-works knowledge'. By modelling this knowledge, CCT attempts to represent the user's mental model of the software system. This model can be based upon either the user's actual knowledge of the software device or on the knowledge an ideal expert-user would have of the software system.

The user's knowledge of the task is distinguished between being 'job-situation knowledge' and 'how-to-do-it knowledge'. Job-situation knowledge is said to be the knowledge the user has about what tasks are carried out within a given domain and using a particular software system. How-to-do-it knowledge refers to the procedural knowledge the user has in order to carry out the tasks. There is clearly some confusion in CCT between 'how-it-works' and 'how-to-do-it' knowledge, since the form of knowledge may be procedural in both cases, in which case the user may only be able to demonstrate how-it-works knowledge by using the software.

Task knowledge

Task knowledge in CCT owes much to the GOMS approach. Following Card *et al.*, Kieras and Polson assume that task behaviour is goal directed and purposeful. Goals can be thought of as being structured into subgoals and each subgoal is accomplished by one or more methods. The goals and methods of GOMS represent the user's job-situation knowledge. Job goals are the goals the user wants to perform using the software. The methods of GOMS are what the user knows about how to achieve those goals. The user's how-to-do-it task knowledge is also identified by the contents of the methods.

Cognitive complexity theory uses production systems to represent in detail the content of a user's how-to-do-it knowledge. Like all production systems, CCT production systems have three components: a collection of rules, an interpreter and a working memory. Each production rule has the conventional form;

IF ⟨condition⟩ THEN ⟨action⟩

The working memory maintains a record of the pattern of current goals that need to be executed to fulfil a particular task. The interpreter cycles between recognize and act modes. In recognize mode it checks all the condition parts of the rules and compares them to the contents of working memory. If the comparison produces a match then the action part of the rule is executed. Only one rule at a time can fire. When the action part of a rule is executed the contents of working memory are modified. Each rule can contain instructions about what to do when the action part is executed. For example, the rules can include instructions to delete the current goal, go to the next part of the method, add a note, add a subgoal, etc.

The goal structure of GOMS is represented indirectly within the production system by the patterns of goals that are stored in the production system's working memory. This is reflected by the add-goal statement in the production-rule actions. The methods of GOMS are implemented in the CCT production system representation as subroutines. Operators are modelled in the production-rule system representation of CCT by 'elementary actions' and selection rules are modelled by the condition part of a production rule.

Predicting training time and productivity with CCT

Training time is predicted using the following formula:

training time $= t.n + c$

where

t = training time per production rule
n = total number of production rules minus the number of common rules
c = time required to complete the non-new part of the task

Both t and c are assumed to remain constant over tasks. This means that each new production rule takes the same amount of time to learn. This assumption is acceptable only if each rule is at the same level of complexity and contains the same amount and type of knowledge. As there are no definitive statements in CCT about the content and level of production rules, this assumption is not sound. For example, two rules to be learned within the same task and using the same interface may be as follows. The task in this example is withdrawing cash from an automatic cash till, and the interface is a text-form-based display with special-purpose buttons and numeric keypad:

Rule 1
  If
      (the goal is to withdraw cash)
  then
      (Do Sequence (insert card)
        (enter PIN number)
        (select CASH ONLY)
        (enter cash amount)
        (withdraw card)
        (withdraw cash))

Rule 2
  If
      (the goal is to withdraw cash)
  then
      (Do Sequence (insert card)
        (enter PIN number)
        (read menu)
        (choose from: CASH ONLY
                  CASH WITH RECEIPT
                  REQUEST STATEMENT
                  OTHER SERVICE)
        (select CASH ONLY)
        (enter cash amount)
        (withdraw card)
        (withdraw cash))

Rules 1 and 2 above are both descriptions of the same task. Rule 1 is at a higher level of description than rule 2. CCT will predict that both rules 1 and 2 will have the same learning time associated with them. Clearly rule 2 is more detailed than rule 1 and would take longer to be learned. Rule 2 could be made even more complex if it were to contain conditional and optional statements that covered what to do if the PIN number were entered incorrectly, and if the cash till had no cash available then this would still be expressable as a single production rule. It is clear that the rules can and will vary in complexity and content. This variability will lead to differences in the learning time for each rule. Consequently, the only way that rule learning time can be considered as constant across rules is if there is an exact definition of a rule that will constrain the model such that all rules are of the same complexity and knowledge type.

Cognitive complexity theory predicts *productivity* by applying the following formula:

Total of the operation execution times
_____

The number of cycles to complete the task × the activation time

The sum of the execution times refers to the production rules that must be executed to complete a task. Execution time is equal to the number of cycles required to complete the task multiplied by the activation time per cycle plus the number of 'add' instructions (e.g. add-goal), multiplied by the time for each add action, plus the intercept parameter (assumed to be zero).

Thus, CCT attempts to make predictions about the time it will take to train a new user to carry out a defined task given a particular sequence for carrying out the task and assuming an optimal training strategy. However, CCT does not define what a task is; it also fails to differentiate between the many different ways that tasks can be performed, and to consider what an optimal training strategy is.

Some observations about CCT

Cognitive complexity theory assumes that people always follow the optimum path to reach a goal. In contrast, people use familiar and easy-to-recall ways of reaching a goal even if they are suboptimum in terms of overall efficiency for completing the task. CCT is based upon GOMS and consequently does not accommodate any problem-solving behaviour. As a result of ignoring problem-solving behaviour, CCT is not able to model the behaviours that occur as a person is learning either to use the system or the task.

The psychological validity of using production rules in CCT at best is weak. As we have already seen, there is no reason to assume that any two production rules will be of equal complexity. There is no evidence to show that CCT can be used with any reliability such that if used by two different people to model the same task, user and software, they would produce the same model, the same production rules and hence the same predictions.

Cognitive complexity theory is at best an evaluation tool rather than a design-generation tool. It cannot be used to help the designer to make decisions about the display of information or the design of icons, buttons, windows, etc. It cannot be used to evaluate finely detailed interaction behaviour. For example, it cannot predict the time it will take a user to select an item from a menu, or if they will understand the meaning of a particular icon or command string. Finally, CCT can make only a limited evaluation of a user interface based on some rather gross predictions of the quantity of knowledge the user must acquire, or the quantity of knowledge that must be used to perform a task with the system. It cannot make qualitative predictions about the different types of knowledge that are required or about the differences between production rules that are more complex, but are of an equal number.

INTERACTING COGNITIVE SUBSYSTEMS AS A BASIS FOR A COGNITIVE TASK ANALYSIS

The GOMS model described in Chapter 9 was based on a simplistic model of human cognition characterized in terms of a model human processor. This model was the basis for making predictions about HCI through associating the demands placed on the model human processor by particular tasks involved in interacting with a given user interface. As was discussed in Chapter 9 the simplicity of the model human processor was one of the major weaknesses of the GOMS approach. More recently, Barnard (1987) has proposed a more elaborate framework for modelling the user's cognitive resources. This is based on a theory known as interacting cognitive subsystems, in which a number of special-purpose processing systems are linked together in a cognitive architecture. This architecture assumes that human perception, cognition and action can be analysed in terms of well-defined and discrete information-processing modules. These modules, it is assumed, are capable of processing information in parallel and each processing subsystem has its own, separate memory record store.

The architecture of ICS is subdivided such that there are a number of functionally independent subsystems each of which operates in a specific domain of processing.

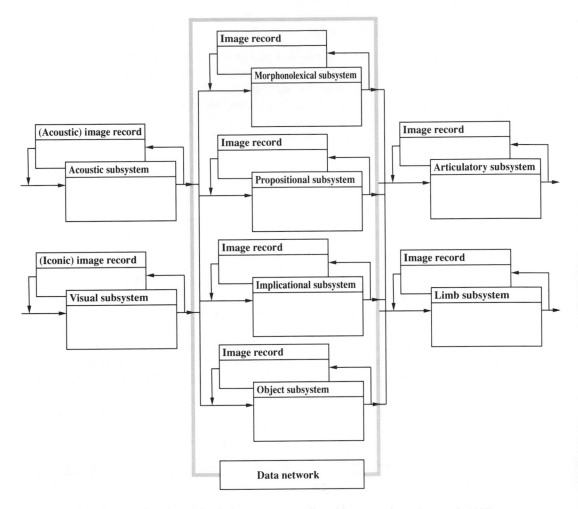

Figure 10.1 Interacting Cognitive Subsystems overall architecture (from Barnard, 1987)

Figure 10.1 shows the architecture of ICS. It can be seen that there are three components to the architecture addressing sensory, representational, and effector subsystems.

Each subsystem has its own associated 'image record' which maintains an episodic memory-trace for that particular subsystem. The sensory subsystems process incoming sense data from a particular modality, such as the visual, acoustic or haptic senses. Each sensory processor is special to a particular sensory modality, and transforms information from that modality into specific mental 'codes' that represent the structure and content of the incoming data. The output from the sensory subsystems is then further processed by one or more of the representational subsystems. There are four of these representational subsystems proposed by Barnard (1987), the morphonolexical subsystem, the propositional subsystem, the implicational subsystem and the object subsystem. Each of these representational subsystems is connected to the sensory subsystems, to each other and to the effector subsystems by a *data network*. This allows each subsystem to operate in parallel with other subsystems. For example, the morphonolexical subsystem incorporates specific processes for handling the surface structure of language; the propositional subsystem and the implicational subsystem process the semantic and conceptual aspects of the information; the object subsystem specializes in the processing of visuo-spatial structures. The effector subsystems include an articulatory subsystem and a limb subsystem which receive output from the representational subsystems and process them to produce motor output in the form of speech and other bodily movements.

From this overview of the architecture of ICS, it can be seen that it provides a much richer description of human-information processing than was provided by the model human-processor of Card, Moran and Newell. The ability to differentiate between different forms of sensory input and to allow parallel processing by all subsystems, especially the four representational subsystems, means that the architecture is capable of modelling human behaviour to a higher degree of sensitivity.

Each subsystem operates in a different way, since it is receiving different forms of input from and producing different forms of output to other subsystems. However, all subsystems share a common internal organization of processing resources. Any given subsystem can only process information represented in a specific mental code. A process known as the copy process creates an episodic memory record of the input to a given subsystem. A number of parallel processors then recode the information within the subsystem to produce the output codes. For example, in the case of the acoustic subsystem, the processing could construct a lexical output for further processing by a relevant representational subsystem, while simultaneously transmitting a locational code to the limb subsystem, then enabling that subsystem to control the orientation of the head towards the sound, to enable a better hearing of the acoustic signal.

Barnard suggests that these transformational processes within a given subsystem can be thought of as production systems, such that if they respond a particular pattern of conditions are met and a particular process will operate to produce an output of a given type. The transformational processors within a subsystem are *serial* in that they can only process a given input stream at any one time. However, the copy process creates a record of all inputs to the subsystem, and these memory records therefore act as a buffer for the subsystem. A more detailed description of the ICS architecture can be found in Barnard (1987).

An example of how ICS might function

This example is taken from Barnard (1987, page 124) and it is presented here to give some feel for how the architecture of ICS might be used to describe part of a task being performed using an interactive computer system. The computer system is a word processor and the task is revising a paper.

> In reading a paragraph, a particularly difficult sentence is noted. This is deleted and a rephrased version entered.

The state of the task and the ICS as depicted by Fig. 10.2 is that the user has completed reading the relevant sentence. The analysis proceeds by showing the

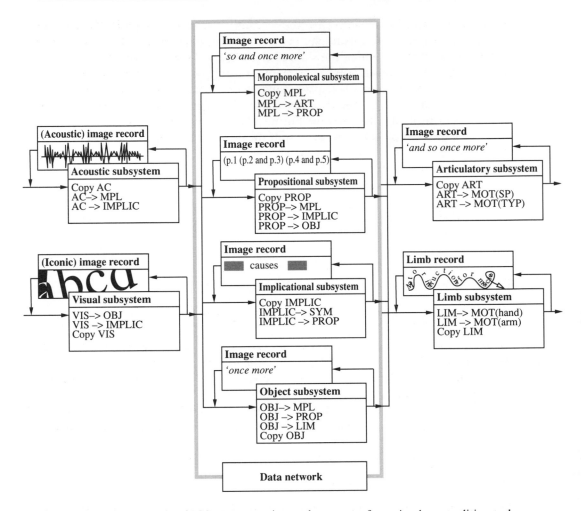

Figure 10.2 An example of ICS representation and processes for a simple text-editing task (from Barnard 1987)

configuration of the different processes involved in reading and interpreting the sentence, deleting it and typing in a fresh version of the sentence.

The text of the sentence is processed by the visual subsystem where a copy process creates an image record of the information in the visual field. In parallel, the VIS → OBJ process recodes the raw visual data into a higher order representation. Such recoding might ignore brightness or colour of the input but identify whether the letters are upper or lower case. The output data is then transmitted over the network to the OBJ → MPL processor (MPL, i.e. morphonolexical) where a copy of the input is made and recorded and the input is recoded into a speech-based code reflecting the surface structure of language. Here the details of the surface structure of the word are discarded. The output from the OBJ → MPL subsystem is then transmitted across the network to the MPL → PROP subsystem. This then processes the semantic content of the sentence and identifies relations among the entities in the text. The output of the PROP (propositional) subsystem is coded into the PROP → IMPLIC form for the implicational meaning of the sentence to be identified. It may be necessary to cycle between PROP → IMPLIC and IMPLIC → PROP processing to enable alternative meanings to be evaluated. The output from this cycle could then be passed to the LIM processor for producing the correct motor movements to delete and insert the text. This, of course, will also involve much more processing by the various subsystems to enable the user to read the menu bar, position the cursor, identify the correct selections and insert the new text. For example, to capture the processes involved in deleting the sentence, we might need to postulate the following processing by the subsystems:

> (:: PROP→IMPLIC ::
> :: IMPLIC→PROP ::)n
> :: PROP→OBJ ::
> :: OBJ→LIM ::
> :: LIM→MOT*

plus 'feedback' via

> *VIS→OBJ ::
> :: OBJ→PROP ::

Where '*' denotes 'external' input/output, ' :: ' denotes transmission over the data network and '(...)n' denotes reciprocal processing between subsystems.

Thus the user would have to elaborate the action sequence by translating the intention to delete into the object and limb subsystems, and monitor feedback about the position of the cursor through the visual, object and propositional subsystems. This constitutes a cognitive analysis of the task in terms of the particular interacting cognitive subsystems of the ICS framework.

Some observations about ICS

The intention of ICS is that it provides more accurate analyses of the cognitive processing required to perform various tasks using a computer system. The analysis is performed first by making assertions about which processors and subsystems would be involved in performing any part of the task, detailing the 'program' to be followed by the user in carrying out that processing, and then making predictions about the complexity and difficulties that might arise in using the computer system because of the processing required by the user. For example, a new user of an accounting system that uses arbitrary names for commands, and has no inherent structure to the menu and the dialogue format, would have to engage in a considerable amount of processing involving all subsystems to identify what a particular menu item might mean.

Interacting cognitive subsystem can be seen as providing a more intensive form of analysis of the complexities of using a computer system than both GOMS and CCT. However, just as CCT and GOMS were seen to be quite demanding for the analyst to use, the added degree of fidelity offered by ICS makes it much more difficult to apply than either GOMS or CCT. Even for a psychologist to identify consistently and completely all the different subsystems and their correct associations for any given task would be a difficult undertaking. For a nonpsychologist to understand even what a particular subsystem does is probably too much to expect. In recognition of this fact, Barnard and colleagues set out to develop an expert system to enable the allocation of subsystems to task components to be done automatically. Such a tool seems necessary if ICS is to be used by anyone other than a well-trained psychologist.

PROGRAMMABLE USER MODELS

More recently, research on modelling in human–computer interaction has considered the possibility for implemented models of users or user interaction. Models such as CCT or TAG have been criticized for their reliance upon an informal notation which has proved to be difficult to use. Also, these and other similar techniques must be applied as an evaluation of a previously-generated interface design rather than to assist in the process of generating the design. Young, Green and Simon (1989) have attempted to produce a psychologically constrained architecture called a *programmable user model* (PUM) which the designer can program to simulate the user performing a range of tasks with a proposed interface. Such a model has not yet been produced but the ideas that Young *et al.* have are worth considering further.

The PUM is one way of conveying psychological considerations to the interface designer about the usability of the interface being designed. A programmable user model is intended to serve two purposes: first, to allow predictive evaluation of the usability of a design before it is actually built; and second, to draw the designer's attention to issues of usability and to provide them with a way of thinking about these issues.

A PUM is meant to be an analytical model of a computer user. The model requires the designer to program certain aspects of the user's intended behaviour. The content of a PUM is user knowledge. It is based upon an idea from Runciman and Hammond (1986) who stated that there are two processors in an interactive system—the user and the computer. As the software developer builds and refines the computer program, they are also implicitly specifying the 'user program'. Making the specification and design of the 'user program' explicit is an attempt to rectify the imbalance in design (i.e. the focus is often on the design of the computer software and not on the issues of usability) and to provide the designer with a way of knowing that the 'user program' is indeed 'executable' by a user in an efficient and error-free manner. Thus a PUM is meant to be seen as an architecture for the execution of a user program.

A PUM is a cognitive architecture and not an artificial user, since building a complete model of an ideal user is unlikely to enable designers to see the problems with their designs and would probably be impossible to construct. It is an approximate model, but it is not primarily calculational (as the GOMS approach is). Rather than providing a tool for constructing an interface, a PUM is meant to be a tool for constructing a model of the user. However, it would be of more use if a PUM could form part of a more powerful and complete interactive system design toolkit. Also, a PUM is not an expert system that attempts to provide a simulation of an expert designer or of an expert psychologist. It does not provide advice or guidelines; instead it draws the designer's attention to the user through the experience of constructing the user model for the design they are working on.

In order to build a PUM the designer would have to work through some kind of programming language. The idea is that this language will be rather like building a knowledge base. This would involve identifying and specifying conceptual objects and the operations performed on them, identifying methods and so on, that would be used to organize these operations, and identifying what other background knowledge would be required. A PUM is seen as being an interpreter of an instruction language. It does not simply execute all specified instructions; instead, it seems as if a PUM incorporates some form of simple planning mechanism that can fill the gaps between and the details of instructions.

A modelling approach based on SOAR (Laird, Newell and Rosenbloom, 1987) has been considered as part of the PUM research. This involves a problem-solving architecture in the form of a series of nested problem-spaces and a learning mechanism that involves chunking. These two features allow learning and problem-solving to be modelled in a PUM. PUM also incorporates ideas from ACT* (Anderson, 1983, and see Chapter 4), interacting cognitive subsystems (Barnard, 1987) and task action grammars (Payne and Green, 1986).

Some observations about PUMS

As PUMs are still very much a research project and have not yet been realized in any demonstrable form, it is difficult to form a clear understanding of what a PUM includes, what its contribution to interaction design might be and what are the likely problems in using the approach. However, the original idea of Runciman and Hammond upon which the PUMs approach is based is certainly novel and interesting. The novelty is in treating design as not just the design of a software program, but also the design of a user program. This is often not realized by interface designers. An interaction involves a user and the software, and the design of the software constrains the person's behaviour and extends their potential in many ways. Failing to accept that this is indeed designing user as well as software behaviour is short-sighted and is likely to lead to the design of many bad interactive systems.

The PUM approach has the potential, therefore, to bring issues about the design of user and software behaviour on to a more even footing. PUMs also acknowledge the need for some kind of task modelling, since both user and system come together to perform some tasks interactively, such as to land an airplane safely or to book a seat at the theatre. PUMs use the term 'scenario' to talk about exemplar tasks that might be used to assess the coming-together of the software program and the user program as an interactive system. However, apart from describing the role of these task scenarios, the PUMs work does not address the issue of how to model or conjoin the task of the user and the software. We will examine this issue of modelling tasks in the following chapters.

CONCLUSION

The different models discussed in this chapter are advances on the earlier models of TAL, GOMS and CLG discussed in Chapter 9. The main focus seems to be to provide designers with models that allow factors affecting the user and task to be brought into the design cycle more explicitly. In all cases, user and task models are being used to evaluate the design. This is important since it allows the designer to identify how the user interface affects the *internal* tasks the user has to perform. Reflecting back, the task–artefact design cycle discussed in Chapter 1 and the models described here all support detailed analysis of the interaction in terms of scenarios and assume a 'psychology of tasks'. ICS provides an explicit psychology of tasks in terms of the psychological processes involved; PUMs hides the psychology from the designer, but forces the designer to take note of its consequences. However, none of the models allows the designer to design with explicit task scenarios. Only CLG, described in Chapter 9, allowed the designer to develop both task scenarios and designs in parallel. In the following chapters, a task–artefact design approach is developed that builds upon these earlier modelling approaches and allows task-based design and evaluation.

Exercises

1 Write a TAG description for a cash dispenser; identify the simple tasks and rule schemas. Identify the consistency of the design by analysing the schemas and rules.
2 Carry out a CCT analysis of a simple system (such as a cash dispenser) and identify what new knowledge a user would have to acquire to use the system. Consider the amount of transfer of knowledge that could be expected to occur.
3 ICS provides a detailed processing model of how a task would be performed. How is this different from CCT or GOMS? What are the consequences of modelling information processing?

11 TASK ANALYSIS AND TASK MODELLING

Summary

- Task analysis (TA) is an important method in HCI. Historically, TA has been developed alongside methods such as workstudy, critical path analysis and systems analysis. TA is very different from the other forms of analysis mentioned above, in that it analyses tasks in terms of human behaviour. In the sixties and early seventies work on TA was strongly influenced by training needs. Both in the UK and in the USA, methods of analysing tasks were developed which sought to identify how people could be trained to perform particular tasks. In the UK, the best developed and most successful approach at that time was hierarchical task analysis (HTA). In the USA, the emphasis was placed on ability profiles and taxonomies of human performance.

- More recently TA has been given greater importance in the context of interactive system design. The GOMS, CLG, TAL, and other approaches to modelling HCI discussed in Chapter 9, require some form of TA prior to either the predictive modelling of behaviour (in the case of GOMS) or the decomposition of a design (in the case of CLG). While approaches such as these, and more recently TAG, CCT, ICS and PUMS (discussed in Chapter 10) assume some form of TA they do not provide any such method.

- Recent work on training requirements for information technology (IT) gave rise to a method of TA known as task analysis for knowledge description (TAKD). This work identified the knowledge requirements of IT tasks at a level of generality that made the description of that knowledge independent of the constraints of the original tasks analysed.

- More theoretical issues relating to TA concern what form of analysis is to be undertaken and how the results of the analysis can be modelled. These two issues influence the type and form of the analysis and determine what kind of data are relevant for the analysis.

- In analysing a task there are four important decisions to be made before the TA can begin: first, the purpose of the task analysis should be made explicit; second,

- the characteristics of the domain need to be identified; third, the tasks themselves need to be identified within the domain, and fourth, the user groups need to be defined.

- In carrying out the TA, the following three questions need to be answered: first, what constitutes data for the analysis, or in other words what information about the task(s) is needed; second, where can that information be obtained, and third, how can that information be obtained.

- Task knowledge structures (TKS) provide a theory of how task structures may be reflected in a person's understanding of a task. TKS describe tasks in terms of the knowledge used or required to perform a task.

EARLY APPROACHES TO TASK ANALYSIS

During the fifties and sixties there were a number of research projects funded in the UK and the USA that were concerned with identifying how people should be trained or retrained. One obvious reason for this in the USA was the continued use of conscription to the armed forces. The armed forces needed to be able to select and train men to use equipment and carry out many tasks that were completely novel to them. Also, as the period of conscription was only short, the amount of time spent training needed to be minimized. In the UK, the funding for TA research was not restricted to the military. The Department of Trade and Industry and the training councils were concerned that methods of training should be developed to enable people to move between industries more effectively as skills shortages and redundancies occurred.

Three prominent researchers of TA for training are Annett and his colleagues, Fleishman and his colleagues and Miller. Both Fleishman and Miller were influenced by the idea that tasks could be analysed in terms of their psychological requirements. The work of Fleishman and Quaintance (1984) and Miller (1975) led to the development of a method of TA that decomposed a task into the *psychological abilities* that were required to perform the task. For example, these abilities included perceptual, motor and problem-solving abilities. A task would therefore, be analysed in terms of the relative ability requirements and would then be classified as being, say, a perceptual–motor task if there were a predominance of these two ability requirements in the task. In some cases, the amount of time spent performing a given component of the task would be used to assess whether the task was predominantly of one type of ability or another. To accompany the analysis of tasks, batteries of psychometric tests were developed to assess the abilities of people who might be required to perform those tasks. If, when tested, a person had a poor level of ability in what was a requisite skill for the task then this indicated that training would be required in this area.

The main strength of this approach is the systematic way in which it has been developed both in terms of the methods of analysis and in terms of the associated psychometric tests. Its weakness is that the theory of psychology on which the approach is based is rather weak, especially in cognitive psychological terms. This means that it has difficulty in analysing such tasks as writing a report, designing a house, or writing a computer program, which are all highly cognitive tasks. Moreover, the ability-profiling approach does not help the analyst understand how the task is carried out, what structure is imposed on the task or what goals and subgoals are being achieved while the task is being undertaken. Consequently, it would be very hard to instruct or teach someone else how to perform the task simply from an abilities analysis. Furthermore, the technique does not lend itself to making recommendations about how to design or redesign the equipment that might support, or otherwise be associated with, the task.

Annett and his colleagues (Annett *et al.*, 1971) developed a method of task analysis known as *hierarchical task analysis* (HTA). The context in which Annett and colleagues were working was training, but the aim was to identify where training was required for tasks, or parts thereof, that were crucial to the successful attainment of a given goal. HTA was directed at decomposing a task into the necessary goals, subtasks, subgoals and procedures for achieving those goals. The approach was influenced by the work on planning and problem-solving of Miller, Galanter and Pribram (1970), whose seminal text in psychology helped set the subsequent course of cognitive psychology. HTA is similar to the task-level descriptions of CLG, at least inasmuch as both the task level of CLG and HTA use tree diagrams to represent the hierarchical structure of a task.

Hierarchical task analysis is concerned with the empirical analyses of existing task performance. Unlike the abilities approach to task analysis, there are no assessment metrics associated with HTA that can be used to identify how well a person might perform a task. The approach of HTA is very much analytical rather than predictive or by assessment. Annett and colleagues developed HTA while analysing such tasks as fault-finding and repair in electrical switchgear.

A problem facing many approaches to TA is choosing the appropriate level of analysis. One feature of HTA is the way in which the analyst is supposed to determine the level at which to stop the analysis. A rule-of-thumb known as the $p \times q$ rule was developed to allow the analyst to determine into how detailed or low a level the task should be decomposed. Briefly, the $p \times q$ rule involves assessing the price to be paid in terms of the effort required to carry out the analysis at a lower level of detail against the cost of an error at that level of task performance. In practice, the $p \times q$ rule was only a rough guide and was not always workable by others attempting to use the method.

More recently, HTA has been applied to process-control and computerized process-control plants such as nuclear power stations. In doing this, the notion of a *plan* has been introduced to HTA. For HTA, a plan is assumed to be a particular collection of subgoals, subtasks and activities that are recognizable as achieving a particular goal.

The strength of HTA is in its empirical content. It requires the analyst to study actual task performers to form a detailed model of the task. It appears to have been used successfully to identify where training is required on tasks such as fault-finding and process control. However, the analysis relies heavily on overt behaviour such as the physical actions of the task performer. In their report of HTA, Annett *et al.* (1971) provided, as an appendix, a sample of the questionnaires and proformas used in the analysis. While this does not constitute a well-developed methodology for analysing tasks it did provide a good case study of how Annett *et al.* had used HTA in a nontrivial example.

One weakness of HTA is its only loose connection to any theory of psychology that would allow the task analysis to result in principled and theoretically-based recommendations. Despite its success in the training area, it is very much up to the analyst's own experience or judgement to make recommendations about where training effort is required and what form of training is most appropriate. In fairness to HTA, it was never claimed that the method would, by itself, produce recommendations: instead, it is a very useful technique of analysis for the experienced trainer to use.

A more recent approach to the use of TA in training involved work on training requirements for information technology (Johnson, Diaper and Long, 1984; Diaper and Johnson, 1989). This gave rise to a method of TA known as task analysis for knowledge description (TAKD). This work identified the knowledge requirements of IT tasks at a level of generality that made the description of that knowledge independent of the constraints of the original tasks analysed. TAKD analysed tasks in terms of actions and objects, and identified generic actions and generic objects which were assumed to be at a level of description that made them independent of the technology and tasks in which they had been observed. The rationale for this was that training might involve using novel tasks and novel equipment. These generic actions and generic objects were taken as being the primitive elements of a knowledge representation grammar (KRG). This grammar was not a formal grammar but simply a set of sentences of the general form

KRG SENTENCE :: GENERIC ACTION, GENERIC OBJECT/GENERIC OBJECT

such that a KRG sentence was simply a generic action followed by one or more generic objects. This form of TA enabled the knowledge required to perform a task to be defined for training purposes, without detailing the particular tasks or equipment that would be used in any training course. Thus any task, or collection of tasks, which utilized the same generic action and object knowledge would be an appropriate training task for acquiring that knowledge. This work was the basis for further work on TA in human–computer interaction which is reviewed in the following section.

TASK ANALYSIS AND TASK MODELLING IN HCI

The approach to TA and task modelling described here is the result of research and development work carried out largely at the Department of Computer Science, Queen Mary and Westfield College, University of London and had its beginnings in research carried out by the author and colleagues at the Ergonomics Unit, University College London. The work commenced in 1982 under a research grant from the Manpower Services Commission to identify the knowledge required to perform basic information technology tasks, such that a national syllabus for training in information technology could be developed. This early work led to the development of TAKD (Johnson, Diaper and Long, 1984). This approach was used to develop both a core and a 12-month syllabus in IT. The TAKD approach was developed to identify training requirements: however, it was soon recognized that TAKD might be of interest to HCI (Johnson, Diaper and Long, 1984). In 1985, research commenced at QMW directed at identifying how TA might be developed and used to complement the process of the design and evaluation of computer systems. The results of that research gave rise to better understanding the role of TA in HCI, and to provide us with an appropriate and well-developed method of TA. More recently, our research on TA has investigated how models of tasks might be used to allow evaluation of interface designs and to form part of an interface-design environment. Tasks can be modelled and formally specified along with other components of the computer system design. The TA method described here is the product of that research effort.

WHY USE TASK ANALYSIS IN HCI?

First, consider why TA is relevant to the design and evaluation of interactive computer systems. People use computers and computerized equipment to help them carry out tasks, as part of their work or in pursuit of other goals outside their working life. Computer systems are designed to help people carry out tasks more effectively and to carry out tasks that were previously not possible. Tasks are, therefore, of central interest to application system developers. A task is the mechanism by which changes are effected in a given domain. For example, the domain may be architecture, and one of the goals of architects may be to design houses and, in particular, the room layout of houses. In this example, the task would be those activities that architects undertake to design the room layout of houses. For example, the architect may take into account building regulations, produce outline sketches and consult the users of the building. Analysing the task of room layout design would identify the activities that architects undertake when carrying out these tasks. Such an analysis would provide an input to the design of an interactive computer system to support architectural tasks if it were able to identify the structure and content of those task activities. Moreover, if the analysis could be used to make principled recommendations that would constrain the design of the computer system, such that it supported and minimized the effort required to perform those tasks without adding superfluous task requirements, then the TA would have contributed towards the engineering of a well-designed system.

A second role for the TA is in providing an idealized, normative model of the task that any computer system should support if it is to be of any use in the given domain. A further purpose of TA is to provide a set of benchmark tasks against which any computer system design can be evaluated.

Thus TA can be used to gain understanding of how people currently work in identified and chosen domains. The domain might be ship-building, authoring or financial accounting. All domains involve tasks that people carry out to bring about changes of state. Changes of state might be, for example, the various changes that occurred during the activities of designing, constructing or fitting-out ships. The tasks would be the activities that brought about the changes.

TA is an analytical process and therefore can be applied to any tasks that currently exist. It would be impossible to perform a TA of designing and implementing a time machine since time travel has not yet been made possible and no workable time machine has been constructed. However, task modelling can be applied to both tasks that have, and tasks that have not been brought into existence. A task model is a hypothesis of how a task is or might be carried out. As such, a task model can be produced as part of the process of designing a new task. For example, while no time machine has ever been constructed, H. G. Wells was able to develop a model of what one might be like and a model of the tasks involved in building and controlling it. In a less fictitious manner, when system designers write a training manual or provide an online help facility, they are producing one form of model of how tasks might be carried out with a computer that has not yet been used to carry out those tasks.

In Chapter 9, TA was mentioned in the context of the GOMS approach which decomposed a task into goals, operators, methods and selection rules. The GOMS analysis was then used with a model of a human processor to predict user-task behaviour in terms of task performance time. This is using TA to evaluate a design decision. Clearly, this requires a detailed model of how the design can be used to carry out the chosen evaluation tasks.

TA is required in all the approaches to modelling in HCI considered in Chapters 9 and 10. However, in all of these approaches no method of TA is described.

A THEORY OF TASKS—TASK KNOWLEDGE STRUCTURES

The task knowledge that people possess is an important subset of their total knowledge. This knowledge should be taken into account in the design and development of interactive software systems, since task knowledge forms a significant part of the total knowledge that the user will recruit when they attempt to use that software to perform tasks. Task knowledge structures (TKS) (Johnson *et al.*, 1988) represent the knowledge people possess about tasks they have previously learned and performed in a given domain. Task knowledge is assumed to include knowledge of goals, procedures, actions and objects. TKS theory provides a method for the analysis and modelling of tasks in terms of goals, procedures, actions and objects. In addition, TKS theory identifies the representativeness (typicality) and centrality (importance) of particular aspects of task knowledge.

From TKS theory, a method has been developed for analysing task knowledge called knowledge analysis of tasks (KAT) by Johnson and Johnson (1990a, 1991). This process of analysis produces a description of a person's or group of people's knowledge of the tasks they currently know how to perform.

The application of the theory of TKS and the analysis method of KAT to the design of interactive software systems can be facilitated by using this analysis in conjunction with conventional design processes (such as structured systems analysis and design methodology, SSADM) or as an information base in conjunction with ad hoc design practices such as rapid prototyping. The analysis of existing tasks and the design or redesign of new tasks are both necessary and supported by TKS.

A family of models for applying the results of KAT to user-interface design have also been considered by Waddington and Johnson (1989b). Design occurs in a variety of ways. However, there is a common set of design decisions across all processes. These include decisions about the scope of the design in terms of which tasks it will address (and which ones it will not address); the functionality of the design (i.e. which functions it will provide to help the users with their tasks); which dialogue style and structure the user will be presented with; what kind of display and which objects will be displayed to the user at particular states in the dialogue; and, of course, which tasks the user will have to perform to use the designed system. All these design decisions relate to the user tasks and influence the ease with which a user is able to carry out the desired tasks with the subsequent system. By expressing the proposed design in terms of user's tasks, the effects of such decisions on the usability of the system in terms of its support of user tasks can be identified. Similar expressions of design in terms of user tasks could also be made as other design choices and decisions are being made, such as the dialogue structure, resulting in a family of task-orientated design models, each making visible how the system could be used to perform an identified task.

Task knowledge structures and HCI

As we have seen, traditionally, TA has investigated what people do (either in terms of overt behaviours or in terms of psychological processes and structures) when they carry out one or more tasks. This involves collecting information about how people perform those tasks. In the context of HCI, GOMS assumes that goals, operators, methods and selection rules comprise a user's cognitive knowledge structures of their tasks, and that these structures are interpreted by various information-processing systems (such as those assumed to operate while information is held in an active state in working memory). By extending the original ideas of Card *et al.* (1983) these four elements could be considered as the basic structural components of any task knowledge that a person might recruit to perform a task. In other words, we might suppose that people not only perform tasks, but also develop structures to represent the knowledge that they recruit to perform a particular task.

Consequently, one assumption to be made is that people have goals, operators, methods and selection rules represented in memory and these constitute the structures of knowledge associated with task performance. These task knowledge structures are then assumed to be processed by various information-processing subsystems such as those proposed by Barnard (1987). In CCT, Kieras and Polson (1986) argue that production rules can be used to model goals, operators, methods and selection rules and that these production rules bear a close relationship to the way a person does (or would) structure their knowledge of the task. From this assumption, Kieras and Polson then claim that counting these production rules provides an assessment of the degree of learning required to use the system, and the complexity of a user interface. In yet a further approach to modelling users and tasks in HCI in the theory underlying task-action grammar, Payne and Green (1986) also claim that people possess task knowledge structures and that this structuring of knowledge is captured by the rules of their grammar.

In all cases, there is a clear belief that people structure their knowledge of tasks in a particular way. There is a further belief that this task knowledge can be analysed, modelled and predicted.

Task knowledge structures is a theory which assumes that as people learn and perform tasks, they develop knowledge structures that are established from previous task experiences and applied to future task performances in a dynamic process, and that this knowledge is structured in a way that makes its recall and processing facilitate quick and efficient task performance.

Using and identifying task knowledge in system design and development

Various attempts have been made to show that models of task knowledge can be used to influence the design of software systems and to improve the usability of such systems (see Chapters 9 and 10). However, there is little evidence that any such models have ever been used in any commercial or real design-and-development projects other than in research settings. Also, there is little evidence that the use of such models produces significant improvements in the usability of software. There are many reasons why this is the case, not least of which is that the people developing these models are researchers with little or no opportunity to be involved in actual design-and-development projects. Often, little effort is made by the researchers to show how such models can, or might be, applied to existing design practice. Without any good case histories of the usage of such models in actual design projects or any identified mapping between the models and their use in design practice, it is almost impossible to see how the models can be used in design practice. Later in this chapter, it is shown how TKS theory and the KAT method can be and have been applied to design-and-development practices.

Transfer of knowledge between tasks

It is clear that people acquire knowledge about tasks and subsequently transfer this knowledge to new or different tasks. Transfer of knowledge is of interest to the application of TA to HCI, and it is a central and often implicit assumption of many of the approaches mentioned in Chapters 9 and 10. Issues of usability and learnability are directly related to the amount of knowledge that the person is able to transfer from one task to another. Pollock (1988) has demonstrated that people who are required to learn to use a second word processor after first having learned a different word processor, recruit and apply knowledge they have acquired about using the first word processor to the second. Unfortunately, sometimes this leads to errors, since the second word processor may behave very differently from the first word processor. This long-established phenomenon, prevalent in training, is known as *transfer of training*.

There is widespread evidence that in those cases where there is an appropriate transfer of existing knowledge from one task situation to a new or different task situation, there are considerable savings of training time to be made in terms of the length of practice or instruction required to achieve a given level of task performance. Where it is possible for a person to employ an effective transfer of knowledge, this can result in the person achieving a higher level of task performance sooner and with less training effort than otherwise would be the case.

The concept of transfer of knowledge is often exploited in the context of HCI, particularly where claims are made that a system is easy and efficient to use because it uses terms that are familiar to the user, or because it uses a style of interaction that is 'natural' or 'familiar'. Most often these claims are vacuous, unfounded and in some cases untrue. Such claims about new computer or software systems are nothing more than sales slogans. However, they are based upon commendable aims, but for the designer to take into consideration what is easy or familiar to the user requires more than a trivial understanding of what the user already knows and how people transfer knowledge from one task context to a new or different task context.

To understand how people transfer knowledge between contexts it is necessary to consider (a) what knowledge is likely to be transferred, (b) what knowledge is appropriate to be transferred (and conversely, not appropriate to transfer), and (c) what facilitates such transfer. In terms of what knowledge is likely to be transferred, Pollock (1988) and others before her have considered the distinctions between the transfer of specific knowledge, such as the position of keys, the name of commands and the sequences of actions, and the transfer of more general knowledge, such as the fact that all word processors have files which can be created, saved, deleted and changed (even though the names and appearances of these will be different from one word processor to the next, as will the way in which the user is required to use them interactively).

The knowledge, both general and specific to the task domain, can be and is transferred. It seems likely that general knowledge can only be utilized in task performance through specific knowledge. If specific knowledge appropriate to the new task context is not available, then specific knowledge from the existing task contexts may be inappropriately transferred. For example, to send a mail item from one user to another on an electronic mail system, the person wishing to send the mail item must (among other things) know that the command for sending the mail is 'send'. This is an instance of specific knowledge of a command name that is required in order to perform the task of sending mail in the context of a particular electronic mail system. The person performing the task may not have this specific knowledge (i.e. may not know that the command name for sending mail is 'send') and yet they may know that the next appropriate action in the task is to send the mail and that some command is required. In such circumstances, they may transfer specific knowledge that is appropriate to sending mail in another context, such as in a paper-based internal mail system, where the outgoing mail-tray is labelled 'post'. Consequently, this person may enter the command 'post' when using the electronic mail system instead of the command 'send'. This is an example of specific knowledge being required but an inappropriate transfer of existing specific knowledge occurring. Note, not all general knowledge is appropriate to be transferred to a new task context and not all specific knowledge is inappropriate.

Facilitation of transfer is defined to include only those situations in which there is an explicit intention to enable existing knowledge to be recruited and/or generalized to a new or different situation. This excludes those cases where transfer of knowledge occurs, but it is not brought about by any intentional act. An intent to facilitate transfer might be realized in the development of a particular training programme by the inclusion of referents to existing knowledge in the new or different task contexts arising from the proposed or developed system. The use of examples in the manual or help facilities to show where existing and new knowledge is assumed to be required. This obviously does not cover all the possible or actual ways in which transfer can be facilitated; that is not the intention of this chapter. What is intended is to point out that transfer can be facilitated. This transfer can arise from a positive intention on the part of the user and can be helped or facilitated by the support the design provides. However, the support for this transfer can only be provided after a specific identification of the knowledge assumed to be required for transfer, where and when this knowledge is currently used, under what conditions, and how it is likely to be used in the new or different context.

There is no simple relation between knowledge and its transfer. Each of the three aspects of transfer mentioned above concerning what knowledge is likely to be transferred, what is appropriate to be transferred, and what facilitates such transfer, should be seen as contributing factors which interact in a complex way. Predicting transfer requires all three factors to be considered. Some attempts to show how a consideration of users' existing knowledge or required knowledge can be identified and applied to improve the design of computer systems, and user interfaces in particular, have been made with some success. For example, Knowles (1988) carried out a detailed analysis of the required and transferred knowledge of tasks in the domain of pattern design in the fashion industry. Her analysis clearly identified where the system designer of a CAD system for pattern design failed to support users' existing and (in some cases) crucial knowledge of the pattern-design tasks, and in other cases introduced new knowledge requirements that were directly at odds with what the user currently knew and expected to find supported by the computer system.

Tasks, task structure and task knowledge

A task is an *activity* that is undertaken by one or more *agents* to bring about some *change of state* in a given domain. Agents can include people, animals, or machines. Tasks can be grouped together in many ways. One grouping of tasks is in terms of a *role*. An agent assuming a particular role (examples of roles are author, referee, editor, etc.) is expected to carry out the set of tasks associated with that role (for example, the role of editor might include tasks of identifying authors, identifying referees, integrating the manuscripts and submitting the complete set of manuscripts to the publisher). One higher order grouping of both tasks and roles is a *job*. A job can be defined in terms of the set of roles that a person is expected to take on and the tasks that are associated with them. For example, the job of accountant might include the roles of administrator, advisor, negotiator, etc.

Clearly all is not as clear-cut as this appears to be. There are many areas in which it is difficult to categorize some task as being discretely within any role; also the same task may be found to occur in several roles. Some roles can be jobs in some contexts (for example, while teacher is a role in the lecturer job context, in another context teacher is a job). These contexts can be determined by organizations and institutions. A task can be more precisely identified and defined by taking account of the context in which it is found to occur.

Structure in tasks

Task activities do not occur independently of one another. Some groupings of task activities are quite probable, while others, which might be logically or physically possible, are never found to occur together in reality. Activities are carried out together in a task ; they cause, enable or are subsequent to other activities.

The *knowledge* used to carry out tasks is assumed to be similarly structured to reflect the structuring observed in task performances. Garner (1974) has expressed similar ideas in describing how people represent physical objects based on the structure and relations of those objects observed in the real world.

All intentional human behaviour requires knowledge in some form, and it follows that if behaviour is structured then this structuring is either determined by or at least reflected in the way that the task knowledge supporting those behaviours is itself structured. One way that activities may be structured is in terms of a task plan which provides a feasible and acceptable structuring on the activities that collectively satisfy a task goal or subgoal. Empirical evidence for the representation of plans in long term memory can be found in work on programming tasks (Green, Bellamy and Parker, 1987). Further evidence for structuring and planning in tasks comes from the work of Byrne (1977) on tasks in domains such as cookery and menu creation.

TASK KNOWLEDGE STRUCTURES

Task knowledge structures (TKS) theory holds that task knowledge is represented in a person's memory and can be described by a TKS which is assumed to be activated during task execution. Contained within TKSs are *goal-oriented* and *taxonomic substructures*; goal-oriented substructures represent a person's knowledge about goals and their enabling states, subgoals and procedures. Taxonomic substructures represent knowledge about the properties of task objects and their associated actions. The goal-oriented substructure can be thought of as including something like the goals, methods and selection rules of the GOMS approach. However, TKS theory makes no assumptions about the processors that operate on these structures. Consequently, TKS does not include the notion of specific operators, or even predictions about processing time. TKS extends the knowledge structures considered by Card, Moran and Newell (1983) by including declarative knowledge (as well as procedural knowledge) about objects, their properties and the actions they can afford.

Task knowledge structures are assumed to be acquired through learning from previous task performances, and are dynamically represented in memory. Empirical support for the assumption that people possess something akin to TKSs can be found in the work of Galambos (1986), who showed that people recognize and use structures of events, such as order, sequence and importance of activities within the event sequence, to understand, explain and make predictions about those events. Further support for the view that knowledge structures similar to those proposed in TKS are represented in long-term memory comes from the work on text comprehension by Graesser and Clark (1985), in which general knowledge structures were hypothesized, whose function in story understanding was to relate goals to causal and enabling states.

Task knowledge structure theory assumes that the knowledge a person has acquired about a task is contained within a TKS stored in memory. The TKS is then activated and processed in association with task performance.

Central and representative knowledge elements of a TKS

A TKS contains knowledge which differs in terms of its 'centrality' and 'representativeness' relative to other knowledge used in the task. The notion of 'representativeness' is similar to that used by Rosch (1985) and colleagues (Rosch *et al.*, 1976) to describe the relations between objects in the world and their categorical representation in memory.

It is assumed that in TKS the taxonomic substructure includes knowledge about *objects* (both physical and informational) and their associated *actions*. Actual objects and actions may differ in how representative (or typical) they are with respect to the task. For example, a task such as producing a design for a ring may include a number of objects such as jewels, shanks and mounts. A representative or typical jewel might be a diamond while platinum might be a typical mount; in contrast, jet might be an atypical jewel. Representativeness is concerned with the instances and their relations to the class, and is a matter of degree rather than an all-or-none property. It can be influenced by cultural and contextual factors.

Centrality is different from representativeness and is concerned with critical points in the task at which success or failure is determined. For example, in designing a ring, if there are no shanks then that task cannot be completed. This makes shank a central object to the task. Similarly, if no action of shaping occurs then the task would also fail to be completed. This makes shaping a central action to the task. Empirical evidence for the notion of centrality in tasks can be found in Leddo and Abelson (1986), who showed that for well-learned tasks, such as borrowing a book from a library, there were certain segments which were central to the task in that they were critical points at which success or failure of the task could be determined. It is assumed that knowledge which is deemed to be central to the task is more likely recruited and transferred to similar tasks in differing contexts (i.e. when the task is being carried out using different technologies), since this knowledge is 'tightly bound' to the task goal.

A SUMMARY OF TASK KNOWLEDGE STRUCTURE THEORY

A TKS is a summary representation of the different types of knowledge that have been acquired through learning and performing a given and associated task. These TKSs are recruited and further processed when the task is performed. A TKS is related to other TKSs by a number of different relations. One form of relation between TKSs are within- and between-role relations. A role can be defined by the collection of tasks that a person occupying that role performs.

Within-role relations   Within a role each task to be performed will have a corresponding TKS. When a person takes on a particular role with a recognized set of tasks, that person must either acquire or already possess the relevant TKSs for that role. Thus a person will have knowledge of the tasks that together define a particular role.

Between-role relations   A second form of relation between TKSs is in terms of the similarity of tasks across different roles. In such cases it is possible that a common

Task	An activity which when undertaken results in a change of state in a given domain and satisfies a main goal.
Goal	A state to be achieved; a goal provides the purpose for which a task is undertaken.
Subgoal	An intermediate state that is achieved in the process of achieving a goal.
Plan	The result of a planning or problem-solving activity which identifies a way to achieve a goal in terms of the final and interim states (ie in terms of goals and subgoals.
Procedure	An executable behaviour comprising actions and objects that results in either a state or interim state (each goal and subgoal must be related to at least one procedure and a procedure may be related to many goals and subgoals).
Action	An operation that is performed as part of a procedure, which can be overt or covert.
Object	An entity within the domain which can be informational, conceptual, or physical and is associated with actions within procedures. Each object has a set of defining properties.

Figure 11.1 Summary definitions of selected user-task knowledge

TKS can be assumed to exist comprising the task knowledge common to each role–task instance.

Other relations Further relations between TKSs include temporal and experiential ones. A TKS may change over time and with the development of expertise. The former is primarily concerned with how TKSs may become elaborated or faded as time elapses and assumes some form of cognitive processor operating on the contents of a TKS. The latter is essentially a problem of learning and knowledge acquisition and assumes the existence of some form of cognitive processor(s) which functions to add and restructure TKSs as expertise is acquired.

The representation of knowledge in a TKS

Within each TKS different types of knowledge are represented. There are four components to a complete TKS model. These are as follows:

1 A goal-oriented substructure.
2 Task procedures.
3 A taxonomic substructure compromising the generic task actions and objects.
4 A summary task knowledge structure.

Summary definitions of the elements of a TKS are given in Fig. 11.1.

The *goal-oriented substructure* identifies the goals and subgoals identified within the TKS and includes enabling and conditional states that must prevail if a goal or subgoal is to be achieved. Goals and subgoals are states and, as such, are not executable. The goal structure can be thought of as containing a plan for carrying out the task. For a goal or subgoal to be executed there must be an appropriate procedure. *Task procedures* are different from goal structures insomuch as they are executable. There may be alternative procedures for achieving a particular goal or subgoal; consequently, there is also conditional and contextual knowledge associated with each procedure. The procedures rely on knowledge of *objects* and *actions*, which, when combined, constitute a given procedural unit.

Properties of objects are represented in a *taxonomic substructure*. The taxonomic substructure identifies object properties and attributes including: the class membership, the procedures in which it is commonly used, its relation to other objects and actions, and some reference to the properties of representativeness and/or centrality associated with the object in a given task context.

The taxonomic substructure contains the category structure for the objects. The category structure is divided into superordinate, basic and subordinate category levels. These levels are not static, so that between individual people at different levels of expertise what constitutes a superordinate, basic or subordinate object will vary. The basic level is the level at which a person identifies objects and represents their knowledge about the object. It is at this level that the object properties and features are defined. The taxonomic substructure details the features of objects including their representativeness (typicality) and centrality (importance).

Exercises

1 What evidence is there that tasks are structured?
2 What are the elements of a task knowledge structure and how are they related?
3 What are the notions of centrality and typicality?
4 What is the role of task analysis in HCI?

12

KNOWLEDGE ANALYSIS OF TASKS

Summary

- Knowledge analysis of tasks is a method of task analysis that is developed from the theory of task knowledge structures.

- Knowledge analysis of tasks involves collecting data from a variety of sources, such as task performers, instructors, supervisors, and others, directly or indirectly affected by the task. To collect these data a variety of techniques can be used, including protocol analysis, observations, questionnaires, interviews and experimental methods.

- Having collected adequate data to identify the knowledge elements of a task, an analysis of those data is required. The data for each task and each role are analysed in terms of TKS elements. A second stage of analysis is then performed to identify generalized TKS elements that are common to many tasks and/or many task performances.

- From a knowledge analysis of tasks a task knowledge structure is produced to model people's knowledge in terms of goal structures, procedual substructure and taxonomic substructure.

A METHOD OF TASK ANALYSIS: KNOWLEDGE ANALYSIS OF TASKS

To identify the knowledge people possess about a task, a methodology of task analysis has been developed known as knowledge analysis of tasks (KAT). KAT has been developed from TKS to identify the elements of knowledge represented in a task knowledge structure.

Before a TA is undertaken, the purpose of the analysis should be clearly defined as this can influence the extent of analysis that is required. Any TA is comprised of three major activities; first, the collection of data; second, the analysis of that data; and third, the modelling of the task domain. Each of these is considered in turn in subsequent sections of this chapter. However, before the analysis can begin, the

165

analyst has to identify the domain(s) of interest and select an appropriate or representative sample of tasks for the analysis. The domain may sometimes be predetermined in the case of systems design, since the initial feasibility study or market research report could have specified the domain and identified sample tasks. However, selection of tasks is important and, like any sampling activity, the results of the analysis will be seriously affected by the choice of tasks. For this reason, it is necessary to identify at the outset what the criteria or rationale for selecting particular tasks are. It is difficult to lay down criteria in advance for all possible task analyses, since there are many contextual and pragmatic constraints that may affect the sampling. However, these constraints should be clearly specified. Other *criteria* for sampling which can be considered in every case are as follows:

- *People and roles*   In any task there are likely to be a number of different people who perform the task. To avoid any variation due to individual differences, the analysis should include a number of different individuals performing the same task. As well as individual differences there may be role differences, such that a different role would have different requirements or methods of performing the task. It is therefore important to identify the different roles associated with the task and sample a variety of individuals enacting these roles.
- *Organizations*   A task may take different forms when it is performed in different organizations. The constraints of the organization and its particular style should therefore be considered. It is advisable to sample the same task across different organizations, depending, of course, upon if you are designing a computer system for use by a single or by many organizations.
- *Technology*   One of the most influential constraints on a task is the technology on which the task is carried out. It is important to identify those aspects of a task that are independent of the particular technology upon which the task is undertaken, and those which are dependent. If the intention is to replace the technology, then the new technology should not have to support artefacts of the old. Therefore it is important to sample across different technological versions of the same task.

In addition to the three general sampling criteria above, the tasks themselves need to be clearly identified. The best way to proceed is to have as complete a description as possible of the families of tasks within the identified domain. This can become part of the first stage of the analysis, in which a taxonomy of tasks in the domain is identified and then used as a basis for selecting representative tasks from each task family in the domain. Identifying the tasks within the domain and families of tasks is considered in the section on data collection below.

IDENTIFYING KNOWLEDGE

From the theoretical assumptions about task knowledge structures described in Chapter 11, we can now consider which aspects of task knowledge should be identified by a task analysis. In identifying the knowledge that people utilize in successful task completion, the analyst first needs to identify the person's *goals*, *subgoals* and *subtasks*; in other words, how the person conceptualizes the *goal structure* of the task. Second, it is necessary to consider the ordering in which the subtasks are carried out: this is determined by the *task plan*. Third, the different *task strategies* (a strategy is a particular set of procedures) must be identified along with the circumstances under which those strategies are employed. Fourth, it is necessary to identify the *procedures*. Finally, the *task objects* and *actions* are identified and categorically structured and this structure is a further important aspect of task knowledge which must be identified.

COLLECTING TASK DATA: APPLYING KNOWLEDGE-GATHERING TECHNIQUES TO TASK ANALYSIS

This section first briefly considers general guidelines for TA. This is followed by a survey of the different techniques of knowledge gathering. The section concludes by identifying which techniques can be used to identify TKS elements.

General guidelines for task analysis

Task analysis essentially involves obtaining *different types of information about a task(s) from different sources using appropriate methods*. TA is an iterative process where the analyst is constantly seeking to identify new information, confirm existing information and reject false information. These heuristics are further qualified by four general guidelines as follows:

1 Identify the purpose of the analysis.
2 Check the analysis with the task performer(s).
3 Analyse more than one person and one task.
4 Make use of more than one technique for gathering knowledge.

Knowledge-gathering techniques—a brief survey

Structured interviews and questionnaires

A structured interview is where the analyst has prepared a number of questions that are felt to be relevant to the task and domain. These prepared questions are used by the analyst to guide the interview, but the analyst should be prepared to deviate from both the prepared questions and the order of presentation. A questionnaire is, of course, prepared in advance and is inflexible. However, there are many varieties of questionnaire, such as fixed order, multiple orderings, yes/no questions, open answer questions, forced choice questions and many others.

Interviews and questionnaires are suitable for extracting rules, general principles behind task execution and background information, covering low probability events and the reasons underlying behaviour. Interviews may take less time to carry out than other techniques but they rarely provide detailed knowledge descriptions, and should be supplemented with direct or indirect observation of the task performance of a number of individuals. Interviews are a useful technique for providing an initial overview of the task or set of tasks in the domain.

Interviews have a higher success rate than questionnaires, since the return rate of questionnaires is rarely better than 25 per cent. However, many more questionnaires can be sent out than interviews held. A feature of questionnaire design is that each questionnaire should be short enough to allow it to be completed in 30 minutes or less. If it takes longer than this to complete, the return rate will drop considerably.

Observational techniques

Observational techniques involve collecting data from a visual study of the task performer's behaviour. The observation should focus on the performers actions and changes of state that occur in the domain. These are particularly appropriate for providing corroborating evidence, and gathering more detailed knowledge, when knowledge is context bound and when the task involves many individual steps. However, these techniques are time consuming, cannot be used in isolation and require inference on the part of the analyst to identify the structure of the task and certain types of object and action. *Direct observational techniques*, for example looking over the person's shoulder, is intrusive and may seriously influence the person's behaviour. *Indirect observation*, for example video recording, is less intrusive but requires time and effort in setting up and analysing.

Concurrent and retrospective protocols

Protocols are verbal reports given by the person performing the task; they can be either concurrent with the task performance, or retrospective. Protocols provide detailed information on many aspects of a task, including task goals, task plans, procedures, actions and objects. However, protocols require some inference on the part of the analyst. The responses must be carefully coded and the enterprise is time consuming. Furthermore, it is not always wise to rely solely on verbal reports, since people are not always able to give accurate, precise or reliable verbal reports about their own behaviour. In *concurrent protocols* (CPs) subjects report what they are doing while they are doing it. CPs are appropriate when there is insufficient time to carry out retrospective protocols and when the analyst is interested in what a subject is doing at a given time. It should be noted that CPs may interfere with normal task behaviour in a serious and not always obvious way. In *retrospective protocols* (RPs) the subject is required to generate a durable memory trace while completing the task, and then the contents of the trace are verbally reported after the task has been completed. An RP could be given while the task performer observes their own task performance, for example, using a video recording. RP reports are appropriate when the analyst requires more reliable information than is available through a CP and when the subject can be called back to go over the task recording. Additionally, RPs are appropriate when the analyst is concerned with the reasons for, and explanations of, any behaviour, cognitive aspects of tasks, such as planning knowledge, and feelings and emotions the person entertains about the task. Both CPs and RPs are normally collected along with direct or indirect observations. CPs and RPs can be used conjointly. For example, a CP could be collected using a video and audio recording. This recording can then be played back to the task performer, giving them an opportunity to add to, correct, or otherwise provide a further RP of the task.

Experimental techniques

Next follows a summary of several experimental techniques which may be employed in identifying the similarity of task components, for example the actions and objects, and the features or attributes of those actions and objects. All the techniques described in this section normally require the analyst to have already obtained detailed information about the task.

Kelly's repertory grid (adapted from Kelly, 1955)

The task analyst must have already identified many or all of the components of knowledge associated with a task or set of tasks. This technique involves first selecting a given set of objects (or other task components, e.g. procedures) and then presenting these to the subject, i.e. the task performer, in groups of three. The subject is then asked in what way(s) any two of them are alike and different from the third. This grouping and separating process is repeated until all the items have been presented to the subject. The result is a grouping of similar items that are assumed to share common attributes. One problem with this technique is that the analyst has to be very careful in choosing which three items are presented at any one time, since the contrasting set can have a strong influence on any comparison or grouping. There is also a possibility of forcing a classification outcome which is arbitrary, an artefact of the selection procedure, and not representative of the actual relationships between knowledge components in the task.

Card sorting (adapted from Rosch, 1978)

In this technique the analyst is concerned with the similarity of task components. The task components can be objects, actions, procedures, etc. The procedure of this technique is somewhat similar to that of Kelly's repertory grid (above). Task components are entered on cards, one card for each component, and the subject is instructed to group together 'similar components', or 'components which are the same kind of thing'. Rosch and other researchers generally instruct subjects to 'put together the things that go together'. The result of this technique, as with Kelly's repertory grid, is a structuring of similar components which are assumed to share common attributes. Unlike Kelly's approach, card sorting is much less likely to be subjected to experimenter bias.

Rating scales

Rating scales can be useful in identifying representativeness and centrality. For example, each object, or other task component, is presented to subjects who are instructed to judge the given item for its representativeness or centrality on an appropriate scale. For example, the highest number of the scale may be related with the greatest representativeness or centrality. An alternative to this procedure is to instruct the subjects to sort or rank each item into an order of relative representativeness of or centrality to the task.

Frequency counts

With frequency counts the analyst must note on how many occasions a task knowledge-component is either used or referred to in the task(s) or across tasks. The assumption is that a knowledge component that is more central or representative will have a higher frequency-score than a component of lesser centrality or representativeness. Frequency counts provide an index which can be used to compare individual differences across different people performing the same task, and also across tasks. Such comparisons provide some indication of differences in task organization and task plans across individuals. Frequency is only one criterion of representativeness, and some task knowledge-components may occur infrequently but are representative of or central to a task. However, centrality can be determined by checking for the presence of the task item across many instances of the task.

Other useful techniques

Other techniques which might be used in addition to, or incorporated into, the above techniques are as follows:

- Knowledge competitions
- Group discussions
- Multichoice questions
- Analyst carrying out the task following instruction
- Asking for sample outputs
- Cooperating subjects (two or more subjects working in groups)

For further details on these techniques see Welbank (1983).

In the next section the different components of a TKS are considered in terms of the particular data-collection techniques that can be used to identify that component.

IDENTIFYING TASK KNOWLEDGE STRUCTURE COMPONENTS USING KNOWLEDGE ANALYSIS OF TASKS

Knowledge analysis of tasks is concerned with identifying a person's task knowledge in terms of actions, objects, procedures and goals. The techniques considered above are now classified according to which aspects of TKS knowledge they most readily identify (see also Fig. 12.1).

Identifying objects and actions

Identification of objects and their associated actions used in carrying out the task can be obtained by the following techniques:

1 Searching through textbooks, manuals, rule books and other documented reports of the domain and tasks.
2 Questionning the task performer in a structured interview or questionnaire.

Actions and objects
selecting from texts or manuals
structured interview
questionnaire
direct observation
concurrent or retrospective protocol

Procedures
direct observation
concurrent protocols

Goals and subgoals
structured interview
retrospective protocols
direct observation
questionnaires
constructing tree diagrams

Figure 12.1 Summary of the most commonly used techniques for identifying TKS elements

3 Asking the task performer to list all the objects that are involved in the task, and the actions carried out on them.
4 Directly or indirectly observing the person carrying out the task, noting which objects they manipulate and in what ways.
5 Noting all the objects and actions mentioned by the person in either concurrent or retrospective protocols.

Identifying task procedures

This section summarizes techniques for identifying a person's knowledge of the procedures and strategies used in the task as follows:

1 Asking specific questions in the structured interview or questionnaire. For example, asking a person if they can identify any regular parts of the task. It is also useful to ask specific questions of the sort 'what do you do if ...', for example, '*X* goes wrong or fails'. The analyst should also ask why particular procedures are used. A further question to ask is what indiciates the end of one part of the task, and what triggers the start of another, since it is important to be able to identify the pre-conditions and post-conditions for a particular procedure.
2 Protocols and observation can also be used, although some prompting may be required to get the person to report on the various properties of a procedure.
3 Card sorting. This technique can identify the structure of a procedure. It involves putting known task procedures on individual cards, which the person then sorts into an appropriate order for task execution. It can identify sequential, iterative, parallel and unordered parts of the task.

Identifying goals and subgoals

The identification of goals and subgoals can be obtained by one, a selection of, or all of the following four techniques:

1 Asking specific questions in questionnaire or interview about what are the goal and subgoals of the task.
2 From a textbook, instruction manual, or any other available written material, which decomposes the task into goals and subgoals
3 Asking or aiding the person to construct a diagram (e.g. a tree structure or flow diagram) of connected goals and subgoals of the task.
4 Identifying different 'phases' of the task from observations and/or concurrent/ retrospective protocols. When using observations, a phase or part of the task may be identified by pauses. In concurrent or retrospective protocols, it is important to make a note of such statements, as 'now, I intend/want to . . .', etc. The analyst should be sure which referents belong to 'this', 'that', 'it', etc.

Various techniques for collecting task analysis data have been described, together these techniques form part of the KAT methodology. The next section is concerned with analysis of and generalizing from the collected data.

IDENTIFYING REPRESENTATIVE, CENTRAL AND GENERIC PROPERTIES OF TASKS

Some task components are more representative or typical of a task than others. Central task components are those which are necessary to successful task execution. without these crucial elements, the task goal will fail to be achieved. Generic task components, on the other hand, are those which are common across a number of task performers. The term 'generic', in the context of KAT, relates to general (rather than specific) elements of tasks that have been identified by the analyst. The essential function of identifying generic task components is to reduce variation across subjects, across the technology and across instances of similar tasks in the domain(s).

Identifying representativeness and centrality

Task knowledge components can be structured in terms of their representativeness in and centrality to the task. Identifying task element representativeness and centrality can be achieved using one or more of the following methods:

1 *Representativeness*   Count the frequency of a particular task component in the analysis. The assumption here is that the more representative components will be the most frequently occurring.
2 *Representativeness and/or centrality*   The analyst may use rating scales where the name of each task knowledge component is presented on a separate card or other medium, and the person is asked to judge the relative representativeness/ typicality or centrality of each component on a given scale (e.g. on a scale of 1 to 5).
3 *Representativeness and/or centrality*   Presenting task components on cards as in 2, the subject is then required to sort the cards into an order of increasing representativeness or centrality of the task.
4 *Centrality*   The analyst instructs the person to recall from memory all the task components. The order in which they are listed may reflect the order of centrality

of each component within the task. The resulting lists recalled (one from each person) can then be correlated to determine the degree of agreement of task component centrality across the sample population.

In the next section, we consider how to identify generic actions and objects by abstracting from instances of tasks, people and technology and thereby reducing the variance in task performance.

The following steps are recommended for use in identifying generic actions and objects:

1 The analyst constructs two separate lists, one for the actions and one for the objects that have been identified in the analysis. These lists will contain disparate, and often repetitive, information from each task performer and from a range of tasks. For example, in a task analysis of an architectural task, involving 'designing the room layout of houses', two lists were produced containing all the actions and objects from each architect. Examples of the objects were plans, symbols, windows, pipes, appliances, doors, pens and rulers, and examples of the actions were draw, rehang, check, reposition, etc.

2 The lists constructed in 1 are reduced to comprehensive and nonrepetitive lists with each action and object appearing once only but noting the frequency of each action or object in tasks and across people. The original lists do provide a measure of frequency of the respective objects and actions in the task and hence may be of use in the identification of representative actions and objects.

3 Generic actions and objects are chosen. This can be achieved by assuming a critical value of threshold of frequency across subjects and tasks. The analyst must decide at what level the frequency threshold is to be set in order to judge if something is or is not generic. (Caution must be taken in setting this level as some or possibly all the objects and actions may already be generic by virtue of being identified.) For example, it may be decided to treat an item as generic if it is referred to by two or more task performers. If this yields an unmanageable (i.e. too large) list of generic actions and objects then the threshold may be raised. Setting the threshold relies to some extent on the analyst's intuition and experience. However, the analyst can systematically experiment with different threshold values. Threshold setting is an iterative process. The essence of the approach is to treat frequency across people and tasks as an indicator of generic terms.

Alternatively, the analyst can use a more objective approach involving grouping like terms. The assumption here is that the comprehensive and nonrepetitive lists contain all actions and objects involved in the task and that these can then be grouped together to identify generic elements.

Grouping all like elements involves:

a) The analyst(s) associating a particular element with other similar elements. Similarity is determined by attempting to re-express the original task description in terms of the alternative or target element. If the alternative term was 'adequate' then the two are said to be similar.

b) Following the analyst's grouping, additional judges can be used to enhance the robustness of the analyst's groupings. The analyst asks one or more judges to sort objects and actions into groups with the instruction to 'group together the actions' (or objects) that go together, or are the same kind of action (object)'. The results of each judge's sorting can then be correlated to identify the agreed, common groupings.

c) After the groupings have been produced, the next step is to identify a generic label or term which might cover all the individual elements in a particular set. These labels can then be used to represent the generic task elements.

In an analysis of an architectural task, 'design house room layout', the threshold-level method was used to identify generic actions and objects. This procedure was used since there was a time constraint, and generally it is quicker to use a threshold value than to group like terms. By using this method, many generic actions and objects were identified, examples of which are 'draw' and 'plans', respectively. The 'grouping like terms' procedure has advantages over the threshold method since it provides an opportunity for the task performer to judge whether the generic actions and objects identified are indeed generic. If the threshold method is used then some checking of generic elements can be achieved by involving the task performers in a validation process (see 4 below).

4 The fourth step is the validation of the generic elements. To validate the generic elements, list all the actions and objects separately from the generic labels. The task performers are then instructed to identify to which generic group each specific action or object belongs. If the action or object lists are not adequately covered by generic labels then the task performer is free to supply alternative group labels.

TASK MODELS

The results of the KAT analysis can be used to produce a model of the task(s) in terms of TKS. Tasks modelled in terms of TKS will involve the following components:

- A goal structure
- A procedural substructure
- A taxonomic substructure

Each of these components of the TKS reflects the different types of knowledge that are required by the task.

Goal structure

The goal-structure component of the model identifies the relations between different goal states. There are two general forms of relations; hierarchical and control relations. Hierarchical relations show how a goal can be decomposed into further collections of subgoals. Control relations show how goals and subgoals are related to each other for execution; they include sequential, parallel, unordered and optional relations. Both hierarchical and control relations can appear in all parts of the goal-structure components of the TKS model. Goal structures can be represented diagrammatically using tree structures to represent hierarchical components and transition networks to represent control relations.

Alternatively, goal structures can be represented textually using a functional language or pseudocode or frames. In all cases, goals and subgoals are expressed as activities and objects with relations between them.

Procedural substructure

The procedural substructure component of the TKS model reflects the detailed executable form of the task. The procedural substructure is directly related to the lowest level goods of the goal structure. They contain actions and objects and the realtions between them. The relations include sequential, parallel, iterative and conditional control relations. These control relations exist within a procedure body and determine how the actions will be executed with respect to the objects. Procedures can 'call' other procedures and form parts of the bodies of other procedures just as in programming languages. Each procedure is defined by a pre-condition which determines the context that must exist before it can be executed. Upon execution of a procedure a defined post-condition will result. The pre- and post-condition of procedures are defined in the procedural substructure and provide a way of representing the relation between the goal structure and the procedural substructure. Procedural substructures can be represented by using pseudocode, production system, or by frame representations.

Taxonomic substructure

The taxonomic substructure of the TKS model represents the structure of objects and their attributes/features. It defines the hierarchical relations between objects in terms of their categorical or 'class' membership. In addition, each object in the taxonomic substructure has a collection of features and attributes associated with it. These features and attributes include the links to superordinate and subordinate categories (or classes) of the hierarchy. Objects also have features and attributes that identify the typicality (representativeness) of the object and its centrality in the context of tasks. Because the taxonomic substructure is task oriented, actions and procedures associated with the object are also defined in the taxonomic substructure. Further attributes of an object included in its representation can be added to further detail the object as necessary, but these are optional, whereas the others are all compulsory. Objects can be represented using frames or schemas, or through an object-oriented language. Objects are related to actions and procedures by their features and attributes.

Task knowledge structure can be used to model tasks analysed using the techniques and methods of KAT applied to existing or currently performed tasks. In addition, TKS can be used to model new or changed tasks as they are being designed/created. The TKS model can be used as an explicit representation of the scenarios upon which the design is based, and which the design gives rise to. TKS models both model knowledge that people may already possess and/or the knowledge that a designed system would require them to possess.

In this way, TKS models can be developed prior to, along with, and as a consequence of, system designs. TKS models used prior to the design of a system is the conventional approach to using task analysis to inform the design by modelling the existing tasks. TKS models used along with system design is novel, and allows the

designer to develop the scenarios of the interaction along with the development of
the rest of the design. TKS models used to reflect the consequences of a design are in
keeping with the other models, such as GOMS, TAG and TAL, in providing a model
from which the design can be evaluated in terms of how it changes the nature of the
tasks.

In Chapter 13, some examples of the use of TKS models in design are given.
Different forms of representing the three major components of a TKS model are
used, but in each case they reflect the same detail. Which form of representation is
chosen partly depends upon the users of the TKS model and their familiarity with
particular forms of modelling. For example, not all designers can understand formal
system or formal methods. Consequently, many designers would not understand a
TKS expressed in terms of, say, an algebraic specification. A further consideration is
that the form of representation also carries with it more or less precision and more or
less power. These issues are considered further in the following chapter.

Exercises

1 Analyse an existing task, (e.g. programming a video recorder) and document
   your method of analysis. From the analysis produce a TKS model of the task as
   it is currently performed.
2 Design a new (and hopefully easier) way to perform the same task, and extend
   the possibilities of the user by allowing further, related tasks to also be performed. Produce TKS models of your designed tasks.
3 How can TKS models be used to reflect external and internal tasks?

13 TASK ANALYSIS APPLIED TO INTERACTIVE SYSTEM DESIGN

Summary

- Task analysis and task modelling are considered from the perspective of the software development process. Surveys of designers reveal that TA is used to develop ideas for user interaction and also where TA can be used in the design process.

- Two case histories of designing user interfaces are described which highlight how TA can be applied to design.

TASK ANALYSIS AND SYSTEM DESIGN—A BRIEF REVIEW OF DESIGN PRACTICES

In an attempt to identify the design characteristics for effective tools for user-interface designers, Rosson, Mass and Kellogg (1989) carried out a study of the target users and their tasks, namely, software developers and their design practices. While many researchers have speculated about how interactive system design should take place, few have analysed how it is carried out in practice.

Rosson *et al.*'s (1989) study is particularly interesting, since the purpose of carrying out the study was to identify the requirements for HCI tools in design practice. In a similar study, Bellotti (1989) investigated the use of HCI methods and techniques in design, leading to the development of a framework for applying HCI techniques to design. A distinction between these two studies is that Rosson *et al.*, contrary to Bellotti, do not consider the various techniques, methods and tools that are currently on offer from HCI researchers. However, Rosson *et al.* do consider how design ideas are generated and developed. Rosson *et al.* studied 22 designers working on 22 projects in IBM and elsewhere (17 of the projects were from within IBM). Structured interviews were carried out with the designers to identify the following information: background information, general design process, user-interface component, idea generation and also how design ideas were initiated, refined and developed. From the background information the researchers identified the size, scale and type of projects on which designers had recently been working. Projects ranged from having small (one person) to medium (two to five persons) and large (more than five persons) design teams, and were classed as being either research, site-support or product-type projects. The majority of research-type projects involved one-person and the majority of product-type projects were two- to five-person projects.

In considering the design approach, 12 of Rosson *et al.*'s designers followed a phased development approach comprising design, implementation and testing phases in that order (rather like the lifecycle approach) and then followed an incremental development approach comprising simultaneous design and implementation (rather like the prototyping approach). The incremental approach was found to be more common in research-type development projects than in product development projects and this was also correlated with size of project team (i.e. the incremental approach was more common in one-person projects). This was also true for site-support projects (i.e. large project groups used a phased approach and one-person projects used an incremental approach).

With respect to user testing, three designers reported that they made no special effort to obtain feedback from end-users or to test the design with end-users. Of the projects that carried out some user testing, eight had undertaken some form of early design testing. However, in five cases this was informally done and analytic design testing was only undertaken in three cases. All designers who carried out user testing thought that late (i.e. post-implementation) testing did not contribute much to the design, since this always took place after the system had been completed. Despite this view, late testing was most common among those designers who carried out any end-user testing. The timing of end-user testing was unrelated to either the type of project, or, surprisingly, the design approach used, whether phased or incremental. However, the type of testing (informal or analytic) was related to the project type. All product-type projects used analytic testing while none of the research projects did. Also, most of the projects using a phased development approach used analytic testing while none of the incremental development approach projects did. It seems that user testing is seen by these designers as a method of evaluating designs rather than of generating design recommendations, and that HCI methods which would contribute to design generation would be welcomed.

Since the user interface is a major focus of HCI research, it is interesting to examine how Rosson *et al.*'s software engineers carried out user-interface design. One observation from this study is that the majority of designers did not see the user interface as being in any way separate (in terms of when, how or by whom it was designed) from the rest of the system. Only 9 of the 22 designers reported that the user interface had been designed separately from the rest of the system (usually first). Those designers who used an incremental development method tended to treat the user interface as nonseparable. Interestingly, the use of software tools for user interface design was related to this division. Designers who viewed the user interface as a nonseparable part of the system reported either using general-purpose tools (for example, graphics libraries, screen input/output utilities) or creating their own tools (for example, for designing and displaying icons). In contrast, those designers who viewed the user interface as a separable aspect of design reported using special-purpose tools. Another aspect to emerge from this study was the extent to which the design of the user interface had been driven by any design principles (see Fig. 13.1 for a summary of the design principles reported). All 22 designers reported at least one principle.

Input/output
Minimize input movements (3); maximize input channels (2); visually attractive (2); careful use of language (3); screen and key consistency (3); highly visual interface (2).

Dialogue
Process continuity (1); modeless or mode feedback (2); use of menus, prompts (3); context-dependent messages (2); user control (1); natural response time (1).

Conceptual model
Use of analogy, metaphor (4); match user expectations (4); start with user model (1); make examples concrete (1); minimize semantic primitives (1); novice–expert path (3).

General
Easy to use, user-friendly (8); personalize (1); make it simple (3); follow standards (3); understand user needs (2).

Figure 13.1   Reported principles for user-interface design with frequency reported shown in parenthesis (from Rosson *et al.*, 1989)

However, there is an interesting distinction between the kinds of principle reported by the designers. The reported principles were classified into one of four categories of focus: input/output, dialogue, conceptual model and general. It seemed that designers who were concerned with the development of new functionality reported principles related to the conceptual model of the design, while designers not concerned with new functionality reported principles in the input/output category.

How designers form and develop ideas is of concern to many HCI researchers, since it is at the development of the design idea that HCI should have the most impact. To this end Rosson *et al.*'s survey examined how designers generated and developed their ideas. The techniques these designers had used are classified in Fig. 13.2 according to their use in generating or developing ideas.

By far the most commonly reported category of idea-generation methods involved some form of user-task analysis, while trial and error was the most often reported category for development of ideas. It is at this point that Rosson *et al.* have little more to offer in the way of tools and methods to support user-task analysis.

The designers interviewed in this study all thought that they needed more detailed information about users and tasks. One result of Rosson *et al.*'s study was a recommendation that HCI methods which would contribute to design generation would be welcomed. Furthermore, it was also found that the use of prototyping itself did not ensure that user testing was carried out. One reason for this is that user testing requires clear design requirements based on users and tasks to enable the testing to be useful, and these were not available. Also, the testing would be easier to perform if the prototyping could be easily related to user tasks (e.g. if the prototype could be used to simulate how an identified user task would be performed). We can conclude from the results of this survey that designers do use TA to generate ideas, and they do engage in user testing. However, there is no clear evidence that the consequences for user tasks are kept in mind throughout the design process.

As we have seen from Rosson *et al.*, several techniques were found to be used by designers for 'idea generation'. Of the interviewed designers, 53 per cent used TA; 23

Idea generation	Idea development
User-task analysis	
Take user perspective (2)	Take user perspective (2)
Generate task scenarios (6)	
Interview, observe user (7)	
Research the problem (2)	
Rely on domain experience (2)	
Key user on design team (2)	
External source	
Other systems (10)	
Literature, trade press (4)	
Current research issues (2)	
Interaction with others	
Discussion, brainstorm (9)	Discussion, brainstorm (3)
	Explain to coders (1)
Meta-strategies	
Distraction(6)	
Incubation (2)	
Concentration (2)	
Clear-cut mind (1)	
Design activities	
Logical analysis (3)	Logical analysis (3)
Notes, charts, diagrams (5)	Notes, charts, diagrams (5)
	Write specifications (3)
Trial and error	
Build prototype (4)	Build prototype (10)
	Make paper mock-ups (2)
	Implement (1)

Figure 13.2 Reported techniques for generating and developing design ideas, with frequency reported shown in parenthesis (from Rosson *et al.*, 1989)

per cent used external sources such as available literature; 16 per cent used meta-strategies such as concentration; 13 per cent used interaction with others; 12 per cent used design activities like charts and diagrams; and 6 per cent used trial and error.

The most commonly reported category of idea generation methods involved some form of TA while trial and error was the most often reported category for development of ideas (see Fig. 13.3).

Rosson's survey provides an excellent view of design practices that show how user-interface designers actually approach design. This survey adds to our understanding of design methods and design practices. From it we can conclude that the future generation of tools and methods to support design and software development must include some aspects of HCI. In particular, there appears to be some requirement for tools and methods that focus on TA.

There are two aspects to TA (see also Chapters 11 and 12): first, gathering information and analysing the users' tasks; and second, the generation of task models

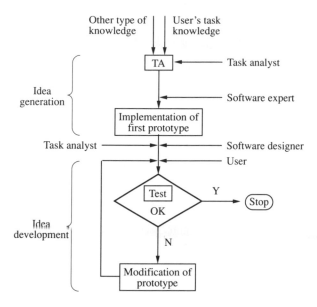

Figure 13.3 Task and analysis and its relationship to idea generation and development

and task scenarios. Rosson *et al.* suggest a tool might be developed which allowed designers to generate task models, perhaps using storyboards, and then to elaborate and modify these into running prototypes. The reality of providing such a tool requires the development of methods of TA and an understanding of the relations between the output from TA and design development.

In a further survey of design practices by Johnson and Johnson (1990b) directed at identifying if and how TA might fit into design practices, more detailed findings were obtained from a small group of designers. Detailed structured interviews of three designers were carried out to identify what design experience they had, what design practices they followed, what TA they performed, what their perception of the need for TA was, and what they thought they would require in the way of tools and methods to support their use of TA in design.

Much of the data from this survey is in agreement with Rosson *et al.*'s study. The designers in question worked as part of small teams and worked on product-development projects. All designers had some knowledge of at least one design method, and all had some knowledge of structured systems analysis and design method (SSADM) (Downs, Clare and Coe, 1988). All designers followed a phased or lifecycle design process with some iteration between and within phases. The phases of design that the designers reported following were: requirements, design specification, design implementation, validation, update and maintenance.

Particular problems related to design were identified by the designers. These are shown in Fig. 13.4 together with the phases of design in which the problems occur. The majority of problems identified by designers were concerned with the information and contact they had with users. In many cases they had little or no information about the users' tasks and had often gathered information from previous experiences of developing similar products for other users. Often the user require-

Requirements
Identifying requirements
Documenting requirements
Obtaining end-user information
Obtaining UI requirements
Reliance upon designers' experience of product range
Relating requirements to any users
General purpose rather than specific requirements
Prioritizing requirements

Design specification
Translating requirements into design detail
Variability in methods of specification
Wholistic vs. partial decomposition
Checking against requirements

Implementation
Design still evolving
Specification and implementation not sequential or discrete
Checking against requirements and/or specification
Lack of testing and feedback from user

Validation
No testing or user feedback during design development
Concentration on function testing not usability of UI testing

Figure 13.4   Identified problems in phased design practices (from Johnson and Johnson, 1990)

ments were derived from a log of problems with the current system, together with added information about what it was thought the system could or should do. At best, the designers had implicit and indirect information about the users and their tasks.

The designers studied by Johnson and Johnson all thought that they needed more detailed information about users and tasks. Two designers wanted tighter documentation of user requirements with more general information about users and tasks. The other designer wanted the TA to include information about what the user needed and expected to see and interact with at the user interface.

The kind of information designers wanted to know about tasks included the structure of tasks, in terms of task goals; how users normally went about achieving these goals; the frequency with which particular procedures were carried out; the circumstances under which one procedure was used rather than another; and the inputs and outputs for each procedure.

In considering where TA might contribute to design, all the designers felt that it would have most impact during the feasibility and requirements stages of design. TA at these stages could be used to identify the functionality of the system. The user-interface requirements and the output from TA could also be used in the design of the interaction dialogue.

Task analysis could help designers to identify what users expect to have available to them at any time, the structure and sequence of their usage of system facilities, the names and form of representation to be given to screen-presented objects and events, and the information that should be available in a given context (i.e. screens) and the structure between contexts (i.e. moving between different screens). Although the designers thought that the TA may not give the detail of screen layout or interaction style, it would provide an initial input and guide for user-interface design.

All designers in the Johnson and Johnson survey thought that the TA should be integrated with a functional requirements specification to provide more complete user requirements. Some designers thought that the TA would need to be in such a form that it could be used to validate the design specification and implementation.

The survey also asked designers in what form would they find information about tasks and users most useful to them. The designers went to some lengths to say that the form of presentation of the results of the TA should support a mapping and checking operation between user tasks and proposed designs. It was pointed out by the designers that the form of design models used can vary depending upon what design tools and methods are used, who the designer is, the subject of the design and the group the designer is in. However, the importance of having the results of the TA in a form that could be mapped on to such aspects of design as functionality and dialogue design was stressed. Furthermore, it was suggested by all three designers that the TA should be in a form that would enable it to be checked and verified with the users. Consequently, the results of the TA may have to be presented in various formats that are conducive to optimum checking with users and for mapping on to the functional design and other design models.

AN APPLICATION OF TASK ANALYSIS TO INTERACTION DESIGN

Up to now, TA in design has been considered theoretically and empirically. Now some case studies are provided. An example of a TA performed by a group of MSc students at QMW using KAT is presented, followed by a more serious study in which the design of a computer-aided design system for use by jewellery designers is described. The purpose of the first case-study was to produce a simple design for a computer rendition of the Rubik's cube puzzle. This was undertaken as a teaching exercise to explain to postgraduate students about the design and construction of user interfaces. The application area was chosen by them to satisfy a number of constraints including the timescale of the project, the availability of the application domain to analysis and the potential for graphical interaction.

Case study 1: Rubik's cube

For those who may not know what the Rubik's cube puzzle is, the aim is to make each of the six faces of a cube be a single colour, where each face of the cube comprises nine separate cubes (Fig. 13.5). These cubes within the main cube have different colours on each face. The person has to twist and rotate each layer of the main cube until a colour match has been reached on each face.

Two sources of data for the TA were used: an instruction book that explained how a person was supposed to play the game, and also people actually playing with a

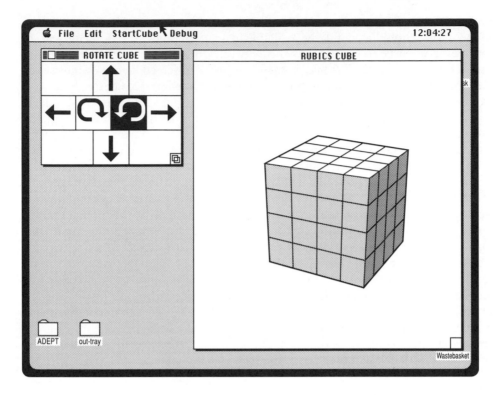

Figure 13.5   Rubik's cube

Rubik's cube. The book provided a basis for identifying the particular aims and objectives of playing with the cube and some understanding of strategies and procedures that could be followed in completing the cube. This book was used to develop a background understanding prior to a more detailed analysis of people actually solving the puzzle using the cube.

Both concurrent and retrospective protocol analyses of six people separately attempting to solve the original puzzle were carried out. Each person was first required to perform the task of solving the puzzle as many times as they were able in 10 minutes. They were required to speak out loud about what they were doing while they were performing the task. Each person's performance was recorded on a video tape with an accompanying audio track. Immediately after the 10-minute interval, each person was required to give a retrospective protocol in which they were asked to describe how they had solved the puzzle, and to use the cube to demonstrate this. This protocol was also recorded on the audio/video recorder.

Results of the task analysis

The data were analysed to identify the goal structures, procedures, and the taxonomic structure of objects and the actions of the task. The following *higher level goals* were identified:

- Complete top layer.
- Complete middle layer.
- Complete bottom layer.

where each layer represents one layer of the $3 \times 3 \times 3$ cube.

Lower level goals (subgoals) associated with each of these higher level goals were also identified; an example of the lower level goals for the 'complete top layer' goal were identified as follows:

- Find the face which is already most complete.
- Form a cross on the target face with adjacent edge-pieces matching the colours of adjacent faces.
- Put all four corner pieces into correct positions.

A face is one side of the cube where two faces meet and this constitutes an edge piece; a corner piece is where three faces meet.

Procedures associated with these goals and subgoals were identified, together with the context in which they were used. For example, the procedure for finding a face which is already most complete was as follows:

> Find face(s) with most top edge-pieces matching the face
>> IF more than one face is like this
>>> THEN choose the face with the most edge-pieces that have adjacent edge-pieces matching the adjacent face.
>> IF more than one face has equal numbers of matching edge-pieces
>>> THEN choose any one of these faces.

The *actions* included

> choosing a face
> searching for a face
> saving a face
> rotating a piece
> rotating a layer
> rotating a cube

The *objects* included:

> cube, layer, face, edge-piece

among others. A *typical instance* of the face object was the target face.

Having analysed user-task knowledge at an appropriate level of generality that had been agreed with the user group, the next stage involved using the information obtained from the TA, in conjunction with design principles, to develop design models. Design models can, as has been seen earlier in this chapter, be in a variety of forms: formal specifications, informal specifications, screen drawings, storyboards, simulations and prototypes. One form of design model developed from TA is an informal specification of the system and user interface related to a model of the tasks the system is designed to support. Thus an informal specification following the approach of Waddington and Johnson (1989a,b) was produced. This specification was developed alongside the prototype design. The specification and the prototype evolved together, each contributing to the development of the overall design.

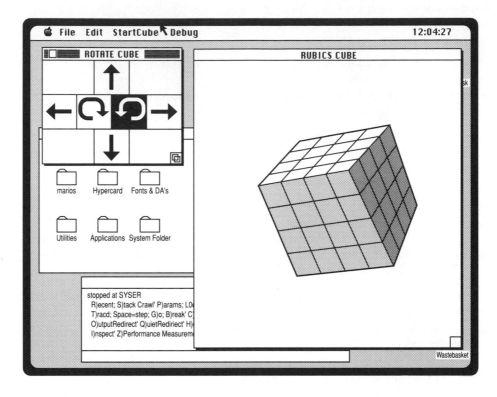

Figure 13.6   Interactive computer program for Rubik's cube puzzle

Figure 13.6 shows one design of an interactive computer program for the Rubik's cube puzzle. This particular design is just one of several that were produced from the TA. The differences between the designs are due to the designer's interpretation of how best to support and improve the various aspects of the users' tasks. For example, one design provided a display of a 3D cube which could be rotated on axes running from opposite diagonal corners of the cube. In contrast, another design gave a display of a 3D cube which could be rotated together with a 2D plan view of the complete cube. In this second design, the designers were trying to improve the user's task by giving, at all times, a view of all faces of the cube. Other differences in design were the way that the user could carry out actions on the cube, such as rotating a layer, face, piece or the entire cube. One design used selectable options from menus in which the user could choose to rotate any of these components. Another design providing a direct-manipulation interface was found to be the easiest and most enjoyable to use, although it did have a longer learning curve than the menu-based design.

The direct-manipulation interface most closely resembled the user's existing model of how to manipulate the cube. However, the selectable parts of the cube were not readily identifiable, hence the longer learning time. The designs also included many task features such as the angle of presentation of the cube to the user. This reflected the *typical* viewpoint that had been identified in the task analysis. Similarly, speeds of rotation were chosen to be within the ranges that users had used. While there were many more features that were taken from the TA, one feature that was added was the reconstruct–deconstruct option. This would automatically rewind or solve the puzzle (and was the only way I ever managed to do it).

Case Study II: Computer-aided design for jewellery design

Task analysis has also been used in more realistic design projects in which the design has had to be carried out in tight time constraints and within limited resources. A case history of a commercial design project in which KAT was used is presented below.

A commercial design project was undertaken by consultants associated with the London HCI Centre at QMW. The project produced a prototype user-interface and recommendations for the design of a direct-manipulation interface to a computer aided design (CAD) system to be used in the jewellery industry. The purpose of the system was to allow jewellery designers to undertake some aspects of the design of jewellery products such as 'rings'.

A systems analysis had already been carried out by the client and this had produced a functional specification for a database. However, it did not describe in any detail the nature of the jewellery design tasks. A TA was carried out using KAT to gain some understanding of how jewellery design tasks were carried out by an experienced and practising jewellery designer. Only one expert jewellery designer was contacted because of time constraints (a maximum of 15 person-days was all that had been allowed to complete the design and prototyping) on the contract, no other experts being available at the time. The consequences of this were that the results of the TA might not be generally applicable to all aspects of jewellery design. Accessing many experts to validate and augment the analysis obtained from any one expert is strongly recommended by Johnson and Johnson (1991). However, the client required a prototype system to demonstrate the potential capabilities of applying interactive computers to jewellery design. It was felt that the results of the TA would serve the purposes of providing a suitable input to the design of an early prototype and providing a basis for making some user-interface design recommendations. It also proved to be an ideal opportunity to show that TA does not necessarily increase the overall timescale of a project, can be usefully carried out in short timescales and provides useful information with minimum additional overheads to the project.

The task analysis

The methods used for data collection were a structured interview supported by a written questionnaire and observations of selective parts of jewellery design on a few examples. This technique of data collection was used in preference to others, such as collecting detailed protocols, because of the time constraints of the contract. Two visits to the jewellery designer's premises were organized. During the first visit, the expert was interviewed and observations were made. The interview was recorded on audio tape and the expert explained the task verbally, provided drawings and gave demonstrations of parts of tasks (notes and comments were made from the observations). From these data, an initial analysis of the task was undertaken. During the

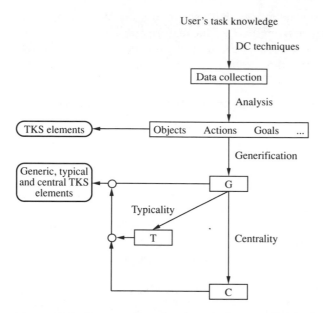

Figure 13.7 Process view of task analysis as applied in the CAD case study

second visit, a questionnaire was completed and further interviews and observations occurred. The second visit also gave us the opportunity to show the initial results of our TA to the expert and to consolidate issues which had not been fully covered during the first visit. In addition, a third meeting with the client and the expert was also held to check the results of the TA and to agree on the format of the TA report. Each meeting lasted approximately four to six hours.

Results of the task analysis

The use of KAT in this project is summarized in Fig. 13.7. The data-collection techniques were as described in the preceding paragraph. The analysis identified and described in detail TKS elements in the form of goals, subgoals, procedures, objects and actions. A process of generalization was carried out, and typical and central elements were identified.

   After carrying out the data-collection part of the TA procedure and identifying in detail all the relevant TKS elements, a task model was built which represented the interconnections between the TKS elements. The task model included a network of goals, subdivided into subgoals which are carried out by procedures (Fig. 13.8a). Procedures are structured sequences of actions upon objects. The task modelling and the generalization, typicality and centrality analyses (Fig. 13.8b) contributed to the production of design recommendations and to the prototyping and design of the functionality, dialogue and presentation of the user interface.

Contributions of task model to the design of a computer-assisted jewellery-design system

The TA contributed to the design of the system in a number of ways. For example, the results of KAT helped us to identify how much information should be provided on the screen at any one time, as well as to give recommendations and suggestions on how to present information on the screen, and to design the dialogue. Moreover, typical objects were used to define default values; central objects were treated as essential to the functionality of the design; generic objects were used as menu or window titles; and specific objects were used as the items of particular menus or windows. An example of part of the user interface design is shown in Fig. 13.9.

The TA enabled us to identify all the information necessary to be represented at any one time for a particular task. As can be seen from Fig. 13.9 the amount of information is large, and would be complex if not well structured. The structure of this information was directly derived from the TA by identifying classes of action that are carried out on classes of object, the procedures used for particular activities and, importantly, the context in which those procedures occurred.

'Lookalike' screen dumps or storyboard-interaction scenarios were developed by using the information derived from the TA together with our experiences in designing user-interfaces. These designs were then passed to the prototype implementors who constructed a prototype user interface on the basis of these designs. The KAT methodology provided an invaluable source of information for generating the initial user-interface design to a significant level of detail.

SUMMARY OF CASE STUDIES

Knowledge analysis of tasks contributes to design-idea generation in both these case studies in three ways; first, to identify the functionality of the system; second, to identify stylistic and presentation characteristics of the user-interaction requirements; and third, in the design of the dialogue, KAT helped to identify what users expected to have available to them at any time, their likely usage of system functions, the names and form of representation to be given to screen-presented objects and events, and the information that should be available in a given context (e.g. screens) and the structure between contexts (e.g. moving between different screens).

There are at least three different aspects of the design of software systems to which the TA contributed, namely, the design of *functionality*, *dialogue* and *presentation*. There is quite a clear distinction between presentation and functionality, since presentation is concerned primarily with the visual appearance and screen layout of the user interface, whereas functionality has to do with the performance and capability of the system. The dialogue is concerned with accessing the functionality through the presentation 'layer' of the user-interface design. The dialogue must support users in achieving their goals and, to do this, it makes use of both the functionality and presentation aspects of the design.

An illustration of the differences between the functionality, dialogue and presentation aspects of design can be given using the jewellery-design system, described earlier.

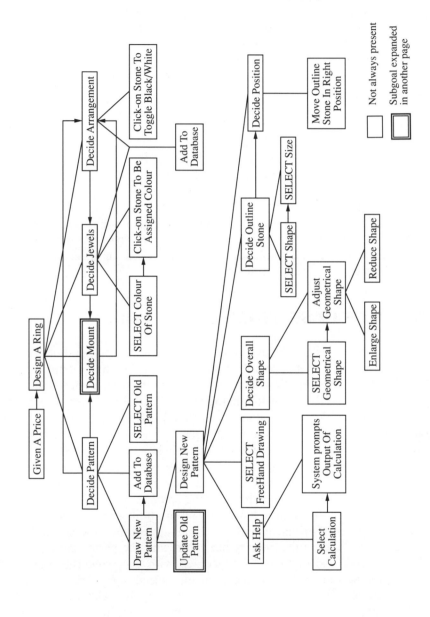

Figure 13.8a   A task model showing network of goals and subgoals

Generification/Typicality (T)/Centrality(C)

Generic objects	Specific objects	Generic objects	Specific objects
Shape	Round (T) Oval Square Rectangle Heart Marquise Drop Hexagon Trillion Baguette	Calibration units (mm)	for Size = 1 to 6 step 0.25 (T) (round and square) 4 x 2, 3.5 x 1.75, 3 x 1.5, 5 x 3, 5 x 4, 6 x 4, 6 x 5, 7 x 5, 8 x 6, 9 x 7, 10 x 8, 12 x 10 (oval and rectangle and baguette) 4 x 4, 6 x 6, (heart) 5 x 2.5, 8 x 4 (marquise) 6 x 4, 8 x 6 (drop) 5 x 5 (hexagon and trillion)
Setting	Claw (T) Channel Grain	Jewel	Diamond (T) Zirconia Ruby Emerald
Colour	White (T) Red Green Blue ⋮		Sapphire ⋮
		Metal	White Gold Yellow Gold (T) Platinum
Orientation	Plan (T) Side View (T) Isometric View (T) 360 degrees rotation (of ring's components and of the whole ring)		Silver
		Ring's component	Head (T) Shank (T) Jewels/Stones (T)
		Mount	Two Piece Mount (T)
Price			One Piece Mount
Pattern(C)		Position	Central Stone Row Of Stones
Jewel choice			Symmetrical Stone 12 o'clock position/1, 2, 3, etc.
Calibration tool		Magnifying tool	

Figure 13.8b   Generalization, typicality and centrality analyses.

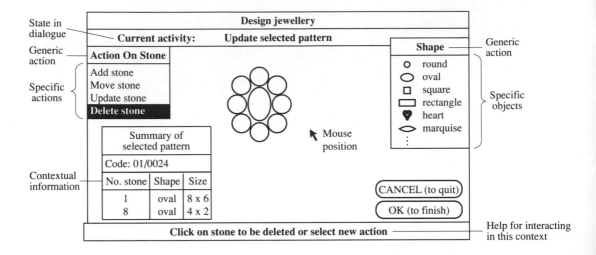

Figure 13.9 Example of user-interface design with generic, typical and specific objects and actions in a system for jewellery design

The system *functionality* for a jewellery CAD system might include create, edit, select, display and delete bejewelled products.

The *dialogue* is concerned with the structure of the permissible links between different states of the system. Dialogues include the interaction necessary to access a particular function of the application, and the interactions that occur in applying the available functions in the context of particular tasks.

The *presentation* includes the design of pop-up menus, windows, icons, buttons, text fields, command names, etc. The presentation aspects of the design are the media through which the state of the application, accessible functions and feedback are presented to the user.

If task analyses are to be used on a regular basis in all kinds of design projects then some form of tool support is required, since becoming a skilled task analyst requires some experience and training.

14 INFORMAL AND FORMAL SPECIFICATION OF USER-INTERACTION TASK SCENARIOS

Summary

- Informal specifications of user interaction can be produced which show how the design can be used for particular task scenarios. This can be done at a number of different design stages.

- Formal specifications of user interaction are more difficult to produce and to interpret but they offer greater precision and completeness. There are many different approaches to formal specifications. However, to produce specification of designs in terms of task scenarios requires a specification of task elements and user interface components.

INFORMAL SPECIFICATIONS OF TASKS AND USER INTERFACES

One important aspect of the design of interactive systems is the specification of the design. In HCI the most difficult thing to specify is the nature of the interaction. As we have seen in Chapters 9 and 10, many of the models developed in HCI such as CLG also capture some form of specification of the design of the user interaction. Partly because it has been found to be so difficult to produce a complete specification of the user interaction, rapid prototyping and simulations have often been used in the place of any specification. However, the role of a specification is to provide a documentation of the design which can then be reasoned about, evaluated, agreed upon, or simply passed on to different members of a design team as a reference document. While rapid prototyping provides a demonstrable view of the design, it does not meet all the purposes of a specification. Also, it is often the case that no matter how rapidly the prototype can be produced, there is some reluctance to change the design once it has reached an implemented form and furthermore prototyping represents a trial and error, rather than a principled, approach to design.

As we have seen from the surveys of Rosson *et al.* and Johnson and Johnson, the use of TA in design is acknowledged and is seen as providing an important input to the generation of design ideas. However, if a design idea is to be developed then the designer must have some way of reflecting upon the consequences of the design for the users' tasks. One approach is to provide a way of including a task perspective in the design specification.

Waddington and Johnson (1989a, and b) developed an informal notation which produced a family of related, frame-based, task-oriented models. There were three overall aims in developing this notation: first, to ensure that the usability of an interface design is borne in mind at all times by the designer; second, to allow the designer to see how, at the conceptual level of the user interface, task behaviour is mapped on to interface behaviour. The notation is intended to allow designers to explore alternative interface designs to see which most suitably reflects the expected task behaviour. The third aim was to model design decisions in such a way as to allow predictions of usability to be made at different stages of design. The technique was developed from TKS theory and comprises three forms of task-oriented design modelling: general, specific and interface modelling, which are assumed to correspond to different stages in a phased or lifecycle approach to design. However, there is no sequential dependence between the models, and there is nothing to prevent them being used independently.

The models and notation attempt to relate TA, as described by TKS theory and carried out using the techniques of KAT, to system design and development by providing a form of expression for a system design that focuses on the user tasks such that the design can then be related to the results of the TA. The notation was developed to allow both for designs developed directly from a TA and also for designs that create new or modify existing tasks in a nontrivial way. Thus the notation does not constrain the designer to merely implementing existing tasks; it supports the design of new tasks, and new ways of interacting with the world. The first component of the family of models is the generalized task model (GTM). This model captures the general properties of a system design and ignores any detail about how the design will be implemented, how resources (including users) will be allocated in the design, and what kind of interface will be constructed. It captures the structure of the tasks that the general system design is assumed/intended to cover.

THE GENERALIZED TASK MODEL

The results of a TA can be used as input to the design activity, and the results of the design activity are then reflected back in terms of the structure of user tasks as defined by TKS theory, by a generalized task model (GTM). The GTM represents the general system design in terms of the structure of tasks in the domain and independently of the detail of the individual tasks analysed to produce it. In other words it is a *generalized system task model*. However, because of its task structure, it can be interpreted to allow other tasks from the same task domain to be described using its elements. For the purpose of exposition, the principles of producing a GTM are demonstrated using the example task of 'arrange a project meeting', from the domain of office-based messaging.

In an office environment, one would typically find roles such as secretary, coordinator, personal assistant, manager, etc; however, the GTM describes *generic roles*. This allows for the possibility that the generic role may be undertaken by any of the particular roles peculiar to the environment. The generic roles identified in the example task are 'arranger' and 'attendee'. The task is subsequently modelled from each role perspective separately. The two roles are clearly not independent (nor would they be in the case of most tasks involving more than one role), and the GTM captures the interaction of roles within a task as will be shown. The task behaviour associated with each role is first described in terms of the *goals* and *subgoals* which must be satisfied to accomplish the task. The notation for goals and subgoals in the GTM is ⟨goal name⟩ (⟨object⟩ (⟨specific object type⟩)). In the example, (Figs 14.1 and 14.2) 'arrange a project meeting' is the goal which is shared by the arranger and attendee roles. However, the subgoals for this goal then vary in the case of each role.

The subgoals are indented to show that they are subordinate to the goal. Notice also that the subgoals are parametrized in the same way as their goal. This is because they inherit the parameters from their goal. The subgoals are connected by different kinds of relationship. Two possible relationships are 'causes' and 'enables'. 'Causes' means that the finishing of one event causes the commencement of the next event; 'enables' means that the finishing of one event satisfies the necessary and sufficient conditions for another event to commence, but this event is not triggered by the first event; 'finishes' simply means that after this event the task could terminate successfully. Other relations between goals and subgoals include concurrency (in which two or more events must occur at the same time); temporal order (in which the two or more events must be carried out in a given order); unorderedness (in which one or more events can be carried out in any order); and optionality (in which one or more events may be omitted without preventing the main goal from being satisfied). In addition to these relations are the notions of pre- and post-conditions which respectively determine the state that must exist before a given event can occur and the state that results after a particular event has occurred. (Note, in the GTM, pre- and post-conditions are not often used because the level of description of the system is too high to make them useful. However, there is nothing in the model to prevent them being used. These properties and relations also hold for 'procedures' and 'actions'. Additionally, procedures and actions have control information represented in the model to describe how the procedure or action is to be executed. These control structures include sequence, iteration and branching.

In Figs 14.1 and 14.2, the GTM for the two roles of arranger and attendee are described. For each role the goal structure, procedures, action and objects, are specified. The abbreviations used in the specification are not part of the specification format. They are simply used here to save space in writing out the specification. Where no relations is shown between two actions, this signifies that there is a strict temporal-sequence order. For example in Fig. 14.1, in the procedure Consult (LOC, ITS, Message) the actions identify, search, retrieve, and store-In are all carried out in the sequence in which they are listed. Furthermore, the model shows that the procedure Consult involves four actions and it is used in each of the subgoals of the main goal. In contrast, the procedure Complete is also used in all three subgoals but it has only one action to its body. Also, procedures Decide, Notice and Record, are only used once in the task. Notice too, that procedures can take different parameters depending upon the subgoal that they are used.

```
Key
LOC = location
ITs = information tokens
ISs = information sources

Role   Arranger
Goal          Arrange (Meeting (Project))
Subgoal            plan (Meeting (Project))_causes
Procedure              Consult (LOC, ITs, Message)_enables
Action                     identify (LOC, ITs, Message)_enables
                           search (LOC, ITs, Message)_causes
                           retrieve (LOC, ITs, Message)_enables
                           store-In (ITs, Message, LOC)
                           Complete (ITs, Message, ISs)_enables
                           fill-In (ITs, Message, ISs)
                           Decide (ITs)

Subgoal            COMPOSE-AND-SEND-MESSAGE (Meeting (Project))_
Procedure              Consult (LOC, ITs, Message)
Action                     identify (LOC, ITs, Message)_
                           search (LOC, ITs, Message)_
                           retrieve (LOC, ITs, Message)_
                           store-In (ITs, Message, LOC)
                       Select (Medium, Message)
                           identify (LOC, Constraints, Medium)_
                           choose (Medium, Constraints)
                       Complete (ITs, Message, ISs)_
                           fill-In (ITs, Message, ISs)
                       Execute (Transaction-Requirements, Message,
                       Medium)

Subgoal            RECEIVE-AND-PROCESS-REPLY (Meeting (Project))_
                   FINISH or fails
Procedure              Notice (Message, Medium)
                       Execute (Transaction Requirements, Message,
                       Medium)
Action                     Consult (LOC, ITs, Reply)
                           identify (LOC, ITs, Reply)_
                           search (LOC, ITs, Reply)_
                           retrieve (LOC, ITs, Reply)_
                           store-In (ITs, Reply, LOC)
                       Complete (ITs, Meeting, Reply)_
                           fill-In (ITs, Meeting, Reply)
                       Notice (New-Information, Reply)
                       Record (ITs, New-Information, Reply)
                           establish (ITs, New-Information, Reply)_
                           enables
                           fill-In (ITs, Reply, New-Information)
```

Figure 14.1 An extract from the GTM for the arranger role in a meeting-organizing task designed to be carried out on an electronic mail system (from Waddington and Johnson, 1989b)

In these examples some procedures are not decomposed into action sequences. This is because not all procedures can be decomposed into sequences of actions—they appear to be more conditional. The GTM models such cases by using production rules of the if—then—else format allowing us to model conditions within the task structure.

The *objects* on which the actions are predicated in both Figs 14.1 and 14.2 are

```
Role    Attendee
Goal            Arrange (Meeting (Project))
Subgoal             RECEIVE-AND-PROCESS-MESSAGE (Meeting (Project))_
Procedure           Notice (Message, Medium)_
                    Execute (Transaction-Requirements, Message,
                    Medium)-
                    Complete (ITs, Meeting, Message)
Action                      fill-In (ITs, Meeting, Message)
Subgoal             COMPOSE-AND-SEND-REPLY (Meeting (Project))_
Procedure              Consult (LOC, ITs, Reply)
Action                     identify (LOC, ITs, Reply)_
                           search (LOC, ITs, Reply)_
                           retrieve (LOC, ITs, Reply)_
                           store-In (ITs, Reply, LOC)
                       Select (Medium, Reply)
                           identify (LOC, Constraints, Medium)_
                           choose (Medium, Constraints)
                       Complete (ITs, Reply, ISs)_
                           fill-In (ITs, Reply, ISs)
                       Execute (Transaction-Requirements, Message,
                       Medium)
```

Figure 14.2   Continuation of the extract from the GTM for the arranger and attendee roles (from Waddington and Johnson, 1989)

shown in the notation of the GTM by appearing as parameters to those actions. So, for example, the first procedure associated with planning a project meeting entails the arranger consulting a *location* for *information tokens* associated with the *message*, where each of these parameters is an object.

All objects consist of properties (shown on the left-hand side of Fig. 14.3) which may assume values. All objects have some properties in common. Two of these are

```
Message
location: envelope|computer|person|otherPeople
          |notePaper
informationSource: LongTermMemory, ContactList,
                   Diary, Reply.
                   PreviousCorrespondence
header: <from: <Self> address: <SelfAddress>
        to: date: <Today> re: >
body: <dictated by current goal>
footer: <signature>
typical instance: notePaper telephone message
Central to: Organizing meetings
```

Figure 14.3   An example of an object definition. Not all the properties (slots) of the object are shown (from Waddington and Johnson, 1989a)

`location` and `informationSource`. The `location` lists a series of possible, alternative locations where that object may be found. The `informationSource` slot lists a series of objects which may act as sources of information from which the necessary information may be obtained to fill in the values of the object's other properties. Two important slots in the object definition are the typical instance and centrality slot. From TKS theory, typical instance refers to the most representative instance of a message object, while centrality specifies that the message object is a central object to the 'arrange a meeting' task.

An object can include other objects in its definition as properties through the 'has a' relation and can show its class membership through the 'is a' relation. For example, a message 'has a' header, a body and a factor. Properties can also have values. The value of a given property will usually depend on the context (task) in which it is currently instantiated. For example, 'Message: header: ⟨to⟩' may have multiple values if a message is to be sent to many people. However, it will often be possible to associate a meaningful default value with a property. So, for example, a message will usually (but not always) be sent ⟨from⟩ oneself. Hence the default value of 'Message: header: ⟨from⟩' is the current logged-on user. A restricted example of an object definition is shown in Fig. 14.3.

THE SPECIFIC TASK MODEL

The next level of model in this family of models is the specific task model. This model is related to the GTM in that it expresses the content of the GTM at a much lower level of detail. However, the specific task model is *not derivable* from the GTM since it requires many design decisions to have occurred before the specific task model can be produced. This specific task model is concerned with the allocation of function between user and device. In an ideal world it might be possible for the device to support *all* aspects of a user's tasks. However, there are many constraints placed on the allocation of functions between user and device from an HCI point of view. It uses exactly the same notation as the GTM but distinguishes between those parts of the GTM that have full, partial, or no support by the system. Thus the specific task model is an intersection between the design and the user task at a level where the design has indicated where software system is to be developed. For an example specific task model, see Waddington and Johnson (1989a, b).

THE SPECIFIC INTERFACE MODEL

The final model is concerned specifically with interface actions and objects, their properties and the dialogue that takes place at the interface between the user and the device to achieve tasks. This is the specific interface model (SIM). This model is specific to the user interface of the system being built. However, it describes that interface at a certain level of detail. This level is independent of presentation artefacts. So, for example, it includes interface objects without specifying whether an object or action should be represented as an icon, menu item or a character string. The notation used to express the interface design is similar to the interface definition

Objects, actions and properties

Object: Standard__message
Actions: select, specify, send, see, read, forward, reply__to, destroy
Properties: to (*null, 1 or more addressees*)
return receipt (*requested, not__requested*)
re (*null, arbitrary text*)
enclosure (*null, 1 file*)
from (*null, one user*)
at (*null, valid time*)
on (*null, valid date*)
body (*null, arbitrary text less than 32 000 characters*)
sent (*true, false*)
received (*true, false*)
seen (*true, false*)
visible (*true, false*)

Dialogue model and task structure mappings

Task: Arrange a project meeting
Role: Arranger
General goal: Arrange (Meeting (Project))
COMPOSE&SENDMESSAGE (Meeting (Project))
    Consult (LOC, ITs, Message)
        search (ContactList, Message: header: to, Message)
          pre-conditions: (Standard__message:visible = *true*)
              actions: see (Standard__message)
          post-conditions: none

        retrieve (ContactList, Message:header:to, Message)
          pre-conditions: (Standard__message:visible = true)
              actions: see (Standard__message)
          post-conditions: none

    Complete (ITs, Message, ISs)
        fillIn (ITs, Message, ISs)
          pre-conditions: (User:logged__on = true) AND
                        (Standard__message:visible = *true*)
              actions: select (Standard__message:to)
                        specify (Standard__message:re)
                        specify (Standard__message:body)
          post-conditions: (Standard__message:to ≠ *null*) AND
                        (Standard__message:re ≠ *null*) AND
                        (Standard__message:body ≠ *null*)

  Execute (TransactionRequirements, Message, Medium)
          pre-conditions: (Standard__message:to ≠ *null*) AND
                        (Standard__message:re ≠ *null*) AND
                        (Standard__message:visible = *true*)
              actions: send (Standard__message)
          post-conditions: (Standard__message:sent = *true*) AND
                        (Standard__message:visible = *false*) AND
                        (Standard__message:from ≠ *null*) AND
                        (Standard__message:at ≠ *null*) AND
                        (Standard__message:on ≠ *null*)

Figure 14.4   An extract from the SIM for a simulated mailing system (from Waddington and Johnson, 1989a, b)

language of Foley *et. al.*, (1989). It provides an object model by giving a description of each of the interface objects, the actions which may be performed on them and the properties associated with them. It provides a dialogue model by giving a description of the interface actions, the interface objects on which they are predicated and the pre- and post-conditions of interaction. This dialogue model is embedded in the task model which reflects the TKS. Hence a designer can see how task behaviour is achieved at the user interface. As with the GTM and specific task model, the SIM is related to but not directly derivable from the specific task model.

An example extract from the SIM for the user interface to a mail system, Hyper-mail, is shown in Fig. 14.4. (This mail system has been prototyped at QMW on an Apple Macintosh.) In the figure, the two parts of the SIM for the part of the interface to an electronic mail system is shown using an extract from the GTM in Fig. 14.3. In the example in Fig. 14.4, first an interface object is specified, namely a 'standard message' object, together with its properties and the actions that can be carried out with it. Included in the object specification is the typicality and centrality information from the GTM. In this case, these are unchanged from the GTM, but that need not always be so.

The second part of the SIM is a specification of how the object would be involved in the task of composing and sending a message to arrange a project meeting. This is a task scenario taken from the GTM, in which the designer can specify how the object will behave and what the user must do in order to carry out the task. Thus it specifies the interaction tasks at the level of the interface dialogue. The specification is at a level that does not detail the screen layout or the interaction style of the object. This could be included in a lower level model following the same structure and modelling format. The model has the same structure and format as the GTM and now shows pre- and post conditions referring to identifiable states.

This concludes the description of the three design models which form part of an informal task-oriented design-specification approach. These models attempt to provide a description of the design, including its user interface, such that the task support provided by the system can be considered in terms of the tasks it can be used for and the tasks involved in using the design. There are many occasions when such descriptions might be useful, for instance, when providing a means of communication between members of a design team or providing a documented record of the design. It is also possible that, by having the design described in this way, it helps the designer pay closer attention to the consistency and completeness of the design from a task point of view. Of course, providing an informal notation may not be the optimum way to present the task aspects of the design for all purposes. For example, it is probably not the optimum form for gaining user feedback about the quality of the design, since it is likely that users would not understand the informal specification. For these and other purposes, some form of simulation may be more useful. Furthermore, carrying out the TA and producing the informal specification places an extra load on the designer or design team and may require them to develop expertise that they currently do not possess. In recognition of this fact, a number of tools and forms of support for design teams adopting a task-oriented approach to design are being developed.

The use of models and specifications in design is important. They provide the designer with a way of externalizing the current state of their thoughts about the design. Such externalization is commonly used by people in many demanding and creative tasks (for example, musicians use score sheets and audio recording to capture the interim and final states of their compositions). By developing models and specifications that allow designers to externalize their ideas about the user, tasks and the user interface, it should be easier for the designer to maintain a careful consideration of the user, the tasks and the interaction during the demands of design.

A FORMAL SPECIFICATION APPROACH FOR TASK-BASED DESIGN

While the family of models described above provides the designer with a means of informally describing the system-design items of the user tasks, it does not go as far as it might in providing the designer with a method of specifying the design.

A more formal basis for the notions of task structure as expressed in TKS (Johnson *et al.*, 1988) has been developed by Gikas, Johnson and Reeves (1989). The formalism has been developed to allow a more precise way of specifying and checking the contents of the model are in line with the theory. It also allows a more precise definition of the theory to be stated. Most importantly, it provides the designer with a way of formally specifying and reasoning about the design in terms of user tasks. Rather than simply introducing the formalism, we will work through a simple example of a task that has been formalized.

An example of the elements of a TKS related to the task of entering details of new reports on to a database in a library is developed below.

In the task scenario:

- The person responsible for entering the details obtains or accepts a journal from the information officer.
- For each journal or magazine, a contents list is typed in along with the name of the publication, the names of the authors, titles of the articles and an abstract or précis of the article itself. Other details such as when it was accepted, revised or submitted are also added. All these details are publicized on the 'library' bulletin board. A part of the task structure for this task might be as in Fig. 14.5. As it stands, the task structure of Fig. 14.5 is completely informal. The relationships between the individual components are described informally. To make the task structure independent of particular interpretations it can be given unique semantics. To do this requires a formal framework for TKS models.

Formalizing the library task TKS

The example library task can be formalized in several stages. First, the temporal relationships between goal and subgoals can be formalized, including the enabling and causal relationships between them. Next, the procedures can be formalized in terms of pre- and post-conditions. Finally, the various objects and their properties that are referred to in the structure can be defined. Having done this, the procedures can be further defined in terms the objects and actions. By formalizing task structures in this way it is possible to check that the model is consistent and complete at all levels.

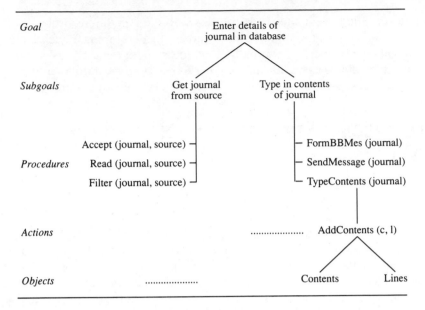

Figure 14.5   A schematic view of the parts of the TKS for the task of entering the details of new reports on to a library database

The formal languages used

To describe the relationships between goals and subgoals and also between procedures, a propositional temporal logic can be used, since this will capture the temporal dependencies between goals or subgoals.

An equational specification language enables us to specify the objects in terms of abstract operations and axioms which define the semantics of the objects. The relationships between objects are made apparent due to the way in which some objects may be parametrized by others. This means that the class hierarchy of objects can be specified. Equational specifications allow us to reason about the theorems describing the behaviour of the objects.

Relationships between subgoals

There are a number of different relations between each set of goals, subgoals, procedures, objects and actions that reflect the different ways that tasks may be achieved. The set of relations include concurrent or parallel, unordered, optional and temporal orderings for each of the above TKS elements. There are two examples of temporal relationships, 'causes' and 'enables'. (For a full account of the formalization of TKS model, see Gikas, Johnson and Reeves (1989).) Temporal logic can be used to formalize the enables and causes relationships, since both relationships are time dependent. Let us see how this would work for each of the above relations, causes and enables, for subgoals.

Let G and T be any subgoals (and hence propositions). We express the fact that G causes T by

$$\neg F(G \wedge \neg FT)$$

and the fact that G enables T by

$$\neg F(\neg G \wedge FT)$$

An approximate English translation for G causes T is 'there is no future time (denoted by F in the formulae above) when G is satisfied and T is never satisfied' and for G enables T we have 'there is no future time when G is not satisfied but T will be satisfied' or 'T will never have been satisfied without already having satisfied G'. Assume that the earlier library task example contains just two subgoals related by 'enables'. This means that the successful completion of 'get-journal' will allow 'type-contents' to begin.

In temporal logic, by the definition above, the relationship can be expressed by

$$\neg F(\neg \mathtt{Getjournal} \wedge F\mathtt{Typecontents})$$

which is to say that there is no future time when `Getjournal` has not been satisfied and later `Typecontents` will have been satisfied.

Relationships between procedures

In specifying the different kinds of relations that exist between procedures, again consider the two temporal relations 'causes' and 'enables'. The notation $f \rightarrow [a]y$ mean that if the pre-condition f is satisfied then, whenever a has been executed, the post-condition y will be satisfied. The pre- and post-conditions can be used to define a procedure's semantics to express the temporal relationships between procedures.

Consider what is meant by saying that procedures p *causes* procedure q or procedure p *enables* procedure q. For p causes q it can be reasoned that: given $f \rightarrow [p]y$ and $f' \rightarrow [q]y$ it follows that p causes q means that if the pre-condition of p is satisfied then at some future time the post-condition of q becomes satisfied, i.e. q does execute if p does, this is formalized as

$$f \rightarrow Fy'$$

Similarly, p enables q means that if p finishes then q can start, i.e. if the post-condition of p is satisfied then the pre-condition of q is, which can be formalized as

$$y \rightarrow f'$$

To return to the library-text example, and using the notational convention that ϕ_A (ψ_A) is the pre-condition (post-condition) of the procedure A, we have:

> Accepting a journal *enables* 'read', i.e. $\psi_{accept} \rightarrow \phi_{read}$
> Reading a journal *causes* filtering, i.e. $(\phi_{read} \rightarrow F\psi_{filter}) \vee (\psi_{read} \rightarrow \phi_{filter})$
> Forming a message *enables* type in its contents, i.e. $\psi_{form} \rightarrow \phi_{type}$
> Typing contents *enables* send the message, i.e. $\psi_{type} \rightarrow \phi_{send}$

TASK-OBJECT SPECIFICATION AND SEMANTICS OF PROCEDURES

The objects of the task structure can be defined in an algebraic way. Consider the three objects: source, contents, journal.

Source
Sorts

      src, str

Operations

newSource:		→ src
mkSource:	src × str	→ src
name?:	src	→ str

Axioms

      N/A

Contents
Sorts

      conts, int, ln

Operations

newContents:		→ conts
addContents:	conts × ln1	→ conts
howMany?:	conts	→ int
content-i?:	conts × int	→ ln

Axioms

    howMany?(newContents) = 0
    howMany?(addContents(c,l)) = howMany?(c) + 1
    content-i?(newContents,i) = EMPTYSTRING
    content-i?(addContents(c,l),i) = if i = howMany?(c) + 1 then l else
        content-i?(c,i)

Journal
Sorts

      jrnl, src, str, conts

Operations

newJournal:		→ jrnl
makeJournal:	jrnl × src × str × str × conts	→ jrnl
setSource:	jrnl × src	→ jrnl
setTitle:	jrnl × str	→ jrnl
setAbstract:	jrnl × str	→ jrnl
setContents:	jrnl × conts	→ jrnl
title?:	jrnl	→ str
abstract?:	jrnl	→ str
source?:	jrnl	→ src
contents?:	jrnl	→ conts

Axioms

    title?(newJournal) = EMPTYSTRING
    title?(makeJournal(j,s,st1,st2,c)) = st1
    abstract?(newJournal) = EMPTYSTRING
    abstract?(makeJournal(j,s,st1,st2,c)) = st2
    etc.

Any other objects that might be needed can be defined in the same way.

The semantics of the procedures using the abstract operations of the objects to define the actions: modal action logic, can be used to do this. The semantics of a procedure takes the form

$$\text{pre}_A \rightarrow \boxed{\text{action}}\ \text{post}_A$$

where pre_A is a pre-condition for the procedure A, post_A is the post-condition for the procedure A, and $\boxed{\text{action}}$ is the set of actions that are executed within the procedure A.

The pre- and post-conditions for any procedure denote the state of the world (before and after the execution of the procedure). Using the above framework, the semantics of the procedure, TypeContents with the pre-condition 'there is at least one entry in the contents' and the post-condition 'the number of the (remaining) entries in the contents has now decreased by one' can be specified. So, if n is the name CurrentNoOfEntries, the pre-condition would be

    f.f(n) ≥ 1

and the post-condition is

    f'.f' = lx.if x = n then f(n) - 1 else f(x)

The $\boxed{\text{action}}$ part is:

    addContents(f(c), f(l))

This completes our formalization of the library task and shows how TKSs can be expressed using a powerful formal system. The reason for doing this (formalizing a task model) is so that the model can be precisely and accurately described using the formal system.

From this example, it can be seen that formal methods can be applied to such aspects of system design as modelling the user tasks and the interaction. There remains much research to be carried before all relevant aspects of users, tasks and their temporal relations can be formalized. TKS theory makes clear the exact and different forms of relation that need to be modelled. The application of formalisms and formal methods to these other relations is not impossible.

CONCLUSION

There is much work still to be done to develop appropriate forms of specifications for user interfaces. If the specification is to be of any use then it must draw out features of the design in such a manner that it provides a perspective for understanding the implications of the design. One perspective that is becoming increasingly important is that of the *internal* tasks required to perform typical and anticipated *external* tasks. A second important feature of the user interface specification is that it should capture information in a clear and precise way. The degree of clarity and precision varies between formal and informal specification depending upon the knowledge of the person reading the specification. Informal specifications require little or no knowledge of logic or mathematics, while formal specifications require a higher degree of such technical knowledge.

A third feature of a specification is that it *can* give the reader a mechanism for evaluating the design. In the examples here, the informal specification can be used to evaluate a design in terms of the complexity of the internal tasks for any given external task. This is done by counting the number of subgoals, procedures, actions and objects used in the SIM. In the formal specification, it may be possible to apply simple, as well as more stringent methods of evaluation. For example, a simple mechanism is to consider the axioms associated with an object and the actions. A more rigorous mechanism might be to prove that a particular task could not be carried out.

Through these features of a specification, the designer would be able to reason about whether or not the tasks (internal and external) could be carried out more easily, if new tasks can be carried out at all, and if the design has any costs for the user and/or implementor. For example, how much the user will have to learn or how many different objects have to be programmed to implement the design might each be used to assess user and implementation costs.

REFERENCES AND BIBLIOGRAPHY

Anderson, J. R. (1974) 'Retrieval of propositional information from long-term memory', *Cognitive Psychology*, **6**, 451–74.

Anderson, J. R. (1983) *The Architecture of Cognition*, Harvard University Press, Cambridge MA.

Anderson, J. R. (1984) *Tutorials in Learning and Memory*, W. H. Freeman, New York.

Anderson, J. R. (1985) *Cognitive psychology and its implications*, 2nd edn, W. H. Freeman, New York.

Anderson, J. R. and Bower, G. H. (1973) *Human Associative Memory*, Winston, Washington DC.

Annett, J. and Duncan, K. D. (1967) 'Task analysis and training design', *Occupational Psychology*, **41**, 211–21.

Annett, J., Duncan, K. D., Stammers, R. B. and Gray, M. J. (1971) *Task analysis*, Training Information Number 6, HMSO, London.

Barnard, P. (1987) 'Cognitive resources and the learning of human–computer dialogues' in *Interfacing Thought: Cognitive Aspects of Human–Computer Interaction*, Carroll, J. M. (ed.), MIT Press, MA.

Bartlett, F. C. (1932) *Remembering: A Study in Experimental and Social Psychology*, Cambridge University Press, Cambridge.

Bell, D. (1989) 'A comparison of icons, labels and icons with labels', unpublished dissertation; Department of Computer Science, Queen Mary and Westfield College, University of London.

Bellotti, V. M. E. (1989) 'Implications of the current design practice for the use of HCI techniques', in *People and computers IV*, Jones, D. M. and Winder, R. (eds), Cambridge University Press, Cambridge.

Bellotti, V. M. E. (1990) 'A framework for assessing applicability of HCI techniques', in *Human–Computer Interaction; Interact 90*, Diaper, D., Gilmore, D., Cockton, G. and Shackel, B. (eds), North-Holland, Amsterdam.

Betts, B., Burlingame, D., Fischer, G., Foley, J., Green, M., Kerr, S. T., Olsen, D. and Thomas, J. (1987) 'Goals and objectives for user interface software', *Computer Graphics*, **21**, 2, 73–78.

Bobrow, S. and Bower, G. H (1969) 'Comprehension and recall of sentences', *Journal of Experimental Psychology*, **80**, 455–61.

Bornat, R. (1988) *Programming from first principles*, Prentice Hall, London.

Bransford, J. D., Barclay, J. R. and Franks, J. J. (1972) 'Sentence memory: a constructive versus interpretive approach', *Cognitive Psychology*, **3**, 193–209.

Broadbent, D. E. (1958) *Perception and Communication*, Pergammon Press, London.

Brown, J. (1958) 'Some tests of the decay theory of immediate memory', *Quarterly Journal of Experimental Psychology*, **10**, 12–21.

Byrne, R. (1977) 'Planning meals: problem solving on a real data-base', *Cognition*, **5**, 287–332.

Card, S. K., Moran, T. P. and Newell, A. (1983) *The Psychology of Human–Computer Interaction*, Lawrence Erlbaum Associates, Hillsdale NJ.

Carroll, J. M. (1990) 'Infinite detail and emulation in an ontologically minimized HCI', in *Empowering People; CHI 90*, Chew, J. C. and Whiteside, J. (eds), Addison-Wesley, Reading MA.

Chomsky, N. (1965) *Aspects of the Theory of Syntax*, MIT Press, Cambridge MA.

Collins, A. M. and Quillian, M. R. (1969) 'Retrieval time from semantic memory', *Journal of Verbal Learning and Verbal Behavior*, **8**, 240–7.

Cook, S. J., Drake, K., Hyde, C., Rosner, P. and Slater, M. (1988) *Report of the prototyping stream*, London HCI Centre, Queen Mary and Westfield College, University of London.

Coutaz, J. (1987) *PAC, an object oriented model for implementing user interfaces*, Laboratoire de Genie Informatique, University of Grenoble, BP 68.

Craik, F. I. M. and Lockhart, R. S. (1972) 'Levels of processing: a framework for memory research', *Journal of Verbal Learning and Verbal Behavior*, **11**, 671–84.

Crossman, E. R. F. W. (1959) 'A theory of the acquisition of speed-skill', *Ergonomics*, **2**, 153–66.

Dance, J. R., Tamar, G. H., Hill, R. D., Hudson, S. E., Meads, J., Myers, B. and Schulert, A. (1987) 'The run-time structure of UIMS supported applications', *Computer Graphics*, **21**, 2, 97–101.

Diaper, D. and Johnson, P. (1989) 'Task analysis for knowledge descriptions: theory and application in training', in *Cognitive Ergonomics and Human Computer Interaction*, Long, J. and Whitefield, A. (eds), Cambridge University Press, Cambridge.

Dix, A. (1991) 'Formal Methods in Human Computer Interaction', Academic Press, London.

Downs, E., Clare, P. and Coe, P. (1988) *Structured Systems Analysis and Design Methods: Application and Context*, Prentice Hall, London.

Ebbinghaus, H. (1885) *Memory: A Contribution to Experimental Psychology* (translated by H. A. Ruger and C. E. Bussenues, 1913), Teachers College, Columbia University, New York.

Fitts, P. M. and Posner, M. I. (1967) *Human Performance*, Brooks Cole, Belmont CA.

Fleishman, E. A. and Quaintance, M. K. (1984) *Taxonomies of Human Performance*, Academic Press, London.

Foley, J. (1987) 'Transformations on a formal specification of user computer interfaces', *Computer Graphics*, **21**, 2, 109–13.

Foley, J., Kim, W., Kovavevics, S. and Murray, K. (1989) 'Defining interfaces at a high level of abstraction', *IEEE Software*, **6**, 1, 25–32.

Galambos, J. A. (1986) 'Knowledge structures for common activities', in *Knowledge Structures*, Galambos, J. A., Abelson, R. P. and Black J. B. (eds), Lawrence Erlbaum Associates, Hillsdale NJ.

Garner, W. R. (1974) *The Processing of Information and Structure*, Potomac, MD.

Gikas, S., Johnson, P. and Reeves, S. V. (1989) *Formal framework for task-oriented modelling of devices*, Computer Science Department Report No. 583, Queen Mary and Westfield College, University of London.

Glanzer, M. and Cunitz, A.R. (1965) 'Two storage mechanisms in free recall', *Journal of verbal learning and verbal behavior*, **5**, 351–60.

Goldberg, A. (1984) *Smalltalk-80. The Interactive Programming Environment*, Addison-Wesley, New York.

Graesser, A. G. and Clark, L. F. (1985) *Structures and Procedures of Implicit Knowledge*, Ablex, Norwood NJ.

Green, T. R. G., Bellamy, R. K. E. and Parker, J. M. (1987) 'Parsing and gnisrap: a model of device use', in *Interact-87 proceedings of the second IFIP conference on Human-Computer Interaction*, Bullinger, H. J. and Shackel, B. (eds), North-Holland, Amsterdam.

Harel, D. (1988) 'On visual formalisms', *Communications of the ACM*, **31**, 5, 514–30.

Harrison, M. D. and Thimbleby, H. (1989) *Formal Methods in Human–Computer Interaction*, Cambridge University Press, Cambridge.

Hebb, D. O. (1949) *The organisation of behavior*, Wiley, New York.

Henderson, D. A. (1986) 'The Trillium user interface design environment', in *Proceedings of Human Factors In Computing Systems; CHI'86*, Addison-Wesley, New York.

Hill, R. D. (1986) 'Supporting concurrency, communication and synchronisation in human–computer interaction—the Sassafras UIMS', *ACM transactions on Graphics*, **5**, 3, 179–210.

Hill, R. D. and Hermman, M. (1989) 'The structure of TUBE—a tool for implementing advanced interfaces', in *Proceedings of Eurographics '89*, North-Holland, Amsterdam.

Howden, W. E. (1982) 'Contemporary software development environments', *Communications of the ACM*, **25**, 5, 318–29.

Hudson, S. E. (1987) 'UIMS support for direct manipulation interfaces', *Computer Graphics*, **21**, 2, 114–19.

Hyde, C. (1989) *CHOICE, London HCI Centre report*, Department of Computer Science, Queen Mary and Westfield College, University of London.

Ince, D. C. (1988) *An Introduction to Discrete Mathematics and Formal System Specification*, Clarendon Press, Oxford.

Jeffries, R., Turner, A. A., Polson, P. G. and Atwood, M. E. (1981) 'The processes involved in designing software', in *Cognitive Skills and Their Acquisition*, Anderson, J. R. (ed.), Lawrence Erlbaum Associates, Hillsdale NJ.

Johnson, H. and Johnson, P. (1990a) 'Integrating task analysis and system design: Surveying designer's needs', *Ergonomics*, **32**, 11, 1451–67.

Johnson, H. and Johnson, P. (1990b) 'Designer-identified requirements for tools to support task analyses', in *Human–Computer Interaction; Interact '90*, Diaper, D. *et al.* (eds), North-Holland, Amsterdam.

Johnson, P. (1982) 'Functional equivalence of images and movements', *Quarterly Journal of Experimental Psychology*, **34A**, 349–65

Johnson, P. and Johnson H. (1991) 'Knowledge analysis of tasks: task analysis and specification for human–computer systems', in *Engineering the Human–Computer Interface*, Downton, A. (ed.), McGraw-Hill, Maidenhead.

Johnson, P., Diaper, D. and Long, J. B. (1984) 'Tasks, skills and knowledge', in *Interact '84*, Shackel, B. (ed.), Elsevier, Amsterdam.

Johnson, P., Drake, K. and Wilson, S. (1991) 'A framework for integrating UIMS and user task models in the design of user interfaces', in *Eurographics Workshop on UIMS*, Duce, D. *et al.* (eds), Springer-Verlag, London.

Johnson, P., Johnson, H., Waddington, R. and Shouls, A. (1988) 'Task related knowledge structures: analysis, modelling and application', in *People and Computers IV: From Research to Implementation*, Jones, D. M. and Winder, R. (eds), Cambridge University Press, Cambridge.

Johnson, P., Long, J. B. and Visick, D. (1986) 'Voice versus keyboard: use of a comparative analysis of learning to identify skill requirements of input devices', in *People and Computers II: Designing for Usability*, Harrison, M. D. and Monk, A. (eds), Cambridge University Press, Cambridge.

Keane, M. and Johnson, P. (1987) 'Preliminary analysis for design', in *People and Computers III*, Diaper, D. and Winder, R. (eds), Cambridge University Press, Cambridge.

Kelly, G. A. (1955) *The Psychology of Personal Constructs*. Norton, New York.

Kieras, D. and Polson, P. G. (1986) 'An approach to the formal analysis of user complexity', *International Journal of Man–Machine Studies*, **22**, 365–94.

Knowles, C. (1988) 'Can CCT produce a measure of system usability?', in *People and*

Computers IV; From Research to Implementation, Jones, D. M. and Winder, R. (eds), Cambridge University Press, Cambridge.

Knowles, C. (1989) 'A qualitative approach to assessing complexity', in *Designing and Using Human–Computer Interfaces and Knowledge Based Systems*, Salvendy, G. and Smith, M. J. (eds), Elsevier, Amsterdam.

Kolers, P. A. (1979) 'A pattern analyzing basis of recognition', in *Levels of Processing in Human Memory*, Cermak, L. S. and Craik, F. I. M. (eds), Lawrence Erlbaum Associates, Hillsdale NJ.

Kosslyn, S. M. (1980) *Image and Mind*, Harvard University Press, Cambridge MA.

Laird, J. E., Newell, A. and Rosenbloom, P. (1987) 'SOAR: an architecture for general intelligence', *Artificial Intelligence*, **33**, 1–64.

Leddo, J. and Abelson, R. P. (1986) 'The nature of explanations', in *Knowledge Structures*, Galambos, J. A., Abelson, R. P. and Black, J. B. (eds), Lawrence Erlbaum Associates, Hillsdale NJ.

Loftus, E. F. (1974) 'Activation of semantic memory', *American Journal of Psychology*, **86**, 331–7.

Long, J. B. and Dowell, J. (1989) 'Conceptions of the discipline of HCI: craft, applied science and engineering', in *People and Computers V, HCI '89*, Sutcliffe, A. and Macauley, L. (eds), Cambridge University Press, Cambridge.

Long, J. B., Nimmo-Smith, I. and Whitefield, A. (1983) 'Skilled typing: A characterisation based on the distribution of times between responses', in *Cognitive Aspects of Skilled Typewriting*, Cooper. W. E. (ed.), Springer-Verlag, New York.

MacLean, A., Bellotti, V. and Young, R. (1990) 'What rationale is there in design?', in *Human Computer Interaction; Interact '90*, Diaper, D., Gilmore, D., Cockton, G. and Shackel, B. (eds), North-Holland, Amsterdam.

Marcus, A. (1991) Graphic designs for electronic documents and user interfaces, Addison-Wesley, Reading MA.

Meyer, D. E. and Schraneveldt, R. W. (1971) 'Facilitation in recognizing pairs of words: evidence of a dependence between retrieval operations', *Journal of Experimental Psychology*, 90, 227–34.

Meyers, L. and Grossen, B. (1972) *Experimental Design and Analysis for the Behavioral Sciences*, W. H. Freeman, San Francisco.

Miller, G. A. (1956) 'The magical number seven, plus or minus two: some limits on our capacity for processing information', *Psychological Review*, 63, 81–97.

Miller, G. A., Galanter, E. and Pribram, K. (1970) *Plans and the structure of behavior*, Harvard University Press, Cambridge MA.

Miller, R. B. (1975) 'Taxonomies for training', in *Measurement of Human Resources*, Singleton, W. T. and Spurgeon, P. (eds), Halstead, New York.

Minsky, M. (1975) 'A framework for representing knowledge', in *The Psychology of Computer Vision*, Winston, P. H. (ed.), McGraw-Hill, New York.

Moran, T. P. (1981) 'The command language grammar: a representation for the user interface of interactive computer systems', *International Journal of Man–Machine Studies*, 15, 3–50.

Murdock, B. B. J. (1962) 'The serial position effect of free recall', *Journal of Experimental Psychology*, 64, 482–8.

Myers, B. A. (1989) 'User interface tools: introduction and survey, *IEEE Software*, **6**, 1, 15–23.

Myers, B. A. (1991) 'GARNET', *IEEE Software*

Naur, P. and Randall, B. (1969) *Software Engineering*, Report on a NATO science committee sponsored conference. NATO.

Newell, A. and Simon, H. (1972) *Human Problem Solving*, Prentice Hall, Englewood Cliffs NJ.

Norman, D. A. and Draper, S. W. (1986) *User Centred System Design*, Lawrence Erlbaum Associates, Hillsdale NJ.

Oborne, D. J. (1985) Computers at Work; a Behavioural Approach, Wiley, Chichester.

Paivio, A. (1978) 'The relationship between verbal and perceptual codes', in *Handbook of Perception Vol. VIII: Perceptual Coding*, Carterette, E. G. and Freedman, M. P. (eds), Academic Press, London.

Palmer, S. E. (1978) 'Fundamental aspects of cognitive representation', in *Cognition and Categorization*, Rosch, E. and Lloyd, B. (eds), Lawrence Erlbaum Associates, Hillsdale NJ.

Payne, S. J. and Green, T. R. G. (1986) 'Task action grammars', *Human Computer Interaction*, **2**, 93–133.

Peterson, L. R. and Peterson, M. (1959) 'Short-term retention of individual items', *Journal of Experimental Psychology*, **58**, 193–8.

Pfaff, E. (1985) *User Interface Management System*, Springer-Verlag, Amsterdam.

Pollock, C. (1988) 'Training for optimising transfer between word-processors', in *People and Computers IV; HCI '88*, Jones, D. M. and Winder, R. (eds), Cambridge University Press, Cambridge.

Pressman, R. S. (1987) *Software Engineering*, 2nd edn, McGraw-Hill, London.

Quillian, M. R. (1966) *Semantic memory*, Bolt, Beranak and Newman, Cambridge MA.

Ratcliff, R., and McKoon, G. (1981) 'Does activation really spread?', *Psychological Review*, **88**, 454–62.

Reder, L. M. (1982) 'Plausibility judgement versus fact retrieval: alternative strategies for sentence verification, *Psychological Review*, **89**, 250–80.

Reisner, P. (1981) 'Formal grammars and human factors design of an interactive graphics system', *IEEE Transactions on Software Engineering*, 5, 229–40.

Rhyne, J., Ehrich, R., Bennett, J., Hewett, T., Sibert, J. and Bleser, T. (1987) 'Tools and methodologies for user interface development', *Computer Graphics*, **21**, 2, 78–87.

Rogers, Y. (1986) 'Evaluating the meaningfulness of icon sets to represent command operations', in *People and Computers: Designing for Usability*, Harrison, M. D. and Monk, A. (eds), Cambridge University Press, Cambridge.

Rosch, E. (1978) 'Principles of categorisation', in *Cognition and Categorisation*, Rosch, E. and Lloyd, B. (eds), Lawrence Erlbaum Associates, Hillsdale NJ.

Rosch, E. (1985) 'Prototype classification and logical categorization: the two systems', in *New Trends in Conceptual Representation: Challenges to Piaget's theory?*, E. K. Scholnick (ed.), Lawrence Erlbaum Associates, Hillsdale NJ.

Rosch, E., Mervis, C. B., Gray, W. D., Johnson, D. M. and Boyes-Braem, P. (1976) 'Basic objects in natural categories', *Cognitive Psychology*, **8**, 382–439.

Rosner, P., Newman, A. and Magennis, M. (1990) *In Touch*, LHC Report, Department of Computer Science, Queen Mary and Westfield College, University of London, U.K.

Rosson, M. B., Mass, S. and Kellogg, W. A. (1989) 'The designer as user: building requirements for design tools from design practice', *Communications of the ACM*, **31**, 11, 1289–98.

Rumelhart, D. E. (1975) 'Notes on a schema for stories', in *Representation and Understanding*, Bobrow, D. G. and Collins, A. M. (eds), Academic Press, New York.

Runciman, C. and Hammond, N. V. (1986) 'User programs: a way to match computer systems and human cognition', in *People and Computers: Designing for Usability*, Harrison, M. D. and Monk, A. F. (eds), Cambridge University Press, Cambridge.

Sarantinos, E. and Johnson, P. (1990) 'Interpreting real life questions and explanations', *Proceedings of the 5th Rocky Mountain Conference on Artificial Intelligence*, New Mexico State University.

Schank, R. C. (1982) *Dynamic Memory: A Theory of Reminding and Learning in Computers and People*, Cambridge University Press, New York.

Schank, R. C. and Abelson, R. (1977) *Scripts, Plans, Goals, and Understanding*, Lawrence Erlbaum Associates, Hillsdale NJ.

Schneiderman, B. (1983) 'Direct manipulation: a step beyond programming languages', *IEEE Computer*, **16**, 8, 101–9.

Sharratt, B. (1987) 'The incorporation of early interface evaluation into command language grammar specifications', in *People and Computers III*, Diaper, D and Winder, R. (eds), Cambridge University Press, Cambridge.

Shepard, R. N. (1978) 'The mental image', *American Psychologist*, **33**, 125–37.

Smith, E. E., Shoben, E. J. and Rips, L. J. (1974) 'Structure and processing in semantic memory: a feature model for semantic decision', *Psychological Review*, **81**, 214–41.

Soloway, E., Bonar, J. and Ehrlich, K. (1983) 'Cognitive strategies and looping constructs: An empirical study', *Communications of the ACM*, **26**, 853–860.

Sommerville, I. (1989) *Software Engineering*, 3rd edn, Addison-Wesley, Wokingham.

Stein, B. S. and Bransford, J. D. (1979) 'Constraints on effective elaboration: effects of precision and subject generation, *Journal of Verbal Learning and Verbal Behavior*, 18, 769–77.

Sternberg, S. (1969) 'Memory scanning: mental processes revealed by reaction time experiments', *American Scientist*, **57**, 421–57.

Thimbleby, H. (1990) *User Interface Design*, Addison-Wesley, Wokingham.

Thomas, J. J. and Hamlin, G. (1983) 'Graphical input interaction technique (GIIT) workshop summary', *Computer Graphics*, **17**, 1, 5–30.

Van Harmelen, M. and Wilson, S. M. (1987) 'Viz: a production system based user interface management system', *Eurographics '87*, North-Holland, Amsterdam.

Waddington, R. and Johnson, P. (1989a) 'Designing and evaluating interfaces using task models', *11th World Computer Congress (IFIP)*, North-Holland, San Francisco.

Waddington, R. and Johnson, P. (1989b) 'A family of task models for interface design', in *People and Computers IV*, Sutcliffe, A. and Macauley, L. (eds), Cambridge University Press, Cambridge.

Wasserman, A. I. and Shewmake, D. T. (1982) 'Rapid prototyping of interactive information systems', *ACM Sigsoft Engineering Notes*, **7**, 5, 171–80.

Welbank, M. (1983) *A Review of Knowledge Acquisition Techniques for Expert Systems*, BT Martlesham Consultancy Services, UK.

Whitefield, A. (1987) 'Models in human computer interaction: a classification with special reference to their use in design', in *Human Computer Interaction. Interact '87*, Bullinger, H. J. and Shackel, B. (eds), North-Holland, Amsterdam.

Young, R. M. (1983) 'Surrogates and mapping: two kinds of conceptual models for interactive devices', in *Mental Models*, Gentner, D. and Stevens, A. L. (eds), Lawrence Erlbaum Associates, Hillsdale NJ.

Young, R. M., Green, T. R. G. and Simon, T. (1989) 'Programmable user models for predictive evaluation of interface designs', in *Human Factors in Computer Systems, CHI89 Wings for the Mind*, Bice, K. and Lewis, C. (eds), Addison Wesley, Reading MA.

AUTHOR INDEX

Anderson, J. R. 23, 32, 35, 61, 67
Annett, J. 153

Barnard, P. 143
Bartlett, F. C. 41
Bell, D. 55
Bellotti, V. M. E. 72
Bobrow, S. 38
Bornat, R. 66
Bransford, J. D. 39
Broadbent, D. E. 16
Brown, J. 16
Byrne, R. 161

Card, S. K. 5, 7, 86, 128
Carroll, J. M. 71
Chomsky, N. 137
Collins, A. M. 46
Cook, S. J. 106
Coutaz, J. 105
Craik, F. I. M. 37
Crossman, E. R. F. W. 64

Diaper, D. 7, 154
Dix, A. 75
Draper, S. W. 4

Ebbinghaus, H. 14

Fitts, P. M. 61
Fleishman, E. A. 152
Foley, J. 103, 200

Galambos, J. A. 161
Garner, W. R. 161
Gikas, J. 201
Glanzer, M. 16
Goldberg, A. 107

Graesser, A. G. 161
Green, T. R. G. 161

Harel, D. 112
Harrison, M. D. 75
Hebb, D. O. 16
Henderson, D. A. 105
Hill, R. D. 101, 102, 106
Howden, W. E. 72, 82
Hudson, S. E. 105
Hyde, C. 108

Jeffries, R. 66
Johnson, H. 181
Johnson, P. 57, 62, 65, 100, 154, 156, 231

Keane, M. 51
Kelley, G. A. 169
Kieras, D. 86, 139
Knowles, C. 66, 140
Kolers, P. A. 65
Kosslyn, S. M. 56

Leddo, J. 162
Loftus, E. F. 24
Long, J. B. 7, 64

MacLean, A. 8, 82
Marcus, A. 71
Meyer, D. E. 32
Meyers, L. 88
Miller, G. A. 20
Moran, T. P. 117
Murdock, B. B. J. 16
Myers, B. A. 101, 102

Naur, P. 72

Oborne, D. J. 67

Paivio, A. 56
Palmer, S. E. 43
Payne, S. J. 86, 135
Peterson, L. R. 16
Pollock, C. 66, 160
Pressman, R. S. 72, 79

Quillian, M. R. 47

Ratcliff, R. 34
Reder, L. M. 40
Reisner, P. 86, 125
Rhyne, J. 104
Rogers, Y. 55
Rosch, E. 162, 169
Rosson, M. B. 85, 177
Runciman, C. 148

Schank, R. C. 49
Schneiderman, B. 105
Sharratt, B. 124, 125
Shepard, R. N. 56
Smith, E. E. 46
Soloway, E. 66
Sommerville, I. 72
Stein, B. S. 5, 38
Sternberg, S. 22

Thimbleby, H. 72

Van Harmelan, M. 104

Waddington, R. 156, 185, 194
Wasserman, A. I. 104
Welbank, M. 170
Whitefield, A. 115

Young, R. M. 115, 148

INDEX

Actions, 170
Active and inactive memory states, 21
Aesthetic perspective, 71
Ambiguity, 38–39
Analogical representations, 54–57
Architectures for user interfaces, 100ff
Associative networks, 30

BNF notation and cognitive grammar, 125–127

Card sorting, 169
Categories and memory, 24–26
Centrality, 172
CHOICE, 108
Chunking, 20
Cognition–definition, 13
Cognitive complexity theory, 86, 139–143
Coherence of user interfaces, 26, 33
Command language design, 18, 29
Command language grammar, 117–125
    interaction level, 123
    semantic level, 119
    syntactic level, 121
    task level, 118
Competence models, 137
Composite user interface objects, 71, 102
Computer science and HCI, 3
Concurrent protocols, 168
Confounding, 96
Consistency, 23, 26, 35–36, 135–136
Controls (experimental), 93–94

Declarative knowledge, 57, 61
Dependent variables, 90
Design practices and methods, 177–183
Dialogues in HCI, 6

Evaluations of user interface designs, 84–99, 125
Elaborated memory structures, 37–39
Ergonomics and HCI, 2
Experimental design, 93–98
    methods, 87–92
External tasks, 6

Facilitation effects, 25, 32
Forgetting, 25
Formal methods and HCI, 74, 201–206
Fourth generation software engineering tools, 79
Frames, 51–52
Free-recall experiments, 16
Frequency counts, 170
Functional perspective on design, 70

GARNET, 102–103
Generic models of system design, 80–81
Generic task components, 172–174
    task models, 194–198
Goals, operators, methods, selection rules (GOMS), 86, 127–134
Goal structures, 161, 163, 171–172, 174

Help facilities, 18
Hierarchical task analysis (HTA), 153–154
Human factors, 2
Human Computer Interaction:
    definition, 2
    framework, 7–8

Icon design, 29–31, 54
Imagery, 54–57
Implementation stage evaluations, 87
Incidental learning, 39
Independent groups design, 96

Independent variables, 89
Individual differences, 4
Inference, 37, 39–41
Inheritance, 48
Interacting cognitive subsystems (ICS),
    143–148
Interaction level of CLG, 123
Interface design language (IDL), 103
Interference effects in memory, 35–37
Internal v external tasks, 6
Interval scales of measurement, 92
Interviews, 169
Intouch, 111–112

Kelly's repertory grid, 169
Knowledge analysis of tasks, 165
    identifying actions, 170
    identifying goals, 171–172
    identifying objects, 170
    identifying procedures, 171
    observational techniques, 168
    questionnaires, 167
    rating scales, 169
    retrospective protocols, 168

Lexical consistency, 136
Life cycle model, 75–77
Long-term memory, 23–24

Meaning and memory, 23–24
Memory for gist, 41–42
Menu design, 16, 19, 20–21, 24–26
Mixed group design, 97
Models of interaction, 115–117
Multiple coding in memory, 30

Nominal scales of measurement, 91
Non-parametric statistics, 98

Observational techniques, 168
Ordinal scales of measurement, 92

PAC, 105–107
Parametric statistics, 98
Plans, 54
Practice effects, 64–65
Primacy effects, 18
Priming, 30, 32
Procedural knowledge, 57–61
Procedural substructures, 175
Production systems, 58
Programmable user models (PUMS),
    148–149
Programming skill, 66ff
Propositional networks, 30
Propositional representations, 45–48

Prototyping, 77–79
Psychological ability profiles, 152
Psychology and HCI, 3

Questionnaires, 167

RAPID, 104
Rating scales, 169
Ratio scales of measurement, 92
Recall v recognition, 29–30
Recency effects, 18
Repeated measures design, 97
Representations, 43ff
Representativeness, 162, 172–174
Retrospective protocols, 168
Roles, 162
Rule schemas, 138

Scales of measurement:
    interval, 92
    nominal, 91
    ordinal, 92
    ratio, 92
Schemas, 49–51
Scripts, 52–54
Semantic consistency, 136
Semantic features/attributes, 45–47
Semantic level of CLG, 119
Semantic networks, 47–48
Semantic-syntactic alignment, 136
Serial position curve, 18
Set grammars, 136
Simple tasks, 137
Short-term memory experiments, 16–19
Skill:
    acquisition, 61–64
    associative stage, 61
    automatic stage, 62
    definition, 60
    cognitive stage, 61
    programming skill, 65–66
Software engineering:
    environments, 72–74
Specification of user interfaces, 193–194
Specification stage evaluations, 85–87,
    125
Specific interface model, 198
Specific task model, 198
Spreading activation, 34ff
SSADM, 181
Subject selection, 94–95
Statecharts, 112
Statistical analyses, 97–99
Structure in tasks, 160
Syntactic level of CLG, 121
System design models, 80–81

Task action grammar (TAG), 86, 135–139
Task action language, 125–127
Task analysis and interface design, 155–157
Task analysis for knowledge descriptions
    (TAKD), 154
Task analysis guidelines, 167
Task artefact cycle, 7, 71
Task knowledge structures (TKS), 156–164
    goal structures, 161, 163
    procedural substructures, 175
    roles, 162
    taxonomic substructures, 161, 175
Task level of CLG, 118
Task models, 174
Task models and design:
    Rubik cube example, 183–187
    jewellery design example, 199ff

Trillium, 108
TUBE, 102

User interface:
    definition, 5
    design, 70–72
User interface design environments (UIDE),
    109ff
User interface management systems (UIMS),
    100, 104–107
User interface toolkits, 107–113

Visual programming, 108–113
Visualization, 54–57
VIZ, 104

Working memory, 21–23